Identity and the
Museum Visitor Experience

Identity and the
Museum Visitor Experience

John H. Falk

Left Coast
Press Inc.

Walnut Creek, California

LEFT COAST PRESS, INC.
1630 North Main Street, #400
Walnut Creek, CA 94596

Left Coast
Press Inc.   http://www.LCoastPress.com

ISBN 978-1-59874-162-9 hardcover
ISBN 978-1-59874-163-6 paperback

Library of Congress Cataloguing-in-Publication Data
Falk, John H. (John Howard), 1948-
Identity and the museum visitor experience / John H. Falk.
p. cm.
Includes bibliographical references and index.
ISBN 978-1-59874-162-9 (hardback : alk. paper) --
ISBN 978-1-59874-163-6 (pbk. : alk. paper)
1. Museums--Educational aspects. 2. Museum visitors.
3. Museum exhibits. 4. Identity (Philosophical concept)
I. Title.
AM7.F33 2009
069'.15--dc22
                                        2009013470

Printed in the United States of America

⊛™ The paper used in this publication meets the minimum requirements
of American National Standard for Information Sciences—Permanence
of Paper for Printed Library Materials, ANSI/NISO Z39.48–1992.

Printed on post-consumer partially recycled paper.
10 11 12 13 5 4 3 2

For Lynn

CONTENTS

PREFACE

The real voyage of discovery consists not in seeking new landscapes but in having new eyes.

—Marcel Proust

The impetus for this book actually goes back to the early years of my career in the 1970s when I believed that it should be possible to develop an empirically based model of the museum visitor experience. For more than thirty years, I have been working towards that goal, trying to understand why people go to museums, what they do once inside the museum, and finally, what meanings people make from their museum visitor experiences. In many ways, this book represents the product of all these many years of research and thinking. Although the model I propose in this book falls just short of that dream of a fully empirical model, it comes close.

As described first in *The Museum Experience*[1] and then again in *Learning from Museums*,[2] both co-authored with Lynn Dierking, I made the case that the museum visitor experience is a complex mix of multiple factors. In these previous books, the depth of my understanding limited me to descriptions of the museum visitor experience, albeit using increasingly sophisticated descriptions. In this book, I present not just a descriptive model of the museum visitor experience, but also a predictive model. The breakthrough came in the last six years when I realized that the key to understanding the museum visitor experience was the construct of identity. As I discovered, this single broad thread runs through all facets of the museum visitor experience. Each of us possesses many identities which we use to support our interactions with the world, including a museum visit. An individual's identity-related needs motivate him or her to visit a museum and provide an overarching framework for that visit experience. However, the social and physical realities an individual encounters while in the museum are not insignificant. Although identity-related needs and interests primarily direct the individual's museum visit experiences, the museum itself is not passive. The realities of the museum also play a role in bending and shaping the individual's museum visit experience. But once away from the museum, the individual's identity-related needs once again hold sway, forming a prism through which all experiences are viewed. The challenge was how to weave all these threads together into a single theoretically consistent and empirically supportable model.

In writing this book I have tried to bring together several major strands of knowledge, in particular, my deep understanding of museum visitor studies and a comprehensive awareness of research in the leisure sciences. I have also brought to bear my understanding of psychology, neurobiology, and marketing research. I have tried to intertwine these basic strands into a single, unified model that attempts to describe as well as predict the visitor experience. It is a model that takes into consideration how long-term memories and meanings are constructed from a visit to a museum. It is a model that postulates that a museum visit itself is strongly shaped by the expectations an individual develops prior to a visit, based upon his or her own identity-related need, as well as by the expectations and views of the larger socio-cultural context. It is a model that describes how the individual's larger socio-cultural context is, in a very real way, strongly shaped by the collective personal experiences of every person who has ever visited a museum, including the individual. Although I present the model linearly, as the medium of a book dictates, beginning with the large-scale context of twenty-first century leisure and concluding at the level of personal memories, it's important to keep in mind that the model could just as easily be run in reverse, starting from a person's memories. And of course, each link in the model has numerous feedback loops to each of the other links.

My goal in writing this book, more than anything, is to help change the quality of how museums understand and support the public's museum visitor experiences. I sincerely believe that this model has the potential to permit museums to proactively manage the museum visitor experience in new and ultimately, better ways. Specifically, the model I propose encourages museums to approach interacting with visitors in more customized and tightly tailored ways to meet the specific needs of individual visitors; it is not about types of visitors, but the types of visitor needs. Basing practice on this new model would also require profound changes in current museum practice—developing exhibits and programs designed to accommodate multiple outcomes and visitor goals. Finally, I believe that using the model would also dramatically change how museums define and measure their impact; bringing institutional missions, practices, and assessments more in-line with the actual public values and outcomes. I appreciate that these are bold assertions. Ultimately, each reader will need to decide if they accept either the model or my assertions of its implications.

Although the model I propose is primarily based upon research that I have conducted in the U.S., results from other countries, in particular the U.K., Canada, Australia, and Colombia support my conclusions. Whenever possible, I have included data from other countries though it's clear that my primary data comes from the U.S. Despite this regional bias, I think the basic framework of my model is likely to be robust in other cultural contexts. That said, it remains for others to determine if the specific motivational categories of visitor I have defined are the same in other countries and situations. Also, despite making the case that the variables of gender, race/ethnicity, social class, and even age provide relatively little explanatory power, I do not want to suggest that these variables have no influence on the visitor experience. They would almost certainly be important in museums that focus specifically on identity-related issues of race/ethnicity, gender, or nationality (for example, the numerous race/ethnicity museums such as the many African American museums and the Japanese American National Museum; gender-focused museums such as the Women's Museum; nationality and ethnicity focused museums such as the American History Museum and the National Museum of Australia or Te Papa). That said, I do not explicitly deal with these variables or these types of museums in this book.

Clearly, the tight focus in this book is on museums. However, I believe that the ideas presented here could be applied to a wide range of other leisure settings and contexts. Although similar ideas have been applied to recreation and leisure settings for years, they have always stopped short of the model I propose. Leisure motivation models now consider the reasons for why the public participates in leisure activities, but they have not pushed beyond this by making predictions about visitor outcomes beyond satisfaction.

Organizationally, I have divided the book into two major sections. The first seven chapters are grouped together into a theory section. I have tried to provide a readable and thorough review of the important theoretical ideas that underlie the model. I am hopeful that others will find the logic behind this model as compelling as I do. The final four chapters form a practice section. Inevitably, some museum practitioners may feel that the practice section does not go far enough in providing the details necessary to fully implement the possibilities suggested by this new model. If this is the case, I apologize but encourage patience as the model is newly minted. In time, I am confident that good examples of practice will emerge. At present, I have tried to suggest how I think the model could be applied.

As is always the case, the ideas in this book do not derive exclusively from my own thoughts. I am particularly grateful to a number of individuals who helped me think about these issues over the past several years—some explicitly, some through their writings, and some just through their inspiration. I am particularly grateful to my long-time Institute for Learning Institute research colleagues Martin Storksdieck, Joe Heimlich, Kerry Bronnenkant, Jessica Luke, Jill Stein, and Nettie Witgert; also my Australian colleague Jan Packer. My colleagues at the California Science Center, in particular David Bibas, Jeffery Rudolph, Diane Perlov, and my dear departed friend Dave Combs provided support and input to my investigations at the Science Center over many years. I am also indebted to my zoo and aquarium colleagues Cynthia Vernon, Jackie Ogden, Kathy Wagner, Carol Saunders, Bruce Carr, and Eric Reinhart who helped encourage, critique, and facilitate my major investigations of zoos and aquariums. I also want to acknowledge my Colombian colleagues Carlos Soto, Sigrid Falla, Claudia Aguirre and Fanny Angulo, as well as the thirteen graduate students from the Universidad de Antioquia, Medellin who helped me validate these ideas within a Latin American context. I wish to thank my Oregon State University colleague Dr. Olga Rowe and my graduate research assistants Nancy Staus and Lyn Riverstone for their assistance with interviews and data collection and also my current free-choice learning graduate students. I am particularly grateful to Michele Crowl and Katie Gillespie who have made important contributions to my research and thinking.

I am particularly indebted to the U.S. National Science Foundation for their continuing support of my research; much of this work could not have happened without NSF funding. Accordingly, I want to thank all of the anonymous reviewers who encouraged the NSF to fund my projects and to the program officers like Barry Van Demon, Sylvia James, David Ucko, and Barbara Butler who guided my efforts for the past many years.

I am particularly appreciative of the comments provided by the individuals who reviewed a preliminary version of this book—two of whom I know, two of whom were anonymous. Thanks to all four individuals, but a special thanks to Roy Ballantyne and to Jay Rounds, both of whom I recommended as reviewers. Not only has their thinking and writings inspired me over the years, I knew they would be totally, and if necessary, brutally honest in their reviews; they did not disappoint. Jay, in particular, deserves a very special thank-you as his comments and suggestions were fundamental to the current version of the model and its presentation in this book. Jay, if it's still not quite right, it's not your fault!

I also thank my publisher Mitch Allen for believing in me and encouraging me to write this book. Also my thanks to Patrice Titterington for her editing efforts that helped make this book readable and to Lisa Devenish for overseeing design, layout, and production.

Finally, as ever, I owe a huge debt of gratitude to my intellectual and emotional partner Lynn Dierking. Her continued support in all ways has allowed me to produce this book and it is to her that I dedicate this volume.

PART I

Theory

CHAPTER 1

Introduction:
Museums and Their Visitors

Everything should be made as simple as possible, but not simpler.

—*Albert Einstein*

It's a cool, rainy Saturday in early November in Baltimore, Maryland. If you are a local resident of Baltimore, what is there to do on such a day when you have relatives visiting from out of town? Not surprisingly, two separate local couples, each with visiting relatives, are converging on one of the major attractions in the area, the National Aquarium in Baltimore. Elmira Harris, her husband, their visiting son, and his wife are in one vehicle and George Johansson, his wife, and his wife's visiting father are in another. Arriving within a half hour of each other, the two groups follow a similar drill—park, pay their admission, receive a map of the Aquarium, and begin their visit.[1]

What can we say about the visitor experience of these two individuals, Elmira and George? Even more importantly, what can we predict about what they'll do at the Aquarium and what meaning they'll make as a consequence of their visit? Within this brief vignette, I've already provided what most museum professionals would currently consider the key pieces of information for answering these questions. To begin with, we know that both individuals visited the same museum, the National Aquarium in Baltimore. We know what the exhibitions at the Aquarium are, what information they contain, and what messages the Aquarium is trying to convey. We know which exhibits are considered the most "attractive" and which are less likely to be seen. For many in the museum community this is all we need to know—visitors come to see the exhibitions, they see the exhibitions, and they leave knowing about the exhibitions. However, years of visitor research has shown that there's more subtlety to the issue; we need to know something about the visitor and the conditions of visit as well.

We know when the visit happened—the same time of year, same day of the week, and at almost exactly the same time of day. We also know that demographically Elmira and George were fairly similar—both were adults, local residents, infrequent visitors to the Aquarium, and middle class with some college education. The only major demographic differences were that George was white and in his 30s and Elmira was African American and in her mid-50s. In addition to this demographic information, we also know something about their reasons for visiting, which was again almost identical—a rainy day excursion in order to entertain visiting relatives. We even know their social grouping—an all-adult, family group. Given all of these commonalities it should follow that how these two individuals and their groups "use" the Aquarium, the pace of their visit, what they will attend to, and ultimately, even the meanings they make from the experience, would likely be similar. But minutes into the actual visit it becomes apparent that many, if not all, of these assumptions may not be valid.

It takes less than a minute for Elmira and her family to scatter. Elmira goes off in one direction, her husband in another, and her son and his wife in a third direction. Elmira heads straight upstairs towards the top-floor rainforest exhibit. Oblivious to the other visitors there, Elmira thoughtfully wanders around the displays in the rainforest area, reading labels, and carefully seeking out and watching the live creatures clinging to branches and tree trunks which like Elmira, also appear oblivious to visitors. After the rainforest exhibition, Elmira circles back down through the Aquarium against the flow of traffic, and takes in each of the various other parts of the Aquarium. She gives each her undivided attention, and she visits each by herself. Only after about two hours does Elmira rendezvous again with the rest of her family. The four family members gather for coffee in the Aquarium coffee shop and animatedly relate what they've seen and discovered.

In contrast, George, his wife, and father-in-law never leave each other's side. They start at the beginning, at the bottom of the long ramping walkway, and slowly move through the first exhibit. As the visit proceeds, their pace accelerates. When they finally reach the top floor and the rainforest exhibition area, they mutually agree to skip it after glancing at their watches. During their visit, the three of them carry on a reasonably animated conversation, most of it having little relationship to what they are seeing or doing at the time. George's father-in-law talks about the challenges he had in getting into town, the fact that the cab ride from the airport to their house was so expensive, and how bad the weather and the traffic was. George is then asked by his father-in-law how things are going with his job. Seemingly grateful to get beyond his father-in-law's travel tirade, George enthusiastically talks about his work. Since he works in biotechnology and investigates how chemicals created by marine organisms can be used in pharmaceuticals, once or twice during the conversation George points to something he sees in one of the exhibits that helps him make a point or relates to the work he does. But after the initial flurry of exhibit-viewing, much of the visit is comprised of the three adults strolling along, chatting, and generally scanning back and forth across the Aquarium's various exhibits. After about an hour, the three decide they've had enough and agree to head over to shops of the Inner Harbor for coffee and something sweet to eat before going back to the house.

Months later when I talked with Elmira and George, their recollections of the museum experience were quite different. Although both were able to share the basic outlines of the experience, which I have described here, the meanings they made from the experience were very different. For George, the Aquarium was a backdrop for his experiences; it was a fun and enjoyable setting in which to fulfill his social obligations for the day. Most of his memories were anecdotes about his father-in-law—some positive and some not so positive; little of what he spontaneously talked about related to the Aquarium exhibits or its creatures. By contrast, Elmira was just bursting with information about what she saw and learned at the Aquarium. Unprompted, she described the toucan, sloth, and iguana she saw, as well as various details from the labels she read. She was quite excited about the prospect of some day being able to travel to the tropics and actually seeing these creatures in the wild (something that is not anywhere on the horizon, but nonetheless still a goal for her). Only with prompting did she talk about her son and daughter-in-law. Clearly, George and Elmira's experiences, as well as their memories of the experience, were very different from each other despite the apparent similarities at the outset.

What are we to make of these two visitors' experiences that occurred on this day? How can we make sense of how different they were given the obvious similarities between their two situations? What do we actually know about why people go to museums, what they do there, and what meanings they make from that experience? The National Aquarium in Baltimore as an institution is quite committed to understanding more about the million-plus individuals who visit every year; they are eager to know why they come and what meanings they leave with. And the same is true for all the other zoos and aquariums in the world which collectively have hundreds of millions of visitors each year. In fact, the entire museum community—zoos, aquariums, art, history and natural history museums, children's museums and science centers, botanical gardens, historical and heritage sites, nature centers and natural parks, and other such institutions—would like to know more about the approximately one billion individuals who visit annually. Despite seeming to possess all the information we needed to understand and predict what the museum visitor experiences of George and Elmira would be like—the nature of the museum, time of day, day of the week, time of year, demographic characteristics of the visitors, social group, and visit motivation—it's clear these pieces of information were inadequate to the challenge. It seems hard to believe that these huge differences in experience could just be a function of Elmira and George's different ages and race/ethnicity, though these seemed to be the only major differences between them. Maybe the task of understanding, let alone predicting the museum visitor experience is fundamentally impossible; it is perhaps impossible to make any useful generalizations about museum visitor experiences given how many visitors there are and how obviously unique each individual visitor is. That said, it certainly would be useful if we could!

FROM NICETY TO NECESSITY

Although it was not always true, today most museums exist in order to attract and serve visitors—as many as possible. Although museums have long wondered about who visits their institutions, why and to what end, today they feel economically, socially, and politically compelled to do so. Today's museum has no choice but to think seriously about who their visitors are and why they come, as well as about who does not visit and why not. Visitors are at the heart of the twenty-first century museum's existence. Understanding something about museum visitors is not a nicety; it is a necessity! Asking who visits the museum, why and to what end are no longer mere academic questions. These are questions of great importance.

If we knew who visited museums and what meanings they took away from the experience, we would know something about the role that museums play in society. Likewise, we could also learn something about the societal role of museums from knowing more about why other people choose not to visit museums. If we knew something about who visited museums and what meanings they made we would also understand something about the role museums play in individual people's lives. Buried within the construct we call the *museum visitor experience* lie answers to fundamental questions about the worth of museums—how museums make a difference within society, how they support the public's understandings of the world as well as of themselves. These are all tremendously important issues, and these alone would be justification for trying to better understand the museum visitor experience. But there are more practical and pressing reasons the museum profession might have for improving its understanding, and if possible, its prediction of the museum visitor experience.

If we knew the answers to the questions of who goes to museums, what people do once in the museum, and what meanings they make from the experience, we would gain critical insights into how the public derives value and benefits from museum-going (or not, as the case may be) which we could use to improve museums. We live in an increasingly competitive world where every museum is competing for audiences and resources not only against other museums, but against an ever-growing collection of for-profits and non-profits. If museums are to maintain their current popularity and success, they will need to get measurably better at understanding and serving their visitors. Today, museums are among the most successful leisure venues in the world, but it is not a given that museums will always be popular and successful. Even if museums as a category remain popular, it is not assured that any particular museum will continue to be successful. The past decade has been challenging for most museums and the coming decade promises to be even more so. Financial support which was once abundant is now more limited; governments are cutting back and grant support is becoming more challenging to acquire. Individual donations are also becoming increasingly difficult to obtain and it requires ever more effort to maintain even current levels of support. As I write this book in 2008, it seems unlikely that any museum will escape unscathed from the worldwide financial and political turbulence. An enhanced understanding of audience, current and potential, has to be at the heart of any twenty-first century museum's business model.[2] Asking who is the museum's audience and how can we maximize the quality of the museum visitor experience should be the two questions that every twenty-first century museum should be asking. And not just once, but continuously! So we can see that making sense of museum visitors like Elmira and George and their families, as well as the many others who choose to devote a piece of their precious time to visiting a museum, is an important undertaking. It is also extremely daunting!

WHAT WE THINK WE KNOW ABOUT THE MUSEUM VISITOR EXPERIENCE

What do we know about our two museum visitors, Elmira and George? Were Elmira and George typical visitors? Could we have predicted that these two individuals and their families would visit the Aquarium on the day in question? What really motivated Elmira to visit? What really motivated George? What would their visit experience be like? What would they look at? What would they think about? What would make them satisfied with their experience? What would they remember? What would they learn? What do we know about the museum visitor experience in general, and based upon what we know, what would we have predicted about the visit experience of people like Elmira and George in particular? These should be fairly straightforward questions and in some ways, they are but in other very profound ways, they are anything but straightforward. As previously shown, our predictions about the museum experiences of Elmira and George based upon the "standard" tools proved to not be very useful. I would argue this is because we currently lack a real model of the museum visitor experience; we know what many of the pieces are, but we lack a comprehensive framework for knowing how all of these various pieces fit together and interact. In this book I intend to show that it is possible to understand the museum visitor experience. It is indeed a quite complex system, but not so complex as to be unknowable. Our inability to more accurately predict the visit experiences of George and Elmira derive not so much from a lack of knowledge about museums and visitors, but because historically we have tended to concretely focus on the pieces of the system, rather than think of the system as a dynamic whole. We have also missed what I believe is the key to the whole system—the important role that personal identity plays in the museum visitor experience.

As with any system, our understanding depends upon the lens through which we look at that system. Currently there are two main lenses that represent the beliefs that museum professionals hold about the nature of museums and their visitors. Both of these lenses reveal some of what's important about the museum visitor experience. Each yields some insights into why people visit museums, what they do there, and what meanings they make from the experience. However, viewing the museum visitor experience through just one of these lenses, no matter which one is chosen, provides only a partial picture. Not only do they individually not tell the entire story, they do not even tell the entire story collectively. The fact that each lens provides only a partial view of "reality" would in and of itself not be such a problem. The real problem is that many in the field have come to believe and accept that the distorted perspectives provided by these two lenses provide an accurate and useful picture of the museum visitor experience.

Lens #1: It's all about the Museum—Content and Exhibits

To many in the museum community, the first and most obvious answer to the question of why Elmira and George visited the National Aquarium in Baltimore is that they, or their relatives, must like fish and other marine wildlife. The Aquarium is a place that displays marine organisms such as fish, marine invertebrates, marine mammals, and somewhat uncharacteristically for an aquarium, rainforest wildlife as well.[3] Visitors come in order to see these creatures, to see the exhibitions, and to learn more about marine life. Confirming the obvious, the research I did many years ago found that more than 90% of all visitors to art museums said they liked art; more than 90% of all visitors to history museums said they liked history; and more than 90% of all visitors to science museums said they liked science. The other 10% said they weren't crazy about the subject but they were dragged there by someone who was.[4] This is an answer that makes perfect sense to those who work in museums. After all, displaying and interpreting subject-specific content is what museums do best. Of course, not everyone who likes art or history or science or animals visits art or history or science museums or zoos or aquariums! For example, more than 90% of the American public says they find science and technology interesting, but only visit science and technology museums even occasionally, let alone regularly.[5] So merely having an affinity for the subject matter only gets you so far in understanding why people visit museums. Let's refer back to our Aquarium visitors, Elmira and George. Both would probably say they were interested in marine life, George by profession and Elmira by avocation, but neither are regular visitors to the Aquarium. In fact, both stated in my interviews with them that they rarely visited the Aquarium, generally only doing so on occasions like the one described when they had an out-of-town visitor.

Having an interest in the subject matter of the museum is clearly important to determining who will visit, but as our own personal experiences and the examples above would suggest, interest in a subject is not sufficient to explain who visits any given museum, let alone predict who visits on any given day. However, the belief that it is all about the content is so pervasive in the museum world that the vast majority, perhaps as much as 90%, of all marketing and promotion of museums is content-oriented. Media placements of all kinds emphasize what's on display at the museum or in the traveling exhibits, what rare item can be found in the permanent collections, and what prominent speaker will be part of special programming. All of this marketing is focused on content, and yet such content-focused marketing only slightly influences public visits. Market researchers tell us that most American museum visitors certainly visit because of the content of the museum, but rarely do they say that the content is the single most important factor influencing their decision to visit a museum.[6] Research on American museum visitors shows that most are only vaguely aware of what's on display at the museums they visit. Most say that what is on display at any given time only partially figured into their decision to visit the museum. For example, Colonial Williamsburg in Virginia, an institution with one of the largest marketing budgets of any museum in America, estimated that only a small percentage of its visitors originally heard about the institution through advertising.[7] Nor were the specifics of what was happening at Colonial Williamsburg almost ever the most important factor in influencing them to visit. Similar discoveries have been found to be true at art and natural history museums, science centers, zoos and aquariums, and natural areas.[8] For all of these institutions, advertising and publicity programs about the specific content of their institutions accounted for less than 20% of visits.

Would Elmira and George have visited the National Aquarium if it was a museum focused on a content area they or their visitors found uninteresting? Perhaps not, but the motivation for Elmira and George's visits to the Aquarium on this particular day was probably not primarily motivated by content. Content was important in the sense that it was an interesting place to go, but it was not the major driving factor in influencing these particular individuals to visit on that particular day. As we'll see, there are individuals for whom the content of the museum is absolutely at the core of what motivates them to visit, but they represent a minority of museum visitors. Museum brochures, advertisements, and promotions do make a difference, but rarely in and of themselves are they the single largest determinant of a visit and rarely will they make someone who never visits a museum into someone who will.

"Well," says the museum professional, "I may grudgingly acknowledge that content may not be the primary driver of why people come to the museum, but inarguably, content well displayed is what drives a visitor's museum experience and determines what they learn and remember." To this I would reply, "Yes, perhaps." Without question, the exhibitions and objects within the museum represent a major focus of a visitor's time and attention, but they are not the only things which attract visitors. According to a major study my colleagues and I did many years ago, approximately 60% of a visitor's attention over the course of a visit was spent looking at exhibits, with the peak amount of content focus occurring in the first 15 minutes of a visit and tapering off considerably by the end of the visit.[9] Of course, this means that approximately 40% of the visitor's attention was directed elsewhere; mostly on conversations with other members of his or her social group or on general observations of the setting. Content does drive much of a visitor's experience in the museum, but by no means all of it. And of course, the content the visitor chooses to focus on may or may not bear much resemblance to what the museum professionals who designed the experience hoped they'd attend to. This leads to the issue of how much of a visitor's long-term memories of a museum experience are actually determined by the quality of exhibit design. Research I conducted with my colleague Martin Storksdieck revealed that for some, but not all visitors, what was learned was related to exhibition quality.[10] In some cases, visitors who saw more high quality exhibitions (defined as those that clearly and compellingly communicated their intended content) learned more, but in other cases, learning seemed to be independent of whether high- or low-quality exhibits were engaged. At the expense of over-generalizing from the single example presented in this chapter, both George and Elmira were exposed to the same exhibits but came away with very different memories and learning.

Although I'm not aware of any study that has rigorously attempted to define clear percentages of memory that relate to exhibit content, all studies that I know of suggest that content does play a role in visitors' museum meaning-making; in some cases, it is a large role and in other cases it is a cameo role. For example, in a study Lynn Dierking and I conducted on the memories children had about past school field trips, we found that memory of what someone did and saw, as opposed to, for example, who they were with and what they talked about, tended to dominate across all age groups, regardless of how long ago was the visit.[11] Just as in our two examples at the beginning of the chapter, Elmira's memories were all about the content of the Aquarium while George's memories only lightly touched upon content. If we had asked both more questions about their visit, we would have revealed more content-related memories. But the message is clear—most visitor experiences are a mix of content-focused and non-content-focused events. Research now reveals that visitors' long-term memories follow a similar pattern.[12]

Two corollaries to the *It's all about the Museum* lens are: 1) Frequent visitors are those who care about and know the most about the museum's content; and 2) Visitors who already know something about the content of the museum before visiting will be those who derive the most learning benefit from their museum visit. Museum professionals have variously defined what it means to be a "frequent" visitor, ranging from those who visit three or more times per year to those who visit at least seven or more times per year. No matter the definition, it has often been assumed that frequent visitors are such because of their deep and abiding interest in and knowledge of the subject matter of the institution. Deep interest in the subject matter is no doubt almost certainly characteristic of frequent visitors, but greater knowledge is less likely the case. Although, on average, frequent visitors probably know somewhat more about the museum's content than first-time visitors (it would be hard for this not to be true since some understanding has to accrue to those who come frequently), there's no evidence that shows that frequent visitors on average have substantially more knowledge than infrequent visitors. My investigations of visitors have shown that a whole range of reasons prompt individuals to visit frequently, only one of which has to do with the museum's content. Again, there are frequent visitors who are quite knowledgeable about the museum's collections and content, but there are just as many who have only a passing knowledge. Like the reasons for visiting in the first place, the relationship between visitors and the content of the museum is not simple and straightforward.

A wide and diverse literature document the vital role that prior knowledge and interest play on learning.[13] In fact, specific research by my colleagues and I have shown that both prior interest and prior knowledge are important and vital predictors of what and how much someone learns from a museum experience.[14] Although George, based upon his educational background and professional knowledge of marine biology, *should* have learned more from his Aquarium visit than Elmira, that did not appear to be the case. In general, prior interest and knowledge of the museum's content strongly correlate with learning, but as demonstrated by our example, this is not always true. The complex reality of the museum visitor experience makes even this important connection only true some of the time. In conclusion, viewing the museum exclusively through the lens of the museum, whether it's the content or exhibitions and programs, provides a surprisingly small measure of understanding about the museum visitor experience. In large part this is because these variables are passive, they are only made active when they are responded to, interpreted, and processed by visitors. Given how diverse the individuals are who visit museums, it should be no surprise that the responses, interpretations, and resulting mental processing are also diverse.

Lens #2: It's all about the Visitor—Demographics, Visitor Frequency, and Social Arrangement

Clearly, one cannot understand anything about the museum visitor experience without knowing something about the people who come to the museum. Over the years, many visitor studies have been conducted in order to better understand museum visitors. Although only a fraction of these studies have been published, virtually every museum, from the smallest historic house museum and volunteer-run natural area to the largest art, natural history, zoo, aquarium and science center, have variously counted and in some measure, attempted to describe their visitors. Overwhelmingly, the many efforts to describe museum audiences have framed their efforts using easily quantitative variables. These measures have typically included the demographic categories of age, education, gender and race/ethnicity, but have also included such easily quantifiable variables as time of day, day of the week, and time of year. Museums have also categorized visitors on the basis of their visit frequency—frequent, infrequent, non-visitor, etc., as well as their social arrangement—family, adult, school group, etc. We know much about certain aspects of the museum visitor, in particular the range of standard population characteristics that government agencies and social scientists have traditionally used to describe and categorize the public.

A predictable outcome of segmenting groups into various measurable categories such as demographics is that patterns emerge, but whether those patterns are actually meaningful is another question.[15] It is perhaps not surprising that a number of demographic variables have been found to positively correlate with museum-going, including education, income, occupation, race/ethnicity, and age. One fairly consistent finding is that museum-goers are better educated, more affluent, and hold better-paying jobs than the average citizen.[16] This is true of visitors to art, history, and science museums as well as visitors to zoos, arboreta, botanical gardens, and national parks. In addition to social class, there are three other demographic variables that appear to also strongly correlate with museum-going—age, gender, and race/ethnicity. Museum-going is not evenly distributed by age. Even limiting the discussion to free-choice visitors, in other words excluding school field trips, elementary school-aged children still represent a significant percentage of all museum-goers. Most children do not come to museums by themselves, they are usually brought by an adult, typically their parents. For many museums, family groups are the largest single category of visitor. Adults between the ages of 25 and 44 and children between the ages of 5 and 12 are disproportionately represented among museum audiences. For example, ten years of demographic studies at the Smithsonian Institution indicated that (excluding school groups) about half of all Smithsonian visitors were between the ages of 20 and 44; 30% were children; 16% were between 45 and 64; and less than 4% were 65 years or older. Visitors to art and history museums tend to be older than this average; visitors to science-oriented museums tend to be younger. In general, museum-going peaks for most adults between the ages of 30 and 50, and then drops off again.

Museum visitors are also not equally distributed across the sexes. Approximately six out of every ten visitors are female and this is true across all kinds of institutions (except war and air and space museums). Beyond age and gender, the other demographic variable that has been intensively studied is race/ethnicity. Considerable attention has been focused in recent years upon whether museums are under-utilized by non-majority populations. In the U.S. particular attention has been focused on African American and more recently, Asian American and Latino populations. Over the last decade or two a large number of studies have documented that African Americans and other minority groups are underrepresented among the American museum-going public.[17] In a study I conducted over a decade ago on African American leisure habits, I found that African Americans utilized museums at a rate 20-30% lower than national norms.[18] However, extreme caution needs to be used when interpreting these data. Although it appears to be true that as a group, minorities are less likely than the European-American majority to visit American museums, this reality is not as simple as it initially appears. I would assert that it can't be assumed, as it usually is, that this fact is somehow related to issues of race/ethnicity.

It is essential to realize that U.S. minority populations (as well as likely those in any other country) are not monolithic. Of the three major minority communities in the U.S.—African Americans, Latino, and Asians—African Americans are probably the most homogeneous despite being anything but homogeneous. For example, a recent epidemiological study in New York City followed up data that African Americans had significantly higher incidences of high blood pressure and heart disease than did European Americans.[19] When the situation was studied in detail, however, it was found that the variations in blood pressure and heart disease were greater *within* the New York City African American population than *between* blacks and whites living in New York City. Race provided no insights into why the data looked the way it did. My research into the museum-going behavior of African Americans arrived at similar conclusions. The overwhelming conclusion of my research was that, overall, African American leisure behavior was very similar to European American leisure behavior, while tremendous differences existed within and across the African American community. Where black-white differences existed, race/ethnicity did not emerge as the best variable to explain these differences. In fact, one could generalize that it is not just race/ethnicity that provides a poor explanation for museum-going, so too do other demographic variables such as age, income, and education.

By way of illustration, we can look at our chapter case study of Elmira and George—how do they fit these demographic profiles? Elmira works as an oncology nurse at Johns Hopkins Hospital and her husband is retired and receives Social Security along with a small pension. By most measures, Elmira and her husband live on a limited income. However, both Elmira and her husband had some college education, but, at least in part due to their race, found it challenging to secure high-paying jobs. (Race/ethnicity does make a significant difference in some circumstances, but twenty-first century U.S. museum-going doesn't appear to be one of them.) In contrast, George and his wife are both professionals and together earn a good income. If we were going to use only demographics, we might predict that George and his wife are more likely to be museumgoers than are Elmira and her husband. In other words, Elmira does not appear to be a likely candidate to be a museum-goer. By contrast, George, except for the slight negative influence of his gender, appears to be the perfect candidate—white, well-educated, affluent, and of the right age. However, it turns out that Elmira is a frequent art museum visitor while George rarely visits museums of any kind. Although these examples do not prove that demographic variables are not useful, they do make the point that these quantitative measures are a very blunt instrument for understanding the museum visitor experience.

Although almost every museum has attempted to count and sort their visitors based upon demographic categories—age, gender, race/ethnicity, income, education, and occupation—these categories yield a false sense of explanation. We think we know our visitors, but I would argue that we do not. As summarized above, we think we "know" that museum visitors as a group are better educated, older, and wealthier than the public as a whole, and also white and female, but what does this actually mean? Although these statistics are on average true, museum visitors are not averages, they are individuals. This demographic data provides insufficient information to predict whether or not people will visit a museum. Likewise, knowing that someone is less educated, younger, and poorer than the public as a whole, and also brown and male, provides insufficient information to predict that these individuals will not visit a museum. After all, on at least one particular Saturday in November, both Elmira and George showed up at the National Aquarium, only one of whom, based upon demographics, might have been expected to visit. Knowing that Elmira was older and African American did not predict that she would not visit the National Aquarium any more than knowing that she had some college education and was female predicted that she would. Knowing a museum-goer's age, gender, race/ethnicity, income, education, and occupation does not now, nor will it ever tell anyone why someone does or does not visit a specific museum; it won't even reveal if they will ever visit any museum. The major conclusion I reached after studying hundreds of visitors, both black and white, for my major investigation of African American museum-going was that *museum-going is far too complex to be understood only on the basis of easily measured variables such as demographics.*[20] And this also includes the latest demographic-based trend which is to segment visitors generationally—Mature/Silents, Baby Boomers, Generation X, and Generation Y.[21] These categories just don't provide sufficient information to be really useful; generational stereotypes yield just that, stereotypes.

The reason measures like demographics yield only the most limited insights into who visits museums is because they are fundamentally unrelated to museums. Variables like age, gender, race/ethnicity, and generation do tell something about individuals but they tell virtually nothing about how these individuals might relate to museums. For a personal context variable to be useful, it needs to have some relationship to the other contexts such as the subject matter of a museum and the design of its exhibitions. Knowing that someone is male, in their late 50s, white and well-educated, or that they arrived at 2:00 PM on a Tuesday afternoon, does not provide much information as to what someone will actually attend to while in the museum. Nor does it provide a clue as to what they will remember from the experience as meaningful because this type of data is divorced from the specific realities of the museum. (Unless it was a museum devoted to telling the story of 50-year-old, white, well-educated males with a propensity to visit museums on later week-day afternoons! Then this data would be highly pertinent information.) At one point, social scientists, including and particularly marketing researchers, became enamored with these variables. It was thought that they provided deep insights, but we should now know that this is not true. These kinds of variables unquestionably describe some characteristics of visitors and they can be "objectively" and easily measured, but what of value they tell us is another matter. After many years of effort, the jury is in—the payoff in understanding of the museum visitor experience is remarkably small. As business consultant Anthony Ulwick observed with regard to segmenting retail consumers using traditional demographic categories, businesses often use "convenient classification schemes and impose it [sic] on customers with the hope and expectation that customers will act according to the dictates of the categories the scheme outlines . . . unfortunately, that hope is simply not justified when companies use traditional approaches."[22] Demographic descriptions of museum visitors do sometimes reveal interesting patterns, but interesting patterns are not the same as useful patterns. Quantitative measures such as demographics provide too little information about visitors in relation to museums to be useful variables for describing and understanding the museum visitor experience.

Demographic variables are not the only easily measured variables that museums have applied to visitor populations. Two other variables that have been commonly used are visit frequency and social arrangement. Unlike demographics, these variables are directly related to key aspects of the museum itself and thus, have been much more valuable in understanding the museum visitor experience. However, since these variables capture only some of the relevant information we need to understand the museum visitor experience, when museums unduly focus on them, misunderstandings can arise.

Let's examine, for example, visit frequency. Certainly the group of individuals who regularly visit the museum must somehow have some attributes that distinguish them from those who visit only infrequently or never. The question is what, other than visit frequency, are these attributes? The problem arises when we treat visit frequency as a category of visitor, implicitly assuming in the process that all frequent visitors are the same, that all infrequent visitors are the same, as are all non-visitors. Visit frequency is not a quality of the visitor; it is an action of the visitor that is indicative of some deeper attribute that is important. The actual number of visits is just an indicator of this underlying quality. If we can understand that underlying quality, we will have something useful. Again, just because visit frequency is relatively easy to measure doesn't necessarily make it worth measuring!

A similar situation has been the increasing appreciation among museum professionals of the importance of attending to the visitor's social arrangement. Virtually all visitors arrive at the museum as part of a social group.[23] Not surprisingly then, making sense of museum visitors should require taking into consideration visitors' social arrangements. This not only makes good sense, it is almost certainly true. As cited earlier in this chapter, much of the in-museum experiences of visitors and many of their resulting long-term memories of that experience involve social events. So clearly, the social nature of the visit is extremely important.

What arises as problematic though is the leap from the fact that social interaction is important to the assumption that a key factor for visitors must be *how* they are socially arranged. For example, it is now widely assumed that family groups (a family being typically defined as a group containing at least one adult and a relatively small number of children; relatedness is presumed but is not necessarily the case) behave differently than all-adult groups and that pairs of adults behave differently than larger groups of adults. Beyond the realities, such as being with other people engenders different behaviors than being alone and being an adult responsible for children in a public setting carries with it certain requirements and constraints that being an adult without children in the same setting does not, exactly how much influence social arrangement has on visitors is open to question. Much like visit frequency, a visitor's social arrangement is likely emblematic of deeper influences that do directly affect the museum visitor experience. However, social arrangement only correlates with these deeper influences, they are not in and of themselves predictive. While family groups overall appear to behave differently than do all-adult groups, the reasons they do so are not necessarily directly tied to their social arrangement. As discovered in the results of my study of African American museum visitors, the variability *within* family groups may well be greater than the variability *between* family and all-adult groups.

Thus, knowing that an adult came to the museum with a child provides only a limited predictive ability for how that adult will describe the meaning they constructed from their visit. We do know that visitors' recollections of their museum experiences are almost always influenced by the social interactions they had with the other members of their social group. However, the nature and direction of that influence can be highly variable. For example, in describing their museum visitor experiences, some parents will dwell almost totally on their children's experiences, others almost totally on their own experiences. Knowing only that the visitor was part of a family group (or part of an all-adult group) provides insufficient information to predict the types of memories. For example, George and Elmira arrived at the Aquarium in identical social groupings, but their museum experiences and their post-visit recollections were strikingly dissimilar. Thinking about visitors exclusively through the lens of social arrangement yields some useful insights about how visitors might behave within the museum, but ultimately these insights are too broad and unpredictable to be useful in understanding the museum visitor experience.

TOWARDS A NEW MODEL OF THE
MUSEUM VISITOR EXPERIENCE

The museum visitor experience cannot be adequately described by analyzing the content of museums, the design of exhibitions, through easily quantified visitor measures such as demographics, or even by analyzing visit frequency, or the social arrangements in which people enter the museum. To get the complete answer to the questions of why people visit museums, what they do there, and what learning/meaning they derive from the experience, requires a deeper, more holistic explanation. Despite the considerable time and effort that museum investigators have devoted to framing the museum visitor experience using these common lenses, the results have been depressingly limited. These perspectives have yielded only the most rudimentary descriptive understandings and none approach providing a truly predictive model of the museum visitor experience.

The Contextual Model of Learning, which some have claimed should now be considered a standard in the field,[24] provides a way to organize the complexity of what people do within a museum by describing the visitor experience as a set of interacting, contextually relevant factors. However, the Contextual Model of Learning is not really a model in the truest sense, it is actually a framework and a descriptive tool. A true museum visitor experience model would be prescriptive and yield not only descriptions, but actual predictions about what museum visitors will do and learn. I would suggest that the lack of a real, predictive model of the museum visitor experience has prevented us from moving beyond the often linear and concrete view of this complex and abstract phenomenon. We have historically over-focused on either the museum side or visitor side of the equation while neglecting the interaction or the unification of the visitor and the museum into a single unique experience. We have also been guilty of unduly limiting the temporal and spatial perspectives of the museum visitor experience. As I have long argued, it is fundamentally impossible to understand the museum visitor experience by only viewing it from within the "box" of the museum.[25] Understanding the museum visitor experience requires panning the camera back in time and space and appreciating that the actual time spent in the museum comprises only a small fraction of what is needed for understanding that experience. For most people, museum-going is just a small slice of daily life, just one of many experiences in a lifetime filled with experiences. Accordingly, we need to try and understand the museum visitor experience within this larger context. If we are to answer our fundamental questions of why people visit museums, what they do there, and what meaning they make of the experience, we must see the museum visitor experience as a series of nested, seemingly interrelated events. In reality, the museum visitor experience is no more than a series of snapshots of life, artificially bounded by our own need to frame what happens in the museum as not only important but separate. However, for the public that visits museums these experiences are often neither readily delineated nor seen as singular events.

Thus, I would assert that the museum visitor experience is neither about visitors nor about museums and exhibitions, but rather it is situated within that unique and ephemeral moment when both of these realities become one and the same—visitors are the museum and the museum is the visitor. This new way of thinking suggests that we stop thinking about museum exhibitions and content as fixed and stable entities designed to achieve singular outcomes and instead, think of them as intellectual resources capable of being experienced and used in different ways for multiple, and equally valid purposes. It requires us to stop thinking about visitors as definable by some permanent quality or attribute such as age or race/ethnicity. Instead, we need to appreciate that every visitor is a unique individual, and each is capable of having a wide range of very different kinds of visitor experiences (even though currently most visitors only select from a very limited palette of possible experiences). Finally, it demands that we come to accept that the long-term meanings created by visitors from their time in the museum are largely shaped by short-term personal, identity-related needs and interests rather than by the goals and intentions of the museum's staff.

The result of this new thinking is a model of the museum visitor experience framed around what I call the visitor's identity-related visit motivations—the series of specific reasons that visitors use to justify as well as organize their visit, and ultimately use in order to make sense of their museum experience. Visitors' identity-related motivations emerge as important because they provide a window into this complex system, a way to reframe the museum visitor experience so that it simultaneously captures important and key realities of the visitor, as well as significant and critical realities of the museum. It is not just about the visitor nor is it just about the museum; it is about how these two realities come together as one. Let me state explicitly that what I'm proposing is not just a way to repackage what we've always said and done. I believe that what I'm proposing represents a fundamental shift in how we frame our thinking about the museum visitor experience. In this new typology, neither the visitor nor the museum and its exhibitions are immutable and fixed; each are fluid and changing—the same individual can engage with the same exhibitions and content in fundamentally different ways depending upon their current identity-related visit motivations. To be useful, I've attempted to simplify this complexity into a manageable package, one that meaningfully and validly connects all of the personal, social, and physical realities of the museum visitor experience. To this end, I've strived in this book to embody the quote by Albert Einstein at the beginning of this chapter, the creation of a model that is as simple as possible, but not too simple.

The essence of the model is that each museum visit experience is the synthesis of the individual's identity-related needs and interests and the views of the individual and society of how the museum can satisfy those needs and interests. The tangible evidence of the confluence of these perceptions is the visitor's identity-related visit motivations. These visit motivations create a basic trajectory for the individual's museum visitor experience. That trajectory is influenced, while in the museum, by the factors outlined in the Contextual Model of Learning. Coming out of the visit, the individual uses his or her museum visit experience to enhance and change his or her sense of identity and perceptions of the museum, as well as, in a small but significant way, how society perceives this and other museums.

Over the next several chapters I will explain the details of this model. I will begin by describing what it is about these places called museums that makes them so attractive to the public and entices large numbers of people to visit them—in psychology-speak, "what benefits museums *afford* the visiting public." Then, I will shift to a discussion of individual identity—a construct which I believe helps us understand when and how the needs of the individual become congruent with what a visit to a museum affords. Finally, and most importantly, I will describe how this model can help us understand what happens at the intersection of these two worlds—the place where the identity-related needs of the visitor merges with the affordances of the museum and results in museum visit experiences, visitor satisfaction, and memories, all of which set the stage for future museum visitor experiences.

This new model of the museum visitor experience, framed through the new lens of visitor identity-related motivations, allows us to begin to make sense out of the many museum visits that happen each year by people such as Elmira and George. This model helps us understand these visits not only retrospectively, but potentially prospectively as well. What I will describe is not only a descriptive framework but a predictive model that we can use to anticipate who will visit a museum, what visitors will do within the museum, and even what long-term meanings they will make of their experiences long after the visit. Presumably, if museum professionals possessed such a model they could use it to influence and ideally, enhance museum practice. In the second section of this book, I will offer some initial suggestions on how the model might be applied to this task. But first, we need to begin to better understand this model. To do that we need to view the museum from the only vantage point that makes sense, the view that the broader public has of the museum. I am not interested in an esoteric philosophical analysis, a la the French sociologist Bourdieu, of the socio-political role of museums in society and the legitimacy or illegitimacy of museum's sources of power and authority.[26] Rather, my goal is much more practical—I am interested in answering the question of why would someone make the decision to visit a museum, particularly as most people do, during their precious leisure time? From an early twenty-first century perspective, what then are the attributes of museums that the public perceives that makes them such popular leisure destinations?

CHAPTER 2

The Museum

The competing demands on museums will increase as the number
and diversity of visitors continues to grow. As they vie as never
before with a broad panoply of new centres of interest, museums
face a host of demands from a clientele ever more avid for
stimulation, entertainment and challenge.

—*N. Graburn, 1998*[1]

Q: What I would like to ask you and what I would want to talk about is
what do you really enjoy doing?

A: I enjoy doing *lots* of things. I enjoy walking on the beach, I enjoy
working outside in the garden, well, I don't really have a garden, but
I have flower pots and I love flowers. I love tutoring the children in
the afternoon in my house. I enjoy cooking. I enjoy being able to help
other people to, you know, to understand a new way of doing things. I
enjoy being able to help people walk through the health system which
is very complicated especially if you don't have money, so that is very
rewarding. I enjoy every part of the day because I am not sure if I'm
going to be here tomorrow, here in life, I enjoy every day like it would
be the last one. I have a couple alarms in the health department so
that helped me to realize that I might not be here tomorrow so I enjoy
everything I do, even if I know I am healthy now but you never know,
things are like that sometimes. … and I enjoy spending time with
my husband. Ron, my husband, he's also involved in the community
very, very much so the time that we have together is at nights and on
weekends sometimes weekends because sometimes he has meetings.
He is coaching the high school for track and football, so you know
sometimes on the weekends he has games. So there are weeks when
he needs to go, I will see him late or maybe the next day if he's going
to these things.

Q: Wow, you both sound really busy!

A: Yes. We have my life, his life, and our life. And it doesn't involve either of us at work. So we have our time together that we enjoy very much.

Q: And what is the "our life"—what kind of things do you do together?

A: We take walks, and we like to take short trips on the weekends; go to different restaurants and walk in the little towns, and take pictures... and sometimes we cook together and we're in the kitchen together and that's kind of fun, and then eat together and talk about what happened in our day and this or that. ...

Q: You mentioned that you travel with your husband sometimes.

A: Yes, sometimes we do just small things like we go to Lincoln City there is an amazing restaurant there called Wildflower, very good restaurant.

Q: So, when you go on those trips do you go to places like museums or historical monuments?

A: Oh yeah, we like to do that a lot.

Q: That's great... What is that you like most about that experience?

A: Well, it's a learning activity because usually if you go to a museum it's something that you will want to know. So you learn about what is in there, history, different information, and it's a learning process. I am very curious, I like to know why things are like they are.

Q: So, that's why you go?

A: Yeah, [because I'm a curious person].

This excerpt is from an interview with Maria, a 65-70-year-old Mexican-American woman. Maria and her husband Ron are well-educated but live on a relatively modest income, and clearly, Maria appears to live a very full and satisfying life. She is active in a wide range of volunteer as well as paid activities in her small town. She tutors Hispanic school children in her home in the afternoons, she works for a breast cancer awareness clinic, and she helps other recent Latino/a immigrants, particularly those with low income, navigate their way through the health care system. Maria also spends time with her husband, cooks, gardens, walks, and visits museums. As this excerpt reveals, like so many others living in the twenty-first century, Maria is a very busy person and when describing the things she likes to do, she doesn't readily distinguish between the work-related aspects of her life and those that are purely leisure-related. Mixed together are activities that are "relaxing" like growing flowers with those that are "active" like walking, and those that are consumption-oriented like going out to dinner and those that are learning-related like going to museums. In contrast with life in the twentieth century, where the boundaries between work and leisure were firmly drawn, in the Knowledge Age of the early twenty-first century, work, consumption, learning and leisure are all tightly interwoven.[2] All of this has major implications for our understanding of the museum visitor experience. In order to fully understand why people choose to visit museums, we need to see museum-going first and foremost as a leisure experience. Thus, to understand museum-going as a leisure experience we need to understand more about the broader leisure landscape of the twenty-first century. Once we have that perspective, we can specifically situate museum-going within that context.

LEISURE IN THE TWENTY-FIRST CENTURY

The public has always strived to devote some part of their life to leisure pursuits, but as the world of work has become centered around mental rather than physical labor, more of the public's leisure time is filled with experiences designed to support a range of mental diversions rather than just physical relaxation. Throughout most of the twentieth century, the public primarily used leisure as a mechanism for escaping from the physical and sometimes, mental exhaustion of work. Classic responses were the escapism fostered by Disney and other theme parks or a week spent on vacation "doing nothing." Although these leisure diversions are still popular, their market share is declining. Their main competition in the early years of the twenty-first century has been an entirely different form of leisure experience which includes adventure tourism such as whitewater rafting or mountain climbing and more intellectual pursuits such as visits to historic and natural settings and museums. In the twenty-first century, larger numbers of people view leisure as an opportunity to expand their understanding of themselves and their world.[3] Rather than relaxing under a palm tree at the beach, people consider their leisure time as an opportunity to be energized by immersing themselves in new ideas, spaces, and experiences.

The dominance of the former model is clearly waning as revealed by a recent Canadian Tourism Council's investigation of American leisure time activities.[4] In this study, Americans said that they were seeking beaches (54%), culture (51%), followed by adventures (41%) on a vacation. Furthermore, 40% of American leisure travelers stated that they travel with the purpose of visiting and educating themselves about their destination's unique attractions. The survey also revealed the growing trend of women traveling alone, more than half (52%) of whom said they were traveling in order to experience other cultures by visiting ruins and museums. These statistics would certainly suggest that a large percentage of Americans, and by extension others within the developed world and among the growing middle classes of the developing world, see culture, learning, and self-fulfillment as major leisure goals. Although there have always been individuals who held such values, the fact that so many people now hold these values is historically unprecedented.[5]

One consequence of these major shifts in both the quantity and quality of leisure expectations has been an explosion in the number of leisure options available to the public. There are more places, ways, and opportunities for leisure than ever before and they all compete for a portion of an individual's limited leisure time. As exemplified by Maria, the typical individual finds his or her leisure time divided between a myriad of activities, most of which need to be "shoe-horned" into busy lives and schedules. Whereas Americans, for example, used to regularly set aside one to two weeks every year for a vacation, now most take vacations in the form of three-or four-day getaways as people feel crunched for time.[6] However, now as before, all leisure decision-making is increasingly a series of value-related cost-benefit decisions in which time plays a crucial role. Whether it's a short trip to visit the downtown mall or a museum, or a long trip as part of a tourist-type experience that might include many activities, including museum-going, people are "calculating" the value of the experience—how will an investment of time in this activity maximally benefit me and my loved ones?

Assigning Leisure Value

One of the consequences of the major economic, social, and political transitions in the twenty-first century has been that more people than ever before in places like Western Europe, Japan, North America, and Australia now enjoy unprecedented levels of affluence, health care, and public safety. The result has been that increasing numbers of people have been liberated from the privations of earlier centuries. Using psychologist Abraham Maslow's hierarchy of needs as a model, most people in the developed world are no longer struggling to achieve the basic physiological and safety needs that occupy the bottom of the needs pyramid.[7] They are now able to focus on achieving "higher levels" of need—love and security, self-esteem, and self-fulfillment, the latter of which is the pinnacle of Maslow's hierarchy. In the twentieth century, a person's struggle to move up Maslow's hierarchy was primarily enacted through work; today these strivings are primarily enacted through leisure.[8] Although millions of people in the developing world still struggle at the bottom of the pyramid, ever-growing middle classes now exist throughout Asia, Eastern Europe, and Latin America. These are the regions of the world that have seen the greatest growth in the creation of museums and other comparable "value-added" leisure options.

What is it that would make a leisure product or service rise above the crowded field? Rather than selecting products merely on their utility, today's consumers make decisions on a product's ability to satisfy personal desires and lifestyles. So complete has been this transformation that today a majority of the world's affluent consumers have largely exhausted the things they *need* to purchase; instead, they now focus on what they *want* to purchase.[9] We engage in leisure experiences that promise to make us happier, better partners or parents, or more knowledgeable and competent individuals. We seek experiences that nourish and rejuvenate the spirit and generally make us feel more fulfilled. But because time is increasingly the single limiting determinant of our leisure, we engage in a blending of goals and activities through a kind of consumptive multitasking.[10] Thus, more and more of our shopping, eating, and vacationing experiences are being packaged in ways that enable us to bundle leisure together with "cultural and intellectual enrichment"—a search for the authentic and the self-fulfilling.[11] We have begun to flee the mega-malls in favor of historic areas with ample shopping opportunities such as Annapolis, Maryland, the Provence area of France, and the wine regions of Napa Valley that allow us to experience a greater sense of place. We find ourselves attracted to ethnic restaurants, especially those with a high degree of realism that "talk" to us through their menus of their cultural traditions, or offer cooking classes so as to keep their cooking traditions alive. Even the historically hedonistic cruise industry now provides evening lectures by experts and guided tours of cultural sites at each of their port-of-calls. Twenty-first century leisure has increasingly become about building and supporting identity-related needs.

Leisure and Identity

Theoretically, it would make sense that leisure time activities which inherently involve a large measure of choice and control should be particularly amenable to identity-building. Leisure researcher John Kelly made this point when he asserted that leisure is particularly potent in the self-affirmation process since it is a self-defined, intrinsically motivated activity.[12] The perception of choice and control appears to be fundamental to a heightened sense of self-actualization, which in turn sustains the integrity of personal identity.[13] In essence, we affirm who we are through the active selection and participation in leisure activities. Perhaps the clearest expression of these ideas was made by two leisure researchers, Lois Haggard and Dan Williams, who stated, "Through leisure activities we are able to construct situations that provide us with the information that we are who we believe ourselves to be, and provide others with information that will allow them to understand us more accurately."[14] In a recent *Wall Street Journal* interview, leisure researcher Geof Godbey wrote that

> leisure should resemble the best aspects of work: challenges, skills and important relationships. Leisure has its hierarchy. At the lowest level, it's a search for diversion, higher up it's a search for pleasure and, at the top it's a search for meaning. It's not that diversion is bad, but in terms of human growth, it's inferior to activities that are more pleasurable—and they're inferior to activities that are more meaningful.[15]

As the twenty-first century progresses, the focus of most of the affluent citizens of the world has continued to inexorably shift from the workplace to leisure, from striving for survival to searching for personal fulfillment and satisfaction. Leisure in the Knowledge Age has become ever more centered upon a quest for something larger and something more personally fulfilling. The quest for identity, enacted through leisure, is and will continue to be a dominant theme of this new century. Each individual is seeking to build his or her personal and group identities, using his or her ever-expanding, but ever more precious leisure time for accomplishing this. In some cases the leisure pursuit of identity is overt, as when visiting an ashram or attending an evening Bible group. More often, though, the leisure-time pursuit of identity is more mundane, embedded in such activities as the weekly visit to the gym to keep in good physical shape or the bi-annual visit to the museum in order to stay on top of what's happening in the world of art or science. And befitting a Knowledge Age, more and more of our identity-laden leisure activities come with some kind of learning overlay. At the gym we are constantly trying to learn what new equipment, exercises, or routines will best maintain our physical health while at the museum we strive to learn about what new trends in art, history, or science will influence our lives in the years to come.

Anthropologist Nelson Graburn anticipated these changes more than a quarter century ago when he stated that "leisure is displacing work from the center of modern social arrangements."[16] Graburn foresaw a society in which leisure-oriented activities, particularly those focused on personal growth and development, would soon become the dominant form of daily activity; we are not quite there yet, but we are getting closer to that reality every day. As we continue to transition into the Knowledge Age, we will find that the most sought-after leisure goods and services will be those with the richest potential for combining a high degree of self-enrichment and self-actualization with a high degree of convenience. I will argue that this brings us full circle back to the central question of this book—how can we understand the museum visitor experience? I believe the only way to really understand the museum visitor experience is to begin with the question of why anyone would visit a museum in the first place. When we look at museum-going through the twenty-first century leisure lens described in this chapter, we can begin to understand why museum-going has become one of the most popular leisure activities in the world. As Nelson Graburn correctly predicted thirty years ago, museums are well-positioned to benefit from the post-industrial societal trend towards more meaningful, learning-oriented leisure.

LEISURE NEEDS AND DECISIONS

As the interview with Maria reveals, like so many others today, she is motivated to visit museums because they satisfy very specific leisure-related needs. In Maria's case, it revolves around her self-perception that she is a curious person and museums represent good places to visit for satisfying curiosity. Leisure researchers became interested in the relationship between leisure and motivation starting in the late 1960s because it promised to help them understand why people engage in leisure behavior.

Leading leisure researcher John Kelly argued that situational factors of association, frequency, location, and scheduling were highly correlated with the kinds of leisure chosen by North American adults. The type of activity was one significant element in the meaning derived from participation. From his mid-1970's perspective, Kelly suggested that cultural activities, especially at home, were most likely to be engaged in for their recuperative values. Sports were considered to have meanings intrinsic to participation; entertainment and community activity were much more motivated by social relations; travel was to be engaged in for its contrast to employment; and family activities were to be motivated by an individual's perceived role, such as what it takes to be a good father or mother.[17] Researchers Jacob Beard and Ragheb Mounir identified six components of perceived motivation/satisfaction of leisure participants:

Psychological–a sense of freedom, enjoyment, involvement, and challenge;

Educational–intellectual challenge and knowledge gains;

Social–rewarding relationships with other people;

Relaxation–relief from strain and stress;

Physiological–fitness, health, weight control, and wellbeing; and

Aesthetic–response to pleasing design and beauty of environments.[18]

One of the most powerful approaches to thinking about the important role that expectations and motivations play in leisure was spearheaded by recreation researchers B.L. Driver and S. Ross Tocher who developed what was known as the "experiential approach."[19] Later extended by Driver and a number of his associates, the experiential approach suggested that a leisure experience should not be viewed merely as an activity such as hiking, fishing, camping, or shopping, but rather "should be conceptualized as a psychophysiological experience that is self-rewarding, occurs during nonobligated free time, and is the result of free-choice."[20] Approaching leisure from this perspective is strikingly different than the typical view which primarily focused on the "what" someone did as opposed to "why." In particular, this view of leisure posited that people pursue engagement in recreation and leisure in order to satisfy inner needs or problems.[21]

In the ensuing years, Driver and his colleagues were able to generate a whole range of motivations that seemed to drive recreational behaviors.

In particular, they defined what they referred to as the myriad "packages" or "bundles" of psychological outcomes people desired from a recreation engagement.[22] In all, they defined 15 major, overarching motivational categories that described why people engage in recreational activities, in particular those in the outdoors. They also developed a range of subcategories within many of these major categories:

ACHIEVEMENT/STIMULATION
    Reinforcing Self-image
    Social Recognition
    Skill Development
    Competence Testing
    Excitement
    Endurance
    Telling Others

AUTONOMY/LEADERSHIP
    Independence
    Autonomy
    Control-Power

RISK TAKING

EQUIPMENT

FAMILY TOGETHERNESS

SIMILAR PEOPLE
    Being with Friends
    Being with Similar People

NEW PEOPLE
    Meeting New People
    Observing Other People

LEARNING
    General Learning
    Exploration
    Geography Study
    Learning More about Nature

ENJOY NATURE
    Scenery
    General Nature Experience

INTROSPECTION
    Spiritual
    Introspection

CREATIVITY

NOSTALGIA

PHYSICAL FITNESS

PHYSICAL REST

ESCAPE PERSONAL-SOCIAL PRESSURES

    Tension Release

    Slow Down Mentally

    Escape Role Overloads

Many of these categories could easily apply to museum-going, but which ones? At the same time, several museum researchers, most independently of each other, attempted to go beyond demographic categorizations of visitors to more thoughtfully determine what motivated people to visit museums, and in some cases, think about the implications on the visitor experience of these motivations. I believe it's worth the time to briefly review some of the key efforts in this regard. As we'll see, all of these studies converge around just a few main reasons that people say motivate them to visit museums—reasons representing a subset of the categories established by Driver et al.

WHY PEOPLE SAY THEY GO TO MUSEUMS: A REVIEW OF THE RESEARCH

Molly Hood

In the 1980s, Molly Hood did a series of ground-breaking investigations of visitor and non-visitor motivations for visiting museums.[23] In line with the research of Beard and Mounir, she argued that there were six major criteria by which individuals judge leisure experiences: 1) being with people, or social interaction; 2) doing something worthwhile; 3) feeling comfortable and at ease in one's surroundings; 4) having a challenge of new experiences; 5) having an opportunity to learn; and 6) participating actively. According to Hood, the selection of leisure time activity normally involves some combination of these six criteria, but normally not all six. In her study of the Toledo Art Museum, Hood identified three distinct populations of visitors: 1) frequent visitors (3 or more visits per year); 2) occasional participants (visiting once or twice per year); and 3) non-participants. Hood found that these three populations had very different leisure criteria profiles.

The frequent art museum visitors both highly valued all six of the leisure attributes and found that museums were places that could provide satisfaction on all six criteria. Of the six attributes, though, three were particularly important to this group—opportunities to learn, challenge of new experiences, and doing something worthwhile during leisure time. Hood found that these particular leisure attributes were less important to non-participants (those who never visited the art museum) while the attributes of being with people, or social interaction, feeling comfortable and at ease in one's surroundings, and participating actively were most important. They perceived that these attributes were usually not present in museums. Finally, occasional participants were much more like non-participants than they were like frequent visitors. They too favored being with people, or social interaction; feeling comfortable and at ease in one's surroundings, and participating actively. Hood concluded that the non-participant and occasional participant groups seemed to equate leisure with "relaxation," rather than the more active, intense, learning-oriented experience favored by regular visitors.

A decade later, as part of a major national research study, I replicated Hood's approach in order to better understand the leisure time use of museums by African Americans.[24] In my study of 728 individuals, which included both African and European Americans and represented the same range of museum usage as Hood's group—from non-users to frequent users—the non-museum goers were not significantly different than those who said they occasionally or regularly visited museums. Meanwhile, my non-user group's most preferred leisure attributes were also different than Hood's; their preferences were: feeling comfortable and at ease in one's surroundings, doing something worthwhile, and being with people. The number one criteria of all my subjects—black and white, frequent visitor, occasional visitor, or non-visitor—was feeling comfortable and at ease in one's surroundings. Not only that, doing something worthwhile emerged as key for all groups—a criteria that only emerged in Hood's frequent visitor group. More than half of all individuals in my sample also valued learning, and nearly all also valued social interactions. Thus, either there were problems with Hood's initial data, my data, or in the span of ten years, leisure patterns in America had changed. My belief, then and now, was that the last explanation was most likely correct.

As outlined at the beginning of this chapter, the last decades of the twentieth century were a period of rapid and profound change in leisure values, including a significant expansion of the value of doing worthwhile, value-added experiences such as free-choice learning. That said, the fundamental assumptions of Hood's research are still valid. People make leisure decisions for one of many personal reasons—reasons that have little to do with their demographics and everything to do with their personal values and interests. As an aside, my research determined that the single largest influence on the relative disparity between white and black museum visitation was historical patterns of leisure behavior. The absence of a childhood museum-going pattern in large percentages of the African American community disproportionately influenced their present museum-going behavior. Of course, latent racism and socio-economic disparities were also part of the reason for current differences in museum-going, but these reasons did not appear to be as important contributors as some had assumed.

Theano Moussouri

For her doctoral dissertation Theano Moussouri investigated the question of why people visit museums.[25] She concluded, based upon a thorough review of the literature, coupled with open-ended interviews with hundreds of visitors to a range of museums in England, that all the various reasons given for visiting museums could be grouped into one of six different general categories. According to Moussouri, these six categories of motivations reflected the functions a museum is perceived to serve in the social/cultural life of visitors. She gave the categories the following generic names: 1) Education; 2) Entertainment; 3) Social event; 4) Lifecycle; 5) Place; and 6) Practical issues.

Education represented a category of reasons related to the aesthetic, informational, or cultural content of the museum and was the most frequently cited motivation for visiting. Most visitors mentioned that they visit museums in order to learn or find out more about something, occasionally something in particular, more often just "stuff" in general. Occasionally, visitors also expressed a desire for an emotional/aesthetic experience. These latter reasons were also grouped under the Education category. Entertainment, the second most frequently cited motivation, referred to a set of leisure-related reasons for visiting a museum. Most visitors mentioned that they go to museums in their free time in order to have fun and enjoy themselves, and/or to see new and interesting things in a relaxing and aesthetically pleasing setting.

Social event was another common reason given for museum-going. Museum-going was widely perceived as a "day out" for the whole family, a special social experience, and a chance for family members or friends to enjoy one another separately and together. A related but separate category was what Moussouri called Life-cycle. Distinct from normal social experience, some people seemed to view museum-going as important marker events, taking place at certain phases in one's life, usually related to childhood (e.g., "I was brought to the museum as a child and now I'm bringing my child to the museum").

Place was that cluster of reasons given by individuals when they categorized museums as leisure/cultural/recreational destinations emblematic of a locale or region. Many people visit museums for this reason, including individuals on holiday or day trips or those who have out-of-town guests. Finally, the Practical side of a museum visit also factored into some people's motivations for visiting. Practical factors such as weather, proximity to the museum, time availability, crowd conditions, and the entrance fee contributed to some visitors' decision-making process.

In follow-up research, Moussouri, statistician Doug Coulson, and I found that the public not only usually had combinations of these motivations, but that the nature of these motivations directly correlated with their subsequent experiences and learning.[26] For example, individuals who had a dominant Education motivation for visiting the museum learned different things than did those individuals who had a dominant Entertainment visit motivation, though both groups learned. These data reinforced the observation of psychologist Scott Paris that motivation and learning within the museum are not only connected, but that in order to understand visitor's museum motivations and learning, one needs to view both of these constructs in their broadest sense.[27] It also led Moussouri, Coulson, and me to conclude that Education and Entertainment were not two ends of a single continuum, but totally independent dimensions. The fact was that, almost without exception, visitors shared *both* a desire to learn and to have fun— though for some learning was more important than fun and for others fun more important than learning. Depending upon that relationship, different uses of time and different learning resulted.

Zahava Doering and Andrew Pekarik

In the late 1990s, Zahava Doering, Andrew Pekarik, and their colleagues at the Smithsonian Institution became very interested in understanding what motivated people to visit the various Smithsonian museums. They developed an empirical list of experiences that they believed captured the things that museum visitors generally found satisfying about their museum experiences.[28] Doering and her colleagues separated visitor experiences into four distinct categories—object experiences–focusing on something outside the visitor, for example, seeing the "real thing" or seeing rare or valuable things; cognitive experiences–focusing on the interpretive or intellectual aspects of the experience; introspective experiences–focusing on private feelings and experiences, such as imagining, reflecting, reminiscing, and connecting; and social experiences–focusing on interactions with friends, family, other visitors, or museum staff.

Their investigations suggested that different types of museums, and different exhibitions within museums, appeared to elicit these experiences to varying extents. In fact, Doering and Pekarik went so far as to suggest that visitors don't enter museums as "blank slates," but bring with them well-formed interests, knowledge, opinions, and museum-going experiences. In particular, Doering and Pekarik suggested that visitors enter with a desire to experience one of these four types of visitor outcomes. They referred to these as the visitor's "entry narratives." If we start with the idea that learning, broadly defined, is a major outcome of museum experiences, then it follows that different learning outcomes are likely to be directly attributable to different entry narratives. In addition, visitors' entering narratives will be self-reinforcing. Entry narratives will direct learning and behavior because visitors' perceptions of satisfaction will be directly related to experiences that resonate with their entering narrative. This idea paralleled the results of Moussouri, Coulson, and myself that visitors' entering motivations influenced their learning outcomes.

Jan Packer and Roy Ballantyne

Jan Packer, in her dissertation research, also investigated the relationship between museum visitor motivation and learning. The resulting paper that she wrote with her major professor Roy Ballantyne reports on a subset of her data, in particular 300 visitors, 100 each at an Australian museum, art gallery, and aquarium.[29] These researchers asked the visitors to rate the outcomes they hoped to derive from their visit. A factor analysis of the resulting responses revealed five categories of visit motivations: 1) Learning and discovery; 2) Passive enjoyment; 3) Restoration; 4) Social interaction; and 5) Self-fulfillment. Packer and Ballantyne described Learning and discovery as the desire to discover new things, expand knowledge, be better informed, and experience something new or unusual. As found by Moussouri in her initial work, this was the most common category. Also closely mirroring Moussouri's data, the second most common category was Passive enjoyment–the desire to enjoy oneself, to be pleasantly occupied, and to feel happy and satisfied. Restoration–the desire to relax mentally and physically, to have a change from routine and recover from stress and tension, was also a very important motivation for some visitors in Packer and Ballantyne's sample. Social interaction–the desire to spend time with friends or family, interact with others and build relationships, also emerged as a category, as it has for all who have investigated museum-going. And finally, Packer and Ballantyne identified a category of motivation they called Self-fulfillment–the desire to make things more meaningful, challenge abilities, feel a sense of achievement, and develop self-knowledge and self-worth. As predicted by Doering and Pekarik and identified by Moussouri, Coulson and myself, Packer and Ballantyne were able to document that visitors' entry motivations correlated with differing learning behaviors in the museum.

Morris Hargreaves McIntyre

A wide range of museums have attempted to segment their visitors in recent years for marketing purposes with an increasing number using motivational rather than demographic categories. Some notable examples include the Shed Aquarium, Chicago and the Canadian Museum of Civilization, Ottawa. However, one of the most comprehensive recent efforts was that conducted by the English consulting firm of Morris Hargreaves McIntyre for the Tate Britain and Tate Modern, both in London.[30] The goals of this study were to analyze the ways visitors construct their experience at the Tate and to understand the motivations, attitudes, perceptions, and reactions of visitors in relation to the Tate.

The research involved over 850 visitors to the two institutions, including questionnaires, observations, and focus groups. The researchers concluded that visitors to the Tate were not a homogeneous group and that visitors' motivations, prior experiences, knowledge and interests, and social arrangements all affected the nature of the museum visit. They ended up segmenting the two Tate museum visitor groups into eight categories, what they called: 1) Aficionados; 2) Actualizers; 3) Sensualists; 4) Researchers; 5) Self-improvers; 6) Social spacers; 7) Site Seers; and 8) Families.

According to Morris Hargreaves McIntyre, Aficionados are visual arts professionals looking for inspiration and escapism. Actualizers by contrast are non-visual arts professionals, seeking inspiration or soul-food from their art visit. Sensualists are also non-visual arts professionals; they are described as "culture vultures," seeking an uplifting and moving sensory experience. Researchers are, like Aficionados, visual arts professionals on research and development visits. Self-improvers are people wanting to develop their knowledge of the visual arts and generally, just wanting to engage in an intellectual adventure. Social spacers are visiting the museum in order to meet with others and generally, their goal is to have a good social experience. Site Seers are mainly tourists whose goal is "to do" the Tate. And finally, they created a separate category for Families which they described as groups with a mixture of ages who want a fun and educational trip for their children. Each of these eight groups had their own unique needs and visiting patterns and were characterized by Morris Hargreaves McIntyre as representing different percentages of the Tate and Tate Modern's audience.

James Bigley, Daniel Fesenmaier, Mark Lane, and Wesley Roehl

Finally, in a little noticed but interesting study, researchers Bigley, Fesenmaier, Lane, and Roehl conducted a study in the late 1980s that examined the motivations for membership and financial donations of the individuals associated with several San Antonio, Texas museums.[31] The study included "members" of a history and natural history museum, an art museum, and a collections-oriented science museum focused on transportation history and technology. Although focused on what we would consider frequent visitors rather than the general public, the fact that they based their research on the hierarchy of needs theory of Abraham Maslow and the recreational motivation theories of B.L. Driver makes their results worth noting.

Using these two theories, the researchers derived a set of seven categories that they called "motivational sub-dimensions" which they believed helped explain the motivations of museum members. These seven categories and some of their attributes were: Family belonging–family togetherness; Cognitive–education, curiosity of experience, aesthetics; Prosocial–community welfare, obligation, preservation; Altruism–empathic concern; Intimate group belonging–group togetherness, need to belong; Self-esteem–achievement, reinforcing self-image; and Esteem of others–status, attention, peer group, power. They created a 12-page instrument designed to measure the prevalence of each of these motivations among the 6800 members of the three museums. In all, 481 members responded to their survey. Their data analysis revealed that at least some of the members possessed all of these motivations; most quite strongly identified with some but not others. Members seemed to cluster into two broad, but non-overlapping groups—those who were primarily motivated by a desire for family belonging and cognitive interests and those motivated primarily by cognitive, prosocial, and altruistic concerns. In other words, there were those who were primarily focused on the education and learning of their family and those who were primarily concerned with promoting their own curiosity and learning, though this latter group possessed a desire to also help others within the broader community have these benefits.

What this particular study revealed, which I think has often been missed in other studies, is that cognitive interests were always a part of the equation. Rather than seeing the issue as education vs. entertainment, the data from Bigley et al shows that the education component was never really absent (at least among the museum's most frequent visitors), although clearly the learning benefit of the museum was more pronounced in some visitors than in others. I think this is a vitally important fact that requires some emphasis, and of course, explanation. I will attempt to explain this through a metaphor. If you interviewed 100 people as they entered a restaurant and asked them why they have chosen to visit that particular restaurant on that day, what would they tell you? Predictably, their answers would cover topics such as the quality and friendliness of the service staff, the price of the food items, the atmosphere and ambiance, how convenient the restaurant is to their home, and the ease of parking. What they almost certainly would not say is that they chose this restaurant "because I was hungry." That's because it is assumed that the reason you go to eat out at a restaurant is to satiate your hunger, hence why mention it? Similarly, visitors to museums frequently neglect to mention that the reason they are visiting is because they hope to learn something. Why mention something that is so obvious? Unfortunately, many museum researchers have missed the obvious, mistaking a lack of statement of the fact as evidence that the fact doesn't exist.

Learning is the large, white elephant standing in the middle of the room! All visitors to museums realize that these are educational settings; they are not confusing museums with theme parks. Some come to learn explicitly, some come to learn implicitly, but all come to learn! Although clearly museums support many leisure benefits, free-choice learning emerges as a major anticipated outcome of virtually all visitors' museum experience.[32] So important is this particular outcome that it warrants a more in-depth discussion than the other possible visitor motivations.

MUSEUMS AND FREE-CHOICE LEARNING

Over the past twenty-five years, museums have emerged as the "poster children" of the Knowledge Age leisure landscape; everyone wants to be like museums. I have argued, and continue to argue that the main reason museums are riding the crest of the current leisure wave is because the public perceives them as optimum settings for free-choice learning. Museums are where the worlds of leisure and learning intersect. Ironically, although learning-oriented activities represent a major and growing part of the leisure landscape, little research on leisure learning has been conducted. Why do people engage in free-choice learning in their leisure time? It's fine to assert that people go to museums in order to learn, but what are they learning? Are people driven to go to places like museums so they can learn the same kinds of things in the same ways that people do in schools? What we do know, based upon extensive public leisure research conducted in Canada, is that most adults engage in leisure time free-choice learning primarily for reasons that lie outside of the goals of most formal education programs.[33] They engage in free-choice learning for reasons other than the school-based goal of mastering a discipline or being able to demonstrate to others a command over a body of facts and concepts. In the world of leisure, the motivations for leisure learning appear to be far more personal.

According to tourism researcher Jan Packer, most people visit museums, parks, and other similar venues in order to "experience learning" or what she calls "learning for fun."[34] According to Packer, visitors engage in a wide range of leisure-learning-related experiences because they value and enjoy the process of learning itself rather than to learn something specific. It's the process, not the end-product, that is important to these visitors. Five propositions about the nature of learning in museum-like settings emerged from Packer's research. These were:

1. Learning for fun encompasses a mixture of discovery, exploration, mental stimulation, and excitement.

2. The majority of people consider learning to be, more than anything else, enjoyable.

3. Although most visitors don't visit with a deliberate intention to learn, they do seek or are unconsciously drawn into an experience that incorporates learning.

4. Visitors identify four conditions that together are conducive to the learning for fun experience.
   a. A sense of discovery or fascination.
   b. Appeal to multiple senses.
   c. The appearance of effortlessness.
   d. The availability of choice.

5. Visitors value learning for fun because it is a potentially transformative experience.

All of these propositions have resonance with the ideas presented so far in this chapter. They also closely mirror how Maria, the 65-70-year-old Latina whose interview appears at the beginning of this chapter, views museum-going. For Maria, like many museum visitors, going to the museum is an effortless, multi-sensory, and enjoyable learning experience. The goal is not so much to learn anything in particular, but to fuel the process of discovery and fascination. Packer's research shows that for an increasingly large number of people such as Maria, learning and leisure are becoming one and the same experience. Museums have become settings that a large percentage of the public have come to see as a place where many leisure goals can be simultaneously satisfied. They are places that support five of Beard and Mounir's six leisure satisfactions: Psychological, Educational, Social, Relaxation, and Aesthetic.[35] But the tie that binds all of these leisure satisfactions together is the unique qualities of free-choice learning.

I believe that additional clarity about why the free-choice learning that occurs in the museum context is so fundamentally different from the typical school or workplace compulsory learning can be provided by building off the ideas of British business education researcher Len Holmes. Holmes theorized that there is an inverse relationship between learning for performance and learning for identity-building.[36] Learning for performance is typical in settings like school and the workplace, but it also occurs in a number of free-choice learning contexts such as sports and the arts, as well as in traditional cultural practices such as weaving and hunting. However, learning can also be motivated for purely intrinsic reasons that have little to do with performance and everything to do with the process of identity-related self-satisfaction. In particular, these ideas would suggest that in learning situations where a high degree of expectation and outside judging exists—such as is typical of the learning worlds of schooling and the workplace—there would be an increased demand for learning outcomes to be demonstrated. In these situations learning for skills and fluency will be prevalent and identity-driven learning will be depressed. By contrast, in learning situations where judging is minimal and intrinsic motivations predominate—such as is typical of the free-choice learning that occurs in museums—learning should primarily be identity-driven. Data from an investigation of the long-term meaning-making of museum visitors collected by my colleague Martin Storksdieck and me appeared to support Holmes' framework, though there were some exceptions.[37] We found that most museum visitors' free-choice learning experiences were driven by internally-defined identity-related goals and not by externally-defined performance goals.

LEARNING AS IDENTITY-WORK

Museum expert Jay Rounds has pointed out that most people who have looked at the relationship between museums and learning typically bemoan the fact that most visitors seem to learn so little—in fact, most museum learning researchers have consistently focused on how museums can try to engineer the setting to rectify this situation.[38] As Rounds writes, these experts "seem to proceed on an implicit assumption that more learning is always better . . . [ideally] visitors [should] learn more 'deeply,' more 'comprehensively,' more 'systematically.'" Rounds wisely points out that unlike the experts, museum visitors are not terribly troubled by the limited extent of their learning. In fact, visitors seem quite content to only learn a few things, and even those things often in quite superficial ways. Following up on these observations, Rounds has speculated that a major reason why people go to museums is not for learning as such, though clearly learning is important, but to build identity in order to engage in what Rounds calls "identity work."

Based on these ideas, Rounds speculates that not all of the content a museum offers will be of equal value for any given individual's identity work. According to Rounds, the visitor must search for the potentially valuable experiences, and avoid wasting time on the others. He or she will rarely be served well by attending to, and affiliating with, all of the contents of the exhibition. Visitors do use museums in order to support their lifelong, free-choice learning, but the purpose of that learning is not to gain competence in a subject as in a school or work-based context. Museum visitors are using learning as a vehicle for building personal identity.

This is not as strange a concept as it might first seem to be. A number of leading theoreticians of learning have talked about the fact that learning and identity are actually two sides of the same coin. For example, the Russian learning theorist Lev Vygotsky, who has achieved considerable attention of late from psychologists and educators, viewed intellectual development and growth as the foundation of what it means to become a person.[39] Vygotsky's approach to learning went beyond traditional cognitive definitions and was intimately linked to the fuller range of learning activities we might see an individual engage in within the museum context. In the interview at the beginning of this chapter, when Maria is asked later to talk about a recent museum visit, she described it as follows:

Q: And when you are there in the museum, what kinds of things do you do?

A: I read everything [laughs]. I like to go [to the Marine Science Center] because there are still things that I don't know so when I walk through [there] sometimes I see a lot of new things even if there are the same displays, they change the displays quite often! For instance, you know they had the little fish, the colored fish—they're gone, where did they go, why did they take them away? So, I learned that now they will have something different there, so it's kind of interesting. I like to go there, it's like my treat. OK, I'm going, before I go home I have to go there. I do not do it very often but I do walk through there every couple of weeks.

Maria seemed to suggest in this excerpt that she was as content to learn about why exhibitions are changed as she was by reading labels; she was as interested in the workings of the museum as an institution as she was in what the staff wanted to inform her about fish. Although Vygotsky was not specifically concerned with identity—he never used the term in his writing—interpreters of his work such as anthropologist and Vygotsky translator James Wertsch believe that his view of learning was consistent with the idea that people would use the museum to help them become who they are not yet, in other words, to forge their identity.[40]

Taking these ideas even further, psychologists Jean Lave and Etienne Wenger, who built upon Vygotsky's ideas and helped to pioneer the socio-cultural approach to learning, state that "learning and sense of identity are inseparable: They are aspects of the same phenomenon."[41] Wenger went on to define identity "as what we know, what is foreign and what we choose to know, as well as how we know it."[42] Wenger describes identity as engagement in the world; the lens through which we determine what to think about as well as with whom to interact in a knowledge-sharing activity. So like Vygotsky, Lave and Wenger's view of learning places identity formation at the center of the process. This may or may not, as suggested by Holmes, be true for the learning that takes place in school or the workplace, but it seems highly likely that identity formation is central to learning during a leisure-time museum visit, an idea that was a least somewhat supported by museum researcher Kristin Ellenbogen's investigations of family use of museums.[43] Ellenbogen concluded that a large part of what families did in museums was build identity; particularly family identity.

However, if we take this idea of learning as identity work seriously, it raises other problems. Nearly all theory about learning, as well as efforts to measure learning, has been based upon fairly narrow notions. Most learning research is still predicated on conceptualizations of learning that make sense within academic contexts—learning is about the mastery of facts and concepts in order to orally, or in writing describe and defend an idea or proposition. However, it appears likely that within the world of free-choice learning, learning is typically, if not primarily, for personal rather than public reasons and often strongly motivated by the needs of identity formation and reinforcement. In this context, learning tends to take the form of confirmation of existing understandings, attitudes, and skills in order to allow the individual to be able to say, "Okay, I now know that I know/believe that." The goal is not "mastery" in the traditional sense, but rather to provide the individual with a feeling of personal competence. We currently are not well-equipped to measure and assess this kind of learning. If museum-going is about free-choice learning, and free-choice learning in museums is about identity formation and maintenance, we need to understand what these processes/products actually "look like" within the specific context of a museum visit.

For many, but not all visitors, as evidenced by the interview with Maria, this identity-related learning is at the core of the value the museum has for the visitor. Over the course of the interview Maria made it clear that her goal for visiting a museum is to attain personal satisfaction, to explore freely, and as suggested by Rounds, selectively graze in the rich intellectual "field" afforded by the museum. Maria's motivations for visiting are curiosity-driven—a curiosity that stems from a deep sense of self. She defines herself as a curious person and uses the museum as a vehicle for satisfying, as well as reinforcing that identity. In fact, it really doesn't matter what museum. As was revealed in later parts of her interview, Maria will go to just about any museum: art, science, history, with or without others, and she'll take whatever is available. (The Science Center just happens to be most readily available to her, and it is also a free museum.) The subject matter content of the museum is thus not the issue; rather it is her desire to go some place that helps her build her curiosity identity. Maria is typical of a large number of museum visitors whose primary reasons for visiting museums revolve around the desire to *explore* new and interesting places and thus, enrich their understanding of the world. *Exploring* is a key identity-related visitor motivation. If you remember the description of Elmira in the previous chapter, her behavior while visiting the National Aquarium in Baltimore was also characteristic of someone who is an exploring visitor. This is not an accident. The visitor experience of explorers, like all museum visitors I would assert, begins with a desire to fulfill some inner identity-related need. These identity-related needs, more than demographics or social group or even museum content, largely drive the nature of the visit.

IDENTITY-RELATED VISIT MOTIVATIONS

While reviewing all of the research summarized above, several important things become apparent:

1. There are some clear patterns emerging related to museum visitor motivations, but little consensus as to how those patterns should be described and categorized.

2. Most visitors to museums are aware of the museum's benefits prior to visiting and enter with expectations related to these perceived benefits.

3. Visitors' entering motivations, their museum behaviors, and their exiting learning and memories are not separate aspects of the visitor experience but rather highly correlated—a single, inextricable whole.

Mindful of these commonalities, I decided to thoroughly analyze data my colleague Martin Storksdieck and I collected from approximately 200 visitors to the California Science Center as part of a series of major National Science Foundation-funded studies. In addition to data we had on the reasons each visitor gave for their visit to the Science Center, we also had data on what they did during their visit to one of the two permanent exhibitions, data on an entire series of responses to an extensive post-visit interview, and for 25% of these visitors, extensive interview data collected approximately two years after the initial visit. In sum, we had a very rich data set with which to try and make sense of the relationships between why people came to the Science Center, what they did there, and what and how they ultimately made meaning from the experience.[44]

As was the case for all who have taken the trouble to ask people why they are visiting, we had many answers, including virtually all the responses my colleagues before me had heard. We commonly heard "It's a great place for kids," "I've heard it's really fun," "I'm interested in science and thought I'd drop by to see what's here," and "I was in the park and thought I'd check it out." Less commonly-heard answers included "I'm a science teacher and I'm always looking for neat new ideas" and "I find places like this really cool, it helps me get my head straight." However, my goal was not to just sort (whether physically or by computer algorithm) these answers into convenient categories, but to organize them in a way that holistically considered the museum visitor experience. Rather than just accepting on face value the reason someone gave for their visit such as, "It was a nice day so I decided to visit the Science Center," I wanted to delve more deeply. What was this person's real motivation for visiting? What evidence could I glean about those motivations from looking at how they behaved and what they said they remembered from their visit? In other words, was it really a nice day that prompted them to visit the Science Center? Alternatively, if it was such a nice day, why not visit the beach or hang out in the nearby park? If a nice day was truly their motivation for visiting, was there any indication that they used this reason to direct how they used and thought about the Science Center that was different from someone who wasn't worried about the weather? My hypothesis was that there needed to be more lurking below the surface. I wanted to determine if visitors' motivations could be related to each person's deeply-felt identity-related needs—needs which they perceived that a visit to the Science Center would support.

After reviewing my interviews of the California Science Center visitors, as well as considering previous research studies, I concluded that the myriad ways visitors described their expectations and motivations for a museum visit tended to cluster into five basic identity-related categories of leisure benefits that they perceived were supported by the Science Center. The Science Center was

1. an intellectually challenging place that had the potential for satisfying personal curiosity and interest in science and technology;
2. an educational place where one's family (particularly children) and/or friends could both enjoy themselves and learn new things;
3. an important new attraction in the Los Angeles area that anyone who wanted to experience that which is exemplary, and most important in science and technology should visit;
4. a place where one could go to further specific intellectual needs, particularly in the areas of science, technology, and education;
5. a place where one could escape much of the everyday "rat race" and be intellectually and spiritually recharged and rejuvenated.

The Science Center, and as I've subsequently determined other museum-like settings as well, was visited because it was perceived by visitors as affording opportunities to fulfill

1. the need to satisfy personal curiosity and interest in an intellectually challenging environment;

2. the wish to engage in a meaningful social experience with someone whom you care about in an educationally supportive environment;

3. the aspiration to be exposed to the things and ideas that exemplify what is best and intellectually most important within a culture or community;

4. the desire to further specific intellectual needs in a setting with a specific subject matter focus; and/or

5. the yearning to physically, emotionally, and intellectually recharge in a beautiful and refreshing environment.

Museums are settings that allow visitors to play the role of one or more of the following: 1) Explorer; 2) Facilitator; 3) Experience seeker; 4) Professional/Hobbyist; and 5) Recharger.[45] These five categories are not exactly identical to the categorizations described by the other researchers as summarized earlier in this chapter. In creating these five categories, I have tried to combine the attributes of the visitor leisure-related motivations discovered by myself and others into a new, and what I believe to be a more conceptually-consistent set of identity-related categories. For example, it is my opinion that the motivation of learning/education is so intrinsic to museums that they are more or less embedded within each of my five categories. For those visitors who seek to explore or satisfy their professional or hobby interests, learning is probably very important. While for others, such as those who wish to sample the environment or recharge their batteries, learning is more of a leitmotif. Either way, learning is still a major reason why these particular settings are chosen by the visitor.

It is likely that none of these categories are totally "pure" in the sense that many museum visitors perceive museums to afford most, if not all, of these attributes. Hence, their visit motivations combine some mix of all these reasons; for example, the museum is not only a good place to explore, it's also is a great place for socializing and for recharging one's life "batteries." That said, it appears that on any given day, most visitors tend to walk through the door of a museum with one or another of these leisure identity-related motivations predominating. My data suggested to me, and my continuing research only reconfirms this initial observation, that each of the five major categories represents a fundamental, separate view by many visitors of what needs the museum best supports on any particular day. And, as I will describe in more detail in the next chapter, this categorization has now been validated by research across a wide range of museums.

What makes this typology important is not that I've chosen to analyze visitors' motivations and needs differently than other researchers based upon my own ad-hoc analysis of the data. This is not just another marketing segmentation study, with clever new labels for visitor groupings. Rather, I believe that my framework is based on a sound combination of theory and data which accurately represents the deeply-held, identity-related perceptions and beliefs of the public for why it is valuable to visit a museum. Consequently, these categories reflect the reasons people have for visiting museums, and they also reflect the basic leisure attributes the public perceives that museums best afford. They provide a glimpse into this hybrid thing I have called the *museum visitor experience*. These categories are not a complete description of museums, since all museums are more multifaceted and capable of supporting more than these five categories of behaviors and benefits. And they are certainly not fully descriptive of every visitor, as each is clearly more complex and capable of enacting more than just these five roles. But what this simplified model does successfully describe is that unique place where, at this moment in history, most visitors and most museums come together.

Thus, visitors enter the museum expecting to satisfy one of these leisure identity-related needs; they proceed to use the museum as a setting for enacting these needs; they exit, and weeks and months later, the meanings they make of their visit are shaped by these expectations. These five categories of visitor motivations do a remarkably robust job of representing the majority of leisure attributes most people currently ascribe to museum contexts. It appears to accurately capture a critical part of the reality of how people who visit museums use the setting. The result is that most visitors describe a successful museum visit as one that allowed them to enact the identities—the traits, roles, attitudes, and group memberships—associated with one or more of these categories. And perhaps most surprising, this way of organizing museum visits provides a framework for understanding how to make sense of a large percentage of the long-term recollections visitors have of their museum experience. To clarify why this is so requires that we look at each of these five categories more closely from the perspective of the individual visitor rather than the museum.

The Visitor

Identity . . . is not a material thing to be possessed and then displayed; it is a pattern of appropriate conduct, coherent, embellished, and well articulated.

—Erving Goffman, 1959[1]

Frances is a woman in her late 50s of Japanese American descent. She has worked for years as a bookkeeper and office manager for a trucking company. The following is an excerpt of a telephone interview.

Q: Do you remember your last visit to a museum of some kind?

A: Do you consider a botanical garden a museum?

Q: Yes, have you been to a botanical garden recently?

A: Well, I go to the Berkeley Gardens almost every week. I was there just a couple of days ago.

Q: Tell me about your visit. Did you go by yourself?

A: I usually go by myself; I was by myself last Wednesday.

Q: That's very interesting. Why do you go to the garden so frequently by yourself?

A: I guess I just really enjoy being there [chuckles], I don't suppose I'd go so often if I didn't.

Q: I'm sorry, of course, you enjoy yourself! Let me rephrase my question. People go to museum-like places for a wide range of reasons. Sometimes it's for social reasons, sometimes it's to find out more about a particular topic, and for others it is just the joy of being in a nice place. I guess I was trying to better understand what specific things might motivate you to visit a place like the Gardens so frequently.

A: Well, I would have to say it's primarily just because it's such a beautiful place and I find that going there helps me unwind. It's not that my job is so terribly more stressful than anyone else's, but life today, you know, is quite stressful. So I find going to the Garden quite relaxing.

Q: That makes great sense. I'm actually familiar with Berkeley Botanical Gardens; I used to work there many years ago. I'm curious where you go in the Gardens in particular. Do you just wander around or is there a special place you like to go?

A: Well, on different days I do go to different places, depending upon what's in bloom. But my favorite place to go, and where I went on Wednesday, if that's what you want to know, is Rhododendron Dell. It's so beautiful and mystical there. The creek runs through the space and there are these nice little benches tucked away where you can sit amongst the ferns and the rhodis and just decompress.

[Later in the interview]

Q: So, what got you started going to the Gardens? Are you a gardener?

A: Well, sure I'm a gardener, but then who isn't. But that's not what got me going there in the first place. I have a friend, she's moved away from Berkeley now. She told me about the Gardens. She said she always went there to unwind and I went there with her one time. It was free back then, but now I'm a member so it doesn't cost much. Besides it's worth it. Anyway, at that time in my life I was actually having lots of problems and I really needed some help. I found the Gardens to be some help.

Q: I don't mean to pry, but would you be willing to share with me what you mean by problems?

A: Well, I actually had two problems. First, I was going through a pretty unpleasant, in fact, nasty divorce. And then I was having some serious health issues. Probably the two were related. Anyway, I was a mess and I really needed some way to try and get out of the bad place I was in.

Q: And you found that the Gardens helped you do that?

A: Definitely, it was amazingly therapeutic. So therapeutic, that it sort of became like medicine to me. Back then, I was going almost every day. Now, I just go, like I said, about once a week. All I have to do is walk in the front gate and I can feel my blood pressure dropping. The place just has a wonderful effect on me. To be honest, I don't know what I'd do without it. Besides, I consider myself a very spiritual person, and the Gardens is a good place in which to feel that.

[Later in the interview]

Q: Anything specific stand out in your memory from last Wednesday's visit?

A: The whole thing.

Q: Okay, tell me more.

A: Mainly, just a feeling of calm I had. It was a hot day, by Berkeley standards anyway, and it was so cool and tranquil in the [Rhododendron] Dell. I remember listening to the creek gurgling over the rocks, seeing the sunlight falling in little spots through the leaves of the trees and just soaking in the silence. As usual, it was after work. Fortunately, I get off work early because the Gardens closes so early. But since it was the end of the day, there was virtually no one there. I probably wasn't actually there for more than about fifteen or twenty minutes, but it was enough to do the job.

Q: And the job was. . .?

A: To rejuvenate me, making me feel less stressed, more calm. To allow me to connect with my inner spirit.

Q: So, it sounds like your expectations for the visit were met?

A: Absolutely, I came to be refreshed, and I was. That's why I go so often. I'd go more often if I could, but once a week seems to be about all I can manage.

Frances's interview is quite interesting as it reveals many layers of complexity about her, her experience at the museum, and her motivations for visiting. Although it would appear that Frances has some basic knowledge about plants and gardening, visiting the Berkeley Botanical Gardens appears to primarily satisfy other, very personal needs for her, particularly what she referred to as her spiritual side. Her self-perception as spiritual appeared to directly contribute to her motivations for visiting the museum; by extrapolation, she perceived that a museum would be a good place to "enact" this personal attribute. She is a person seeking calm and tranquility; museums, particularly botanical gardens, are places with lots of opportunities to find a quiet place away from the crowds. The additional insight into her sense of self revealed how the Botanical Gardens helped her through a very rough part in her life. As a result, she became very attached to the Gardens, almost in a physical sense, and thus seeks it out on a regular basis. Frances appeared to be motivated by some deeply held needs. Given that she returns frequently to this same institution, we are probably safe in assuming that she finds these experiences quite satisfying.

Frances is an example of the category of visitor who uses museums to enact the role of Rechargers. A surprisingly large number of individuals actively seek out museums and other leisure settings in order to engage in what museum and tourism researchers Jan Packer and Roy Ballantyne have described as "restoration" experiences.[2] These are individuals, who like Frances, seek respite from the everyday stresses and harsh realities of the world. Unlike other visitors, the Recharger's motivation for visiting a museum is primarily *not* framed in terms of the content of exhibitions (as in the example of Maria in the previous chapter), or even in terms of fun and enjoyment. Although these visitors may discover things that they enjoy, the Recharger is seeking what psychologist Steve Kaplan calls "re-creation"[3]—it may be a human-made, magnificent architectural space; a natural, breath-taking view; or just the solitude of a quiet corner.

Frances's description of her Botanical Gardens visit provides a fascinating lens through which to better understand the nature of the museum visitor experience. In these long-term interviews, particularly in those like Frances's where an effort was made to inquire deeply into the visitor's reasons for the visit and the satisfactions derived, what stands out is how profoundly personal and strongly tied to each individual's sense of identity are these museum visits. Also striking is how consistently an individual's post-visit narrative relates to his or her entering narrative. In other words, prior to entering the Gardens, Frances would have talked about how this visit was all about her desire to find peace and quiet as "going there helps me unwind." Days later, this was still not only a salient motivation for her, but also the dominant framework through which she made sense of her experience.

Frances's visitor experience emerges as something deeply rooted in her sense of self. This interview is typical of the stories each of the hundreds of individuals my colleagues and I have interviewed about their museum visitor experiences over the past years. These stories reveal how complex, as well as personal, are each individual's leisure-time museum experiences. As Frances's interview clearly shows, each of these unique stories reveal how the museum was used to support some aspect of each individual's personal identity-related needs and desires.

WHAT IS IDENTITY?

What do I mean when I use the term *identity*? Identity is something all of us intuitively understand at some level; it speaks to how others think about us, the "me," as well as how we think about ourselves, the "I." This distinction was recognized more than two hundred years ago by the philosopher Immanuel Kant,[4] but most clearly explained a hundred years later by pioneering psychologist William James. In 1890, James wrote about the self as being both the known self (me) and the self as knower (I).[5] Even though his definition of identity/self is now more than a hundred years old (and is reflective of the values of his time), it remains one of the most cogent and useful definitions ever created:

> In its widest possible sense, however, a man's Self is the sum total of all that he *can* call his, not only his body and his psychic powers, but his clothes and his house, his wife and children, his ancestors and friends, his reputation and works, his lands and horses, and yacht and bank account. All these things give him the same emotions. If they wax and prosper, he feels triumphant; if they dwindle and die away, he feels cast down.[6]

According to James, what determines the boundary between self and not-self is one's emotional attitude about an object or thought. The things, people, or thoughts with which one identifies, are quite literally part of self, so long as what happens to them is experienced as something happening to one's own self. This capacity to identify experiences as ones' own allows each of us to create a story from personal memories, with ourselves as the leading character; a story that extends both back and forward in time. In the years since James, the constructs of "self" and "identity" have been used by a wide range of social science investigators from a variety of disciplines, each modifying James's original definition. Perhaps not surprisingly, there is no single agreed-upon definition of either *self* or *identity,* though there are a number of useful reviews of these various perspectives.[7] Highlighting the complexities of the topic, psychologists Jerome Bruner and Bernie Kalmar write: "Self is both outer and inner, public and private, innate and acquired, the product of evolution and the offspring of culturally shaped narrative."[8] Perhaps more pointedly, social psychologist Bernd Simon states that

> even if identity turns out to be an 'analytical fiction,' it will prove to be a highly useful analytical fiction in the search for a better understanding of human experiences and behaviors. If used as a shorthand expression or placeholder for social and psychological processes revolving around self-definition or self-interpretation, including the variable but systematic instantiations thereof, the notion of identity will serve the function of a powerful conceptual tool.[9]

It is just the conceptual tool we are seeking as we try to understand the nature of the confluence of museums and visitors.

The deeper one delves into the literature on identity, the more muddled becomes the construct; trying to wrap one's arms around identity in a way that makes it a usable research and conceptual tool is a challenging task. For the purpose at hand, I chose to build upon the work of a number of gifted investigators. Like Uri Bronfenbrenner, Dorothy Holland, William Lachicotte, Jr., Debra Skinner, Carole Cain, and Bernd Simon, I subscribe to the view that identity is the combination of both internal and external social forces—both cultural and individual agencies contribute to identity.[10] Like James Gee, Stuart Hall, Etione Wenger, and Kath Woodward, I appreciate that there are layers of separate identities—individual, social, and societal.[11,12] Like Jerome Bruner, Bernie Kalmar, and Ulrich Neisser, I acknowledge the important evolutionary influence on identity of innate and learned perceptions about the physical environment.[13] Identity derives from both genetic and learned influences.[14] Combining these perspectives, identity emerges as something that is malleable and continually constructed by the individual as need requires. Thus, our identity can be defined as something that is always "situated" in the immediate realities of the physical and socio-cultural world. Our identity is a reflection and reaction to both the social and physical world we consciously perceive in the moment, but identity is also influenced by the vast unconscious set of family, cultural, and personal history influences each of us carries within us. Each is continuously constructing and maintaining, not one, but numerous identities which are expressed collectively or individually at different times, depending upon need and circumstance.[15] From this perspective, identity is emergent, rather than permanent; it is something nimble, ever-changing, and adaptive. This view of identity runs quite parallel to emerging understandings of the brain and learning. As I will discuss more fully in Chapter 6, knowledge and memory are also emergent rather than permanent aspects of mind.[16]

Contrary to what was traditionally thought, humans do not possess just one single, omnibus, permanent identity, but each of us work from a malleable set of ever-changing identities designed to fit particular situations, needs, and opportunities. That's not to say that we don't all possess and act upon a few strongly-wired, deeply-held identities such as our gender, nationality and for many people, religious and racial/ethnic identities. I have called these more deeply-held identities the "big 'I' identities" and they form the majority of what most social scientists have focused on over the years. The social science literature is replete with investigations of these kinds of big 'I' identities, and perhaps not surprisingly, they often are described by the same demographic qualities of individuals discussed at the beginning of this book. Clearly, there are people who possess these types of identities and behaviors and are motivated by such big 'I' identities. However, I would assert that for most people, these identities represent a small part of what drives their everyday thoughts and activities. Most people don't get up in the morning and decide whether or not to brush their teeth based upon their racial/ethnic identity. Most people don't decide whether or not to take a vacation based upon their national or gender identity. And most people don't choose which kind of leisure activity to partake in based upon their religious identity. Although we can certainly imagine situations where nationality, gender, religion, and race/ethnicity could directly influence someone's leisure decisions, including the decision to visit a museum, most people do not view their leisure experiences, including museum-going, through the lens of these types of 'I' identities.

The type of identity that does figure prominently into the myriad everyday decisions in our lives, including leisure, are what I have called "little 'i' identities"—identities that respond to the needs and realities of the specific moment and situation. This kind of identity can be thought of as truly "situated" identities. Although these kinds of identities are often just as important to our sense of self as our big 'I' identities, they have received less attention by social scientists. Little 'i' identities include our sense of being a member of a family and the responsibilities that involves. For example, we may not spend a lot of time thinking of ourselves as a good niece or nephew, but when our calendar, Blackberry, or memory reminds us of our Aunt's birthday, we send her a card, and in the process enact our identity as a "good relative."

As we've already seen in the previous chapters, some of us think of ourselves as curious explorers while others like Frances think of themselves as spiritual. These are not identities we normally have a chance to play out during a typical workday or evening at home, but they are identities we eagerly try to enact during leisure time. I am willing to wager that if one of Frances's colleagues had asked her to select several adjectives that best described how she thought of herself, "spiritual" would probably not have been one of the adjectives chosen. In the context of work, "spiritual" wasn't likely to be an identity that made sense to Frances. However, if one of her friends had asked her the same question, I suspect that "spiritual" may have emerged as one of the ways Frances identified herself. These kinds of little 'i' identities are quite contextual but still important and often as, or even more fundamental to one's sense of self as are big 'I' identities.

What is important to appreciate is that everyone has identity needs that are very important to them but which are only expressed in the appropriate time and context. For example, we all know men and women who are "super dads" and "super moms" who seem to devote every waking moment to their children's needs and desires. But for every super parent, we probably know many more moms and dads who clearly love their children but do not consider their children to be their single highest life priority. "Parent" is an important identity for both kinds of mom and dad, but for the former it is more of a big 'I' identity and for the latter, more of a little 'i' identity. Similarly, we all know men and women whose race/ethnicity is a constant reality and issue in their lives—a part of their daily identity. But we also know others of the same race/ethnicity for whom this identity is of secondary importance at best; it is considered a happenstance of birth, no more. One very public example of this point was made by former tennis star Martina Navratilova when she objected to the press's preoccupation with her sexual preference as a lesbian by stating, "But I am also a daughter, a sister, dog lover, a good skier, interested in art, literature and music, a vegetarian and so on."[17] This is why demographics do such a poor job of segmenting individuals; as stated earlier this form of categorization is both too general and too divorced from specific realities to be predictive. To really understand people and their actions, we need to understand the characteristics and motivations that matter in a particular time, place, and circumstance, otherwise we create stereotypes and cartoon versions of reality. This is the reason identity has appealed to so many social scientists for so long. Identity is a construct that has the potential to be a richly predictive variable since it is so specific and central to how actual people actually live their lives.

IDENTITY AND BEHAVIOR

Of course, I have made a huge leap in all of the above discussions by jumping from the idea that people have different kinds of identities to the idea that those identities influence behaviors. Most readers of this book easily took this leap with me, but in case you didn't, what follows is a brief overview of some of the extensive literature that documents this phenomenon.

The idea that identity in humans represents a causative agent in motivation and behavior begins from the premise that we are self-aware, self-motivating organisms. Whether we are truly unique in this regard in the animal kingdom is an issue of great debate, but few would argue with the fact people normally think of themselves as the originator of their own thoughts and actions. Stated another way, we perceive ourselves as directly controlling and directing what we do.[18] The scholarly term for this is self-regulation, which according to psychologists involves goal setting, cognitive preparations for behaving, and on-going monitoring of behaviors.[19] The setting of goals are fundamental to self-regulation and, again according to psychologists, goals are derived from perceptions of what one could/should be and how one could/should act, or for that matter what one is afraid to be.[20] Another way of talking about this is what social psychologist Albert Bandura calls "self-efficacy." According to Bandura, "self-efficacy is the belief in ones' capabilities to execute the courses of action required to manage prospective situations."[21] Over the course of a nearly 50-year career, Bandura has investigated how sense of self directly impacts people's motivations and behaviors. The bottom line, according to Bandura, is that it does![22]

Starting from the premise that our sense of self influences our actions, it's not a big leap to ask the question—how does this sense of self influence our motivations and behavior? Leaping into this breach, many psychologists have tried to codify how this process works. Identity Theory describes a causal and hierarchical connection between an individual's perception of their relationship to a specific social relationship called commitment, self-perception, identity, and role performance in that social situation which make up their behaviors.[23] This model assumes that social interactions are fundamental to all human life, which seems a reasonable assumption, and that identity is a major, if not primary, vehicle for navigating those social situations. This theory also posits that each individual maintains multiple identities which are reflective of the different roles, positions, and responsibilities he or she encounters in life.

In summary, the theory concludes that identities are assumed to motivate behaviors. The resulting behaviors provide feedback which then can reaffirm that the individual is the kind of person defined by those identities. In particular, the theory postulates that the more salient an identity is to an individual, the more sensitive that individual should be to opportunities that allow him or her to enact behaviors that confirm that identity and the stronger his or her motivations would be to actually perform such behaviors.[24] Following up on these ideas, other researchers have pointed out that people should not only be acting out behaviors based upon their perceived identities, but they should be actively paying attention to their own actions in order to actually learn, by virtue of their behaviors, who they are.[25] In essence, this research suggests that we act who we are so we can be how we act!

NAILING JELL-O TO THE WALL

All of what has proceeded in this chapter is fundamental to the task of using of identity as a meaningful research construct for understanding the museum visitor experience. We have now more clearly defined what we mean by *identity* and we have seen that in study after study, identity, whether called self-worth, self-knowledge, or self-efficacy is an important factor in determining motivation and behavior. Still, we have not fully "operationalized" identity in a way that is really useful to our needs of binding together the worlds of museums and visitors. To further that goal we need to be able to use identity for something beyond just a nice device for telling stories, even compelling ones. What we need is the ability to use identity as a tool for gauging how and in what specific ways leisure decisions are made, which in our specific case, means decisions related to visiting a museum. As we described in the previous chapter, the public perceives museums as places that permit (afford) a range of possible leisure experiences. The question then is, in what ways do people's leisure time needs match up with their perceptions of a museum's affordances? I'm proposing that identity represents the key to understanding how these two disparate entities come together; identity is the "vehicle" by which perceptions of personal needs and motivations can be matched with perceptions of institutional capacities and affordances. But, as I have also suggested, identity has historically proven to be a challenging and often slippery concept to investigate; it is extremely difficult to "see" identity, let alone measure it.

The work of German social psychologist Bernd Simon provides one way to solve this problem. Simon describes an approach that allows one to characterize identity in ways that are both observable and measurable.[26] The key to Simon's approach is developing identity as a "mediating variable" rather than as just a vague, descriptive tool that makes sense only in narrative form. Simon operationalizes identity so that it can be used as a causative agent—a variable that possesses real substance and scientific validity and reliability. Like the research summarized above, Simon begins with the assumption that "through self-interpretation, people achieve an understanding of themselves or, in other words, an identity, which in turn influences their subsequent perception and behavior."[27] Quite literally, as situations arise, people address those situations by consciously, and to a degree unconsciously, responding on the basis of how they think about themselves. Simon's thinking is very similar to Albert Bandura's ideas of self-efficacy and Sheldon Stryker's Identity Theory. However, it is at this point that Simon's approach diverges; he argues that these self-interpretations involve a varying number of what he refers to as tangible and measurable "self-aspects."

Simon did not invent the concept of self-aspects; that distinction goes to the American psychologist Patty Linville who twenty years ago hypothesized that self-concept needed to be viewed as a multi-faceted cognitive construct composed of concrete and distinguishable entities she called self-aspects.[28] She defined self-aspects as the individualized and idiosyncratic roles, relationships, contexts, or activities that individuals use to describe themselves. But unlike most earlier investigators, Linville's descriptions of identity were not couched in ethereal and convoluted philosophical terms, but in the framework of modern neuroscience. She argued that to the extent these identity-related self-descriptions are real, each self-aspect should be encoded within the brain. Self-aspects should be mental representations maintained in memory; each embedded within related neural networks. Specifically, each self-aspect was likely a unique neural node interconnected with associated networks of neurons. Each neuronal network would be made up of related cognitive, affective, and evaluative memories, as well as other similar self-aspect neural nodes. Linville went on to theorize that the strength of associations among these various self-aspect nodes should vary, with some self-representations being very important to the person and thus, highly interconnected with other nodes and some less important and only weakly interconnected.[29] Linville's conceptualization of identity in this way permitted Simon and other researchers to practically think about and measure identity-related influences. Although Linville is a social psychologist, her self-aspect construct allows researchers to operationalize a range of different identity-related concepts, including identities that are social as well as asocial, those that occur at the level of the individual or the level of the society, and both 'I' types of identity and 'i' types of identity. Whenever an individual conceptualizes a relationship between themselves and some other entity, then in theory that relationship is encoded in the brain as a self-aspect, and in theory it is amenable to study.

It is this last point that is so critical as Linville's construct of self-aspects provides a way to concretely describe an individual's internal cognitive categorization or conceptualization of self. Reframing identity in this way provides a tangible mechanism for understanding how an individual self-describes himself or herself. Thus, we can use an individual's self-aspects as a tool for understanding how an individual thinks about who they are and thus, why and how they might act. According to Simon, self-aspects can refer to

> generalized psychological characteristics or traits (e.g., introverted), physical features (e.g., red hair), roles (e.g., father), abilities (e.g., bilingual), tastes (e.g., preference for French red wines), attitudes (e.g., against the death penalty), behaviors (e.g., I work a lot) and explicit group or category membership (e.g., member of the Communist party).[30]

Individuals make sense of their actions and roles by ascribing identity-related qualities or descriptions to themselves within a specific situation. Some self-aspects can be generalized across a wide range of situations, such as "I'm a clever person" or "I'm a people-person," but many others are quite narrow and only relate to very particular circumstances, such as "I'm good at spelling" or "I'm a good Polka dancer."

In our example at the beginning of this chapter, Frances appeared to have a set of self-aspects to describe herself with respect to her visit to the Berkeley Botanical Gardens. She indicated that the reason she had visited the Gardens repeatedly, as well as the reason she visited the previous week, was because she finds the setting therapeutic: "So therapeutic, that it sort of became like medicine to me . . . All I have to do is walk in the front gate and I can feel my blood pressure dropping." Frances was using the self-aspect of someone seeking "therapy" to clarify what her needs and motivations were on that day. Frances also used the self-aspect of "spiritual" to describe herself, and by extension saw the Gardens as a place that allowed her to enact her spiritual self.

Was Frances unique or do most people walk around with identity-needs in their heads that describe why they do things? Investigations by Simon[31] and other researchers have actually found that people like Frances are anything but unique; these kinds of self-definitional roles and rationalizations appear to be quite common.[32] Individuals regularly construct identity-related descriptions of themselves, descriptions that are specific to the event or situation they are about to engage in. Not only do people have these descriptions, or self-aspects, in their heads, they actually serve as working models for the person, telling him or her what to expect and how to behave in particular types of situations. For example, in cases of anorexia nervosa, self-images of being fat can drive someone to starve themselves, even though others would judge them as already well beyond a state of thinness. And in a stunning example of the importance of identity-related self-definitions on motivations and behavior, psychologist Carol Dweck and her colleagues have shown that individuals who self-define themselves as persistent learners consistently achieve better in school than individuals who self-defined themselves as smart; both types of self-aspect were independent of how intelligent the individuals actually were.[33] Those who thought of themselves as persistent learners were able to overcome short-term failures, and as self-described, persevere through to success. Self-defined smart individuals were often afraid of failure, and thus failed in the face of adversity. Ideas of self do influence our motivations and our behaviors, frequently in profound and even predictable ways.

SELF-ASPECTS AND MUSEUMS

Here's how I envision most people deciding whether or not to visit a museum. Over the course of a week, or day, or maybe even on the spur of the moment, an individual begins to decide how they are going to spend a chunk of upcoming leisure time. As always, there will be many needs competing for that time; there are work tasks and household chores, social obligations, health and fitness needs, and, of course, personal satisfaction goals. Simultaneously, a range of possible leisure options begin to surface in the person's mind: "I heard there's a sale at the mall and I could go shopping for those shoes I need," "I'm overdue getting together with Fred," "I should spend more time with the children," "Susan told me there's an interesting new exhibition at the museum," and so on. The decision of what to do then emerges through a conscious process of first prioritizing the various identity-related needs the individual has, then matching these needs against the list of possible leisure options conjured up by the person. What makes this task possible for the individual is that his or her leisure identity-related needs are made concrete through the conscious awareness of self-aspects; each self-aspect is associated with one or more identity-related need. Similarly, each of the leisure options is evaluated on the basis of whether or not it supports the self-aspects the person is trying to satisfy. The solution, a leisure choice, is arrived at when the individual's most pressing self-aspects match well with the affordances of a convenient and financially affordable leisure setting. In the case of a decision to visit a museum, the match could be between a desire to satisfy one's intellectual curiosity and a setting that affords unique and intellectually stimulating new things to see and do; or it could be a match between a desire to be a good parent and a setting that affords family-friendly, safe, and educationally enriching activities for children; or it could be a match between an overwhelming need to escape, even briefly, the "rat race" with the prospect of being able to visit a peaceful, secluded setting with good benches and lovely views.

I believe that this is the process that happens many times every year as people contemplate whether or not to visit a museum. Although this description makes it sound cognitive and systematic, it is almost certainly much more haphazard much of the time. Still, some variation on this process must be going on in our brains every time we have to make a leisure experience decision. Depending upon an individual's identity-related needs and interests at that particular day and time, the individual sifts through all the possible leisure options he or she can think of that will enable him or her to achieve those needs. If a museum provides a good fit, then a museum visit is what is chosen; if not, the museum visit is filed away as an option for another day. As described in the previous chapter, the vast majority of visitors to museums already possess a working model of what they believe museums are generally like, and thus, what any particular museum "affords" in the way of leisure opportunities. Museums are places that can be fun, educational, family-friendly, quiet, and exciting; or in Frances's case, museums are places that allow you to connect with your "inner spirit." Based upon the self-aspects the individual hopes to enact during this particular leisure experience—"I'm looking for something fun to do," "I feel a desire to express my curiosity today," "I really need to step up to the parent role this weekend," "I'm feeling really stressed," "I could really use some peace and solitude," or "I'm feeling adventuresome," etc.—he or she searches memory for the perfect match of a setting to fit that need. If a museum fits the bill, then he or she will choose to visit. Thus, even before the visitor steps across the threshold of the museum, he or she has already consciously or for many visitors semi-consciously created a set of expectations for the visit. These expectations represent an amalgam of his or her identity-related leisure desires and needs and his or her socially and culturally constructed view of what the museum affords.

By and large, the vast majority of museum visitors' personal, identity-driven perceptions of their roles and needs are well-matched with the actual realities of the museum. When this happens, visit satisfaction is almost guaranteed. Occasionally a visitor's expectations do not match the reality he or she encounters, and they leave dissatisfied. Amazingly, these cases are relatively rare which bespeaks the high understanding that today's visitors have about the museums they visit. However, what's most striking about this system is that visitors to museums and other comparable leisure settings use these kinds of identity-related self-aspects to not only aid in deciding which place to actually visit, they also use them to make sense of their visit while they are engaged. Hence, a visitor's identity-related visit motivations represent not just the reasons for visiting the museum, they also represent the predominant vehicle for experiencing the museum. And perhaps most striking is that these same entering identity-related visit motivations, as made apparent by visitos' self-aspects, also frame the ways in which visitors make sense of their museum experience after they leave. Visitors use their self-aspects as a framework for reflecting back on the experience and "remembering" what it was like. There is a caveat, though.

Much of the previous discussion assumes that a visitor's identity-related motivations, as evidenced by their self-aspects, are consciously available to them; they can be thought about and articulated. This is, for our purposes at least, unfortunately not always the case. Recent research on the mind is revealing that most of our memories and even "thoughts" occur below the level of awareness. According to most estimates, more than 90% of thought, emotion, and learning occur in the unconscious mind, without our awareness.[34] Similarly, most of the ways we formulate thoughts are non-verbal rather than verbal. Verbal language is part of how we store, process, and represent what's going on in our minds but despite its great importance, it is not necessarily the best device for communicating our inner feelings and needs.[35] By necessity, my emphasis here on conscious and verbally describable self-aspects needs to be appreciated as representing just the proverbial tip of the iceberg with regard to what's going on in the heads of visitors. I am inclined to believe that although only some visitors are like Frances, highly verbal and "meta-cognitive" (i.e., capable of reflecting on and talking about what they're thinking), all visitors share these deep-seated identity-related motivations and all are capable, some only with prompting, of describing the self-aspects that underlie their visit. As my colleagues and I have discovered, you can't just walk up to someone and ask "Why did you go to the museum today?" and expect to get at their identity-related motivations. To access the kind of deeply-considered responses required to elicit a person's self-aspects involves asking the question in the right way. And for some visitors, it requires some probing before they are able to be sufficiently self-reflective to give a good answer. Psychologists have referred to this as the "laddering" procedures—the in-depth procedures for interviewing and analysis designed to uncover the relationship and connections between what someone does and why.[36]

EVIDENCE FOR IDENTITY-RELATED MOTIVATIONS

These ideas represent a neat theory that describes how to reconceptualize the relationship between visitors and museums, but until a few years ago this was just a theory. Then, with support from the U.S. National Science

Foundation and in collaboration with the Association of Zoos and Aquariums and the Monterey Bay Aquarium, my colleagues and I initiated a series of research studies designed to test the validity of this theory.[37]

The first task was to try to develop a way to measure each of these five identity-related categories in order to allow visitors to simply and easily tell us what was going on inside their heads. In a series of iterative tests with several thousand visitors at ten different zoos and aquariums across the U.S., my colleagues Joe Heimlich, Kerry Bronnenkant, Nettie Witgert and I set about creating a research tool that we felt would validly and reliably capture the identity-related motivations of zoo and aquarium visitors.[38] Over 125 different phrases were generated representing different ways people had or could express their identity-related motivations for visiting a zoo or aquarium. These items and a variety of formats were initially piloted and then tested using traditional methods and statistical techniques of instrument development. At the end of this process, the list had been whittled down to 20 statements which were once again refined and retested for reliability and construct validity. The final instrument listed 20 statements representing four examples from each of the five key identity-related motivations; each statement was designed to match the realities of a zoo and/or aquarium visit. The instrument was designed so that each visitor would be asked to select the five statements that best explained why they chose to visit the zoo or aquarium on that particular day. For each of the five statements selected, they then would be asked to rank them in importance on a seven-point Likert-type scale, with 1 being not very important and 7 being extremely important.

With this tool in hand, the next step was to rigorously test the theory that visitors could be meaningfully categorized as a function of their identity-related motivations. Not only was it actually possible to differentiate visitors in this way, but it was actually useful. Data for this phase of the research was collected at four institutions: one large zoo (Philadelphia Zoo) and one small zoo (Salisbury [Maryland] Zoo), one large aquarium (National Aquarium in Baltimore) and one small aquarium (New York Aquarium). These institutions were selected to be as broadly representative of the zoo and aquarium community as possible. (Of course, given that we were collecting data from just four institutions meant that "representative" was a relative concept.) A random sample of adults across all four sites (N = 1,555) completed pre- and post-visit instruments. Subsamples of these visitors participated in additional aspects of the study.

Data was collected during the summer months for all sites except the National Aquarium. Unfortunately, major construction projects over the summer of 2005 delayed data collection at the National Aquarium until fall of that year.

The identity-related motivational assessment was administered pre-visit only and required roughly two to three minutes for visitors to complete. Several different variants of the instrument were created in order to randomly shuffle the order of the 20 items to avoid order biases. In addition, data sets were collected that measured changes in the visitors' knowledge of conservation and their attitudes towards conservation and the role zoos and aquariums play in supporting conservation. A series of one-on-one interviews to determine where (in the zoo and aquarium) visitors went and why was administered to a subset of visitors, and finally, a separate subset of visitors received follow-up telephone interviews or an email online survey to understand long-term memories and determine the impact of the experience on visitors.

Overall, slightly more than half (55%) of all visitors were shown to possess a clear dominant identity-related visit motivation upon entering the zoo or aquarium. An additional 7% of visitors had a dual-dominant motivation, indicating strong motivations in two areas simultaneously. Therefore, more than three out of every five visitors (62%) possessed a strong identity-related visit motivation as they entered the zoo or aquarium. All five of the identity-related motivational categories were represented at all four sites. The relative frequencies of visitors entering with different dominant motivations varied across sites, with each site having a distinctive profile. The number of individuals displaying a dominant entry visit motivation varied from just under half (47%) at the National Aquarium to more than two-thirds of visitors (68%) at the New York Aquarium. Most importantly though, was the strong relationship that existed between an individual visitor's identity-related visit motivations and what they learned at the zoo or aquarium.

As an initial way to determine if visitors' entering identity-related motivations influenced zoo/aquarium outcomes, we conducted a two-step cluster analysis using data from the matched pre-post population. Cluster analysis is an exploratory data analysis tool using a variety of algorithms designed to sort objects or responses into groups; the degree of association between two objects is maximal if they belong to the same group and minimal otherwise. First, a cluster analysis was performed on visitors' cognitive and affective (post-only) responses. The distributions of visitors' post-experience understanding of conservation and attitudes towards conservation fell into six unique clusters. Next, a second cluster analysis was conducted to determine what (if any) relationship existed between those individuals who expressed a dominant preference for one of the five identity-related visit motivations and the individuals falling within each of the six naturally forming "understanding and affect" clusters. The results revealed a striking correlation between visitors' exiting understanding of conservation and attitudes toward conservation and zoos/aquariums and their entering identity-related visit motivations. Individuals who expressed a single dominant identity-related motivation ended up clustering with others with similar motivations; this was true for each of the five motivational groups. As a consequence, five of the distinct knowledge/attitude understanding clusters were made up almost exclusively (80–100%) of individuals with a single entering visit motivation. The remaining cluster was presumably a blend of individuals with dual and/or no strong entering identity-related motivations. This stunning result indicates that something is going on here! The patterns in cognitive and affective understanding that resulted from a zoo/aquarium visit seemed to be directly related to the entering identity-related visit motivation of visitors. Specifically, the experiences of the roughly half of visitors who entered the zoo or aquarium possessing a single, dominant motivation were, as judged by cognitive and affective outcomes, most like the other visitors with the same entering motivation.

Overall analysis of the pre- and post-measures of cognitive and affective learning indicated that zoo and aquarium visitors showed no significant gains in their understanding of conservation, but significant gains in their attitudes towards conservation and the role that zoos and aquariums play in promoting conservation. However, when visitors were grouped by their identity-related motivations, this "one-size-fits-all" analysis was revealed to be somewhat misleading. At least among those visitors who had a single dominant entering motivation, one specific subset of visitors did show significant gains in their cognition, while most did not. Likewise, some visitors changed their affect as a function of their zoo or aquarium visit, while other groups did not. As with knowledge change, using the overall affect score yielded a distorted picture of what happened. Based upon these analyses, three sub-groupings of visitors emerged as particularly interesting. Although in this study, only a relatively small percentage of total zoo/aquarium visitors (7%) came primarily in order to experience the specialness of the setting (i.e., Experience seekers), they were the only definable group of visitors who demonstrated significant gains in both cognitive and affective learning. By contrast, 20% of visitors, those classified by our measures as coming to enact an Explorer or Recharger identity-related motivation showed no significant cognitive or affective gains.

Perhaps the strongest indication of the value of segmenting visitors according to their entering identity-related motivations was revealed by the qualitative interview data collected immediately following the visit and seven to eleven months post-visit. Both sets of data showed a relationship between entering motivations and exiting meaning-making. Although no two interviews were exactly alike, visitors within each motivational category provided interview responses reflective of category-typical identity-related motivations and used their own self-aspects as verbal aids in discussing their memories and learning. As the museum visit experience model predicts and these visitors' recollections confirmed, visitors utilized self-aspects to help shape both their entering identity-related reasons for visiting, as well as a way to help organize their experience and communicate it to themselves and others.

For example, the self-aspect "I'm an animal lover" was reinforced by visiting a location devoted to displaying animals and communicating that animals are interesting and important. The same self-aspect was also reinforced by being in a social context where other people were also admiring and enjoying animals. Similarly, the self-aspect "I'm a good parent" was reinforced by bringing one's child to an educationally oriented setting where the child enjoyed him- or herself and appeared to be "learning." It was also reinforced by seeing other families in the same setting, and doing things that looked to be good parenting behavior.

Not surprisingly then, those individuals who entered the zoo/aquarium with well-formed self-aspects—self-aspects that were meta-cognitively accessible to them as visit motivations—by and large used their self-aspects as a framework for experiencing the social and physical context of the zoo or aquarium. They also used these self-aspects as a cognitive framework for subsequently making meaning of their experience. Explorers related to what they saw and found interesting (and acted out this "me"-centered agenda regardless of whether they were with children or not). Facilitators were focused on what their significant others saw and found interesting (and they, too, acted out this agenda by, for example, allowing their children to direct the visit). Experience seekers reflected on the gestalt of the day, particularly how enjoyable the visit was. Professional/Hobbyists tended to enter with very specific, content-oriented interests and used the zoo/aquarium as a vehicle for facilitating those interests (for instance, photography, or setting up a saltwater aquarium). Finally, Rechargers, like Experience seekers, were more focused on the gestalt of the day. But Rechargers were not so much interested in having fun as they were in having a peaceful or inspiring experience. Also evident among these zoo/aquarium-situated identities were clustering of self-aspects; for example, among Explorers, an interest in animals and a self-perception as someone who is curious and likes to look closely at things; among Facilitators, a desire to be a good parent and placing a high value on learning. Self-aspects emerged as truly contextually constructed products. They appeared to be complex representations of the visitor's self embedded within the particular social and physical context of the situation, in this case, a zoo or aquarium.

The data also revealed that visitors within each of these five identity-related motivational groupings were truly different. For example, although Explorers and Professional/Hobbyists seemed to be similar with regard to their "me"-focused visit, in other dimensions they diverged markedly. Similarly Facilitators, Experience seekers, and Rechargers converged in some areas and diverged in others. These differences were revealed in how the setting was used, in changes in cognition and affect, and in the ways different clusters of visitors talked about their experiences.

The most important generalization was that a large number of visitors arrived at the zoo/aquarium with the expectation that the setting would afford certain things to them. Next, they sought out experiences that reinforced those expectations, and encoded their experiences as having satisfied those same expectations. For a majority of the visitors investigated in this study, their entering identity-related motivations revealed some measure of predictability about what that visitor's museum experience would generally be like. Each visitor's museum experience was of course unique, but each was framed within the bounds of the socially or culturally defined limits of how a zoo or aquarium visit affords exploration, facilitation, experience-seeking, professional and hobby support, and recharging. Other types of experiences were no doubt possible, but they appeared to be relatively infrequently sought out or enacted by these particular visitors.

Since this research was completed, similar data has been collected at a large eastern U.S. botanical garden, at two living history museums, one in the eastern U.S. and the other in the midwestern U.S., at a west coast U.S. science center, aquarium and whale watching excursion,[39] and at a variety of other categories of museums, including a major eastern Canadian art museum and an art museum and science center in Colombia.[40] Although the ways in which the motivations were expressed varied across settings, the basic categories held, as did the importance of these categories for helping to understand visitors' meaning making. An important finding was that in the off-season, the percentage of visitors entering with a single dominant motivation in some settings increased to close to 100%.[41] Meanwhile, I too have continued to collect data from individuals, as well as continued to work on strategies for improving the validity and reliability of data collection strategies. My data now includes individuals visiting a wide range of museum types, including art museums, history museums, natural history museums, zoos, science centers, national parks, botanical gardens, aquariums, flight museums, history museums, and children's museums. All of the data I have collected to date are consistent with the basic findings of the zoo and aquarium study cited above.

As illustrated by the interview with Frances at the beginning of this chapter, like most visitors, she did not arrive at the botanical garden as a blank slate. Typical of a frequent visitor, Frances visits the Berkeley Botanical Gardens with very explicit expectations of what she will see and do there; she already knows that it is a good place to visit. But even Frances's first visit to the Gardens involved pre-formed expectations, in her case influenced partially by the recommendation of her friend and of course, also informed by her own prior experiences and knowledge of such places. From the beginning she was hoping to find quiet and tranquility and some measure of respite from the stresses of her life; initially, these related to her health and her social situation, these days it appears to be primarily related to her job. She came with expectations of what she hoped to get out of her visit, and since her expectations were compatible with what the setting afforded, she achieved exactly what she hoped for. Her satisfaction was directly tied to both her image of the setting and her expectations for her visit. "I probably wasn't actually there for more than about fifteen or twenty minutes, but it was enough to do the job . . . To rejuvenate me, making me feel less stressed, more calm. To allow me to connect with my inner spirit. . . . I came to be refreshed, and I was." Frances had a pre-defined purpose for visiting the botanical garden and then she used the garden as a vehicle for fulfilling that purpose. This can be diagrammed as below:

identity-related needs + perceived museum affordances —> visit expectations —> in-museum visit experiences —> satisfaction and memories —> identity-related needs + perceived museum affordances —> visit expectations —> and so on

Recent research is beginning to show this type of positive feedback system between leisure expectations, activities, satisfactions, and setting image occurs in a variety of leisure situations.[42] And I have come to believe it is very much the norm for most people who visit museums.

The most surprising and, I suspect controversial, part of this model is that so much of what appears to be vital to an understanding of the museum visitor experience is represented by events that happen long before the individual ever sets foot inside an actual museum. Much of the action is not taking place inside the museum; it's happening at the level of an individual's identity-related leisure needs and interests and his or her generic perceptions of the value of museums. That's not to say the "in-museum" part of the above model is unimportant, but that it is remarkably less important than we have historically expected, or wanted to believe. Less important, though, is not the same as unimportant! So before we start fretting too much, let's turn our attention to that most familiar part of the museum visitor experience, the part that takes place within the museum.

CHAPTER 4

The Visit

Man's sense of space is closely related to his sense of self,
which is an intimate transaction with his environment.

—Edward T. Hall, 1966[1]

Q: So, tell me about your visit to the National Gallery of Art a couple of weeks ago. Why did you go? What were the things that motivated you to go?

A: We went to see the Edward Hopper exhibit. I've always liked Hopper. There was one of his paintings I've particularly always liked and when I saw that there was an exhibit of his at the National Gallery I wanted to go. Also, [significant other's] sister and mother also said it was good, that increased our motivation. But I would have gone anyway.

Q: So, what was the painting you've always liked?

A: A particular painting with two women from the '30s. It's called *Chop Suey*, it shows the second floor of a Chinese restaurant and these two women are eating there. I always liked how deeply colored it was; I always liked the colors a lot. It's sort of an everyman kind of painting, in a sort of NY kind of way. Not fancy, but classy.

Q: When did you first see the painting?

A: I think I first saw it when I was a student, but only prints. This is the first time I actually saw the original painting. I've seen it several times in books and I think I even once had a lousy print of it, which I never framed. I really liked it even though the prints I've seen of it were lousy. . . . I hoped the painting was going to be in the exhibit. I thought it was fairly likely given that it is considered one of Hopper's classic paintings. I'm not sure I came away from the exhibit thinking this was still my favorite painting. I saw a lot of other of his paintings I really liked. I'm not sure what my favorite is now.

Q: So, what beside color do you like about Hopper?

A: I had a long dead step-grandmother. She was a real stylish lady of NY. She married a lawyer and went up in class. Her mother was a tailor and made all of her clothes. Then she met and married a well-to-do lawyer and really went up in class. She was always very stylish; she was probably stylish before she got married too, but with money she could be even more stylish. The working-class stylish girls in Hopper paintings remind me of her and I liked her. That's what I like about Hopper; he has all these NY-stylish girls in his paintings.

Q: Did you just look at the art or did you also read any of the text?

A: Yes, I did [read the text]. And I listened to all the interpretive tapes and watched the movie.

Q: Tell me about the movie.

A: The big thing I remembered was that his wife was involved with all of his paintings. His wife was in the movie; they were interviewing her. She was about 85. He was in the movie too, but I remember her doing most of the talking. I also learned that she's the subject of all of his paintings. All the people, even the tiny little people in the corners, are her. He used her as a model. Not sure why I didn't know that before, but that was very interesting; not necessarily profound, but it makes him more real [for me]. All of these exhibits try to do this; they start with the beginning of an artist's life and go to the end. But maybe because of the movie, or maybe because the audio tour was so well-written, in this exhibit you moved through his life and really had a feeling for his life.

Actually, I was kind of ready for him to stop painting because by the end of his life I didn't really like his work that much. He died in the '70s, no I think it was the '60s. I didn't really like the paintings from the end of his life that much. But anyway, because of the interpretive stuff, you really got the flow of his life.

Q: Tell me more about what you liked about his early works and didn't like about his later work.

A: I really love how sumptuous his colors are in the '30s. By the time we get to the '60s, he's using modern colors. They are starker. I don't like them as much.

Q: Tell me more about what it was you didn't like about these later paintings.

A: I like the deep reds of his earlier paintings like in *Chop Suey*—big, old, stuffed living room chairs, 1930s maroon kind of colors. Some of his middle period paintings are like that. He got interested in the 1960s in Formica colors. He seemed like he got interested in those pale sort of colors and I didn't like those as much. Although most of the paintings in the last room had these washed-out colors there were a few that I really liked. Some of these had really interesting characters, women; women posed in interesting light. These few were like some of his earlier paintings and that saved the room for me. His characters didn't look like '30s babes anymore, more like '50s or '60s women. That's okay, that's who was around. But I really liked the '30s women more.

[Later in the interview]

Q: To the extent you can describe a goal for your visit, what was it? In other words, what were you hoping would happen? What would make it a great visit?

A: My goal was to see really beautiful paintings. I would look at the paintings and say, oooh, that's really nice. I wanted to bond with the paintings. And also, I still like Hopper so I wanted to see his art; including paintings I'd never seen before. Though I don't normally go for the interpretive stuff, still it was quite helpful. I really prefer to just be with the art and have the interpretive stuff "osmos" in. But in this case, I found the interpretive material really made the experience better. They told you some detail you wouldn't ordinarily see.

Q: Did you achieve your visit goal?

A: It was a mixed bag. I would rather have waited outside a little longer. It really was too crowded for me. I couldn't stand back and look at the paintings. When I was a kid I went down to the Gallery and looked at paintings by myself. I actually enjoyed this kind of thing. I'd sit by myself and soak them in. I really wish I could do that with these big exhibitions, but you can't because of all the people.

I really like Hopper because his paintings are sumptuous enough that you really could do that [sit back and soak them in]. I will say, though, Hopper's paintings weren't big enough. I wanted his paintings to be bigger.

I love those huge impressionist paintings that engulf you.

If I could have done it my way, I would have been there all by myself and stood back and just looked for a long time, and when I wanted, walk up closer to read the print.

I sure wish they'd make the print bigger on those labels. I'm getting older people's eyesight and have trouble seeing those labels. Then I could see them when standing back. It would be great for people like me.

And then, after about an hour or so, we did something that was really a good idea. We looked across the way and looked at the rest of the gallery and saw that we'd seen it all and we said, "That's good, we're done, let's stop." You get over-exhausted going through an exhibition like that and it's good not to try and see too much. That was great. It was enough to just see Hopper.

Mara is a physician in her late 40s who lives in the Washington, DC area. She is not an art person by profession but clearly, she is an art person by inclination. In so many ways her experience at the museum was quite different from the others we have met so far. Unlike Frances for example, Mara was very much involved in the content of the exhibition. She came not only to have the museum experience wash over her but to see a specific exhibition; in fact, she came in large part to see one particular painting. Although she visited the National Gallery as part of a social group—she began and ended her visit indicating that she was with her partner, Mara's visit experience was fundamentally a solo one. In this way she was like Maria, but unlike Maria, whose goal was to explore the museum and counted on serendipity to help guide her experience, Mara arrived with a very specific goal—she was a fan of Edward Hopper. She knew his work, and was particularly interested in seeing one specific painting of his, which she did. I have categorized individuals like Mara as possessing a Professional/Hobbyists visit motivation; these individuals typically possess above-average knowledge of the museum's content due to either their profession or avocation and they typically visit the museum in order to satisfy a specific goal or objective. In Mara's case, it was to view a specific painting and a specific exhibition, but in other cases, the goal can be to get good close-up photographs of animals or, as is often the case for many museum professionals, to discover how others in the "business" are doing the job.

In talking with Mara, two self-aspects for this visit seemed to emerge from her interview. The first was very specific—"I'm a person who enjoys the art of Edward Hopper." The second was more generic—"I'm someone who really enjoys and appreciates art and art museums." Both of these self-aspects helped form not only her motivation for visiting the National Gallery of Art on this particular day, but it also created the lens through which Mara experienced the museum, as well as a frame of reference through which Mara created long-term meanings about her experience. In particular, Mara's self-aspect as someone who likes Edward Hopper motivated her to extensively explore the exhibition; she read all of the label copy, listened to the audio guide, and watched the movie (not just once but twice). This goal provided Mara with what in psychology is called an "advance organizer" for her experience; it was a cognitive guide to all that she subsequently saw and did while in the museum.[2]

The Hopper exhibition itself also helped frame Mara's experience. Although she entered and left the exhibition with preconceptions about what she did and did not like about Hopper which strongly influenced what she chose to view and think about, Mara discovered aspects of his art and life she had not known. In other words, her identity-related motivations and her prior knowledge and interests strongly shaped how she utilized the museum, but the realities of the museum—the specifics and quality of the exhibition and the interpretive materials—pushed back on her and in turn, modified what she saw and did there as well.

What the preceding interview reinforces is what most museum researchers already know—that the museum visitor experience is highly complex. The exact nature of any visitor experience will vary considerably, even among visitors who enter with the same general identity-related motivations. Understanding something about a person's entering identity-related motivations, as well as their prior knowledge and interests, provides an extremely useful framework in which to unravel the complexities of the visitor experience. Although the experience of every visitor is unique, my research suggests that visitors with similar entering motivations, whether it be as an Explorer, Facilitator, Experience seeker, Professional/Hobbyist, or Recharger, are more likely to have similar in-museum experiences than are individuals entering with a very different identity-related visit motivation. This motivation creates a basic "trajectory" for the visit, with each basic motivational category having a characteristic trajectory. Knowing something about these trajectories thus provides a large part of what we need to discover in order to really understand the museum visit experience.

This initial trajectory though is just that, a trajectory. Once in the museum, the individual can, and does head off in many directions. If we are to fully understand the visitor's in- and post-museum experiences, we also need to know something about what the visitor sees and does during his or her visit and how this impacts the visitor's trajectory. The best guide to these other influences is the Contextual Model of Learning.[3] As previously described, an individual's museum visit will be affected by a combination of contextually-specific events that can be organized within three basic areas, or what Dierking and I referred to as the Personal, Physical, and Socio-cultural Contexts. That said, not all parts of the in-museum experience seem to be equally important. I will briefly outline some of the key influences I think are crucial to our model of the museum visitor experience.[4] The influences I will highlight are unlikely to be surprising, because these are the kinds of factors that most museum researchers, including myself, have spent years studying and analyzing. I will cover them only briefly here, not because they are of little importance but because others have already extensively written about them.

PERSONAL CONTEXT:
PRIOR KNOWLEDGE, EXPERIENCE, AND INTEREST

Considerable research over the past decade has confirmed that the personal interests and knowledge a visitor brings to the museum experience has a major influence on which exhibits, objects, or labels a visitor chooses to view and attend to.[5] Museums are amazingly rich and stimulating environments. For those who have worked in museums for years, it's difficult to appreciate just how overwhelming and novel these settings can be for most people. However, all visitors must develop coping strategies for sorting through the cognitive assault of the museum such as how to make good choices of what to attend to and what to ignore. Museum visitors like Mara have well-honed visit strategies. As visitors go, Professional/Hobbyists are among the most adept at navigating the museum. Visitors with this type of motivation typically rely heavily upon their prior visiting experience; they also rely on their extensive prior knowledge and interest in the subject matter to know how and where to focus their attention. All of these strategies allow Professional/Hobbyists to achieve an almost laser-like focus on what most appeals to them. But even the most naïve museum visitor applies some variation of this strategy, seeking that which is familiar. The need to feel secure in an environment drives all of us to seek that which is familiar; moderate novelty is quite stimulating while excessive novelty is quite disturbing.[6] Consumer researchers have long been familiar with this phenomenon of the "cognitive lock-in" where the public regularly equates product familiarity with product superiority.[7]

A search for the familiar is in fact the dominant strategy for nearly all museum visitors. A visitor's own prior knowledge and interests provide a frame of reference for them to make sense of what the museum contains. This is why the quip by a former science center director, "We teach people what they almost already know" is actually quite true.[8] Just as all knowledge is constructed from prior knowledge, so too is decision-making in a novel setting driven by prior interests and experiences. No matter whether the visitor is an experienced Professional/Hobbyist visitor like Mara or a naïve first-time Experience seeker, much of what a visitor chooses to seek out and attend to while in the museum is driven by what they find most familiar and cognitively comfortable. It is important to note that this frequently results in the visitor attending to quite different ideas and objects in the museum from what the professionals who designed the museum exhibitions and programs intended the public to focus on.

Physical Context: Exhibits, Objects, Labels, and Programs

Well-designed exhibitions and programs—the careful use of color, texture, and lighting combined with skillfully written scripts and labels—are extremely successful at getting and focusing visitors' attention. Without question, the realities of the museum, in particular the exhibits and objects visitors look at, the labels and guides they read and listen to, as well as the programs they watch and participate in, all influence their experience. To suggest otherwise would be unrealistic. Still, as this book suggests and in particular, the research that my colleagues Martin Storksdieck, Joe Heimlich, Kerry Bronnenkant, and I have conducted over the past decade attests to, these experiences do not unilaterally determine how visitors behave in museums, let alone what they ultimately learn and remember from the experience.[9]

As the interview with Mara demonstrates, part of what a visitor attends to is somewhat predictable based upon the design and layout of the museum-designed visitor experience. For example, Mara was quite aware of the fact that the Hopper exhibition was laid out chronologically and designed to show how Hopper's art evolved and changed over time, and this structure clearly influenced her thinking and understanding of his art. Similarly, Mara picked up on a number of key ideas included in the interpretive text and film for the exhibition, for example, the fact that Hopper used his wife as his subject in nearly all of his works. As a consequence, Mara exited the exhibition knowing more about Hopper than when she entered. She described learning about changes in the style and content of Hopper's paintings as well as important (to her) changes in his palette. Seemingly, she had not known about nor appreciated this as being important to understanding Hopper prior to entering the museum, despite feeling like she was quite knowledgeable about Hopper before her visit.

That said, it is fair to surmise that there were many other pieces of information about Hopper in the exhibition that did not emerge in my conversation with Mara—information that might have struck another visitor as important. Perhaps, this information did not seem salient to Mara, or she missed it, or she felt she already knew it and did not feel the necessity to describe it to me. In a similar way, there undoubtedly were many nuances of Hopper's art that Mara missed. My interview with Mara shows just how selective is the exact experience of each visitor. Even a diligent museum visitor like Mara could not absorb everything a major exhibition such as the Museum of Fine Arts, Boston–National Gallery of Art Hopper exhibition was designed to provide. Although Mara entered the museum with a fairly high level of prior knowledge about his art, had a very high level of interest, and went through the exhibit about as thoroughly as could be expected, her recall was good but not excellent, even though only two weeks had elapsed since her visit. (Note: The full transcript of the interview is not presented. Mara provided considerably more detail about the exhibition than I've presented, but much less than what could have been gleaned from the exhibition.)[10]

Unquestionably, good exhibition, film, and program design matters to the museum visitor. For more than a quarter century, museum researchers have investigated museum experiences based on the assumption that an important measure of a well-designed exhibit is how well it both "attracts" and "holds" the attention of the visitor.[11] With similar logic, museum researcher and evaluator Beverly Serrell has invested considerable effort measuring and comparing the amount of time visitors spend looking at exhibits within exhibitions. On average, most visitors only stop and attend to between 20% and 40% of the exhibit elements within an exhibition.[12] And which exhibits a visitor ends up attending to is important. In a study conducted by Martin Storksdieck and myself, we were able to show that for many, though not all visitors, the quantity of what was learned in the museum was directly related to the quality of what was viewed. The number of "good exhibits" (as judged by an independent panel of experts) the visitor actually interacted with directly correlated with how much was learned.[13] In other words, it does matter whether an exhibit is well-designed or not. It is important to note that, although in general, exhibit quality mattered, there were individuals for whom exhibit quality didn't seem to matter at all. As I will describe in more detail later in this book, even this paradox can be at least partially explained by the museum visitor experience model. While Facilitators and Experience seekers are almost always strongly influenced by the quality and focus of an exhibition's content and design, Professional/Hobbyists and Rechargers are much less so; Explorers fall somewhere in between.

Socio-cultural Context: Social Interactions and Cultural Background

As it has been described by Lynn Dierking and myself, as well as countless other investigators over the years, the visitor experience is strongly influenced by the within-museum social interactions of the visitor's social group.[14] If you spend any time watching visitors in museums, you can't help but observe how social the visitor experience is. The overwhelming majority of museum visitors arrive as part of a social group. Since the museum environment itself is a socio-cultural one, all visitors, even those choosing to visit alone, find themselves quickly immersed in the socio-cultural milieu of other visitors, museum staff, and volunteers. Look even closer and you realize that much of the social interaction is a way for visitors to connect and find meaning. As discussed earlier, not all of the social interaction is content-focused. For example, some of it involves bonding between individuals or, for example, within families, behavior management such as checking to see if children are hungry or need to use the restroom. Still, much of the social behavior that goes on in museums is focused on discussing and sharing information about the content of the museum. These conversations can ultimately have more impact on a visitor's memory of the experience than the objects and labels themselves. This socio-cultural mediation, either direct or indirect, plays a critical role in personalizing the visit experience for visitors, facilitating their efforts to learn and find meaning from museums. Even Mara, who said she yearned to be by herself during her visit to the Hopper exhibit, periodically interacted with her partner over the course of the visit; for example, they watched the film together. Probably even more importantly for Mara, she talked about the exhibition and her visit experience with both her partner and her parents both prior to arriving at the museum and in the hours and days subsequent to her visit. All of these interactions helped to frame what Mara ultimately recalled as her "visit" experience. Accordingly, it has been argued that learning is a special type of social behavior and museum experiences represent a special kind of socio-cultural learning.[15] Much as what a visitor sees and does while in the museum are intertwined throughout a visitor's experiential narrative of a visit, so too are the visitor's social experiences.

Finally, the socio-cultural context both defines who we perceive ourselves to be, as well as how we perceive the world we inhabit. In a very real sense, the world in which each of us lives has meaning because of the shared experiences, beliefs, customs, and values of the groups that inhabit it with us. This collection of shared beliefs and customs is what we have come to call "culture."[16] Social psychologists Eugene Matusov and Barbara Rogoff have argued that

> the diversity of goals of different communities necessitates defining
> development in terms of progress toward more responsible participation
> in specific communities of practice rather than assuming that development
> is a generic process independent of the goals and institutions of the
> communities in which an individual develops.[17]

Visitors who possess different cultural backgrounds and experiences are not only likely to utilize the same museum spaces, exhibitions, and programs in different ways, but they are almost certain to make very different meanings from what superficially might appear to be similar museum visitor experiences.

TRAJECTORIES AND STOCHASTIC MODELS

We want to believe that the visitor experience in a setting like a museum should depend upon a range of describable and manageable factors. As outlined in the previous chapter, we like to think of humans as rational and predictable creatures, and more to the point, we envision our creations like the museum as logical and predictable places. However, as Martin Storksdieck and I discovered when studying the behavior and learning of science center visitors, there were a whole suite of often unpredictable and unexpected factors that influenced visitors. We concluded that any model of the visitor experience would have to more closely resemble a stochastic model than a linear, logic model.[18] A stochastic model assumes that "initial states"— for example, entering identity-related motivations and an individual's prior knowledge, interest, museum experience, and social arrangement—are important determinants of a visitor's behavior and learning. However, these are influenced over time through interactions with both predictable and unpredictable events. The collective interactions, rather than just the initial state, determine the ultimate outcomes. In addition, random events such as large crowds, a sick or hungry child, or the sudden appearance of a knowledgeable and engaging staff member, can influence not only which factors come into play as important, but also modulate the relative amplitude of impact those factors have on learning. Stochastic factors influence both the quality and quantity of experiences that results.

We can envision virtually every visitor entering the museum with a generalized pre-museum visit experience "trajectory." That trajectory is determined first and foremost by the visitor's entering identity-related motivation, which is strongly influenced by that individual's prior knowledge and interests. In turn, this is influenced by the companions with whom they choose to visit the museum; these companions also collectively shape their perceptions of what specific leisure-related attributes the museum is likely to afford them that day. In general then, these entering conditions collectively predispose the visitor to interact with the setting in *relatively* predictable ways. However, once in the setting, the visitor is affected by a whole series of additional factors, some of which are under the control of the institution (mediation provided by trained staff, orientation brochures and signage, good and bad exhibits, and the nature of interpretation tools such as labels and audio guides) and some of which are not (social interactions within the visitor's own group and interactions with other visitors outside of his or her own group). All of these factors are potentially influenced by other random events, such as whether there's an interactive exhibit of particular interest to the visitor that happens to malfunction; or at the exact moment a visitor arrives at an important explanatory label, a crowd of visitors standing in front of it causes the visitor to skip the label;

or a child or spouse suddenly needs to go to the restroom; or a volunteer "randomly" selects the visitor to be part of a demonstration; or a text panel includes information the visitor just happened to have read about the previous day; or a sudden flash of bright light over one end of an exhibition hall catches the visitor's attention just as he or she enters a gallery and causes him or her to move in a direction opposite to the flow pattern intended by the designers. All of these events happen every day in museums around the world. What is predictable is that events like this will and do happen, what is not predictable is when they will happen and to whom. The point is that if and when random things like this occur, they influence the trajectory of the visitor's museum experience in both small and at times dramatic ways. The nature of the visitor experience depends on events the museum can design for and count on happening, and upon random events beyond the control of the museum.

For many visitors, particularly experienced visitors like Mara (above) and Frances (previous chapter), their trajectory through the museum is relatively straight and true. They head into the experience with one or more goals and they are sufficiently single-minded in their pursuit of that goal. This is particularly true for individuals with Professional/Hobbyist motivations like Mara and individuals with Recharger motivations like Frances. These are typically experienced museum visitors, regular visitors to one specific institution, or at the very least, regular visitors to similar institutions. Armed with a goal and knowledge of how to navigate around potential obstacles to their goal, the likelihood of perturbation diminishes and visitors with these motivations often move through the museum with a smooth and remarkably predictable trajectory. But this is not the case for all visitors.

DEFLECTED TRAJECTORIES

The complexity of the museum environment, coupled with the uniqueness of each visitor, almost guarantees that the visitor experience will never be totally predictable for all visitors. For many visitors, particularly those with the entering motivations of Explorers, Experience seekers, and Facilitators, the "straight as an arrow" type of visit trajectory is the exception rather than the rule. Visitors enacting the roles of Explorers, Experience seekers, and Facilitators are generally less task-oriented than are those enacting Professional/Hobbyist and Recharger roles. The former groups of visitors are likely to meander through the museum, waiting for something to attract their attention or interest. Once it does, that thing or person will then direct much of their experience. Although the specifics of what the visitor focuses upon are determined by the many possibilities in the museum, the reference point remains fixed by the person's entering self-aspects. The following is an excerpt from a visitor, I'll call her Sara, who entered the museum as an Explorer and because of unforeseen events, slid briefly into the Professional/Hobbyist role before returning to her more typical Explorer role.

Sara is a white female in her mid 30s. She has a high school diploma and attended but did not graduate from community college. At the time of this interview, she was working as a customer service representative for a bottled water company in Los Angeles. Sara was one of the individuals interviewed as part of the major National Science Foundation-funded California Science Center study previously described. She visited the Science Center in the spring with her three children who were 9-, 4-, and 1-years-old at the time. Despite being a "family visitor" Sara was definitely operating with an Explorer visit motivation. During her Science Center visit, she alternated between leading the visit and following her children, though there were periods of time when she and the children moved through the exhibition quite independently. This post-visit interview was conducted in Sara's home approximately two years after the visit. If you pay attention to how Sara initially describes her Science Center visit, it is clear that her self-aspects revolve primarily around her desire to satisfy her own interests and curiosities as is typical of Explorers. However, Sara also reveals that a serendipitous event pushed her into a more focused, content-oriented motivation more typical of a Professional/Hobbyist. It is worth noting that despite being a "family" visitor, Sara does not spend much time enacting a Facilitator motivation. Although she displays a continuous concern for her children and their well-being, they do not primarily motivate her behavior, or her memories of the experience as they would for someone who was enacting a true Facilitator motivation.

Q: When you went [to the Science Center], the purpose of the visit was what?

A: Well, to see what I could learn. Now that my daughter, she's in the 6th grade and she's transitioned to junior high so they have a lot more things going in those grade levels and I didn't want to be an ignorant parent with questions she'd ask, not that I'm the most intelligent person but you know science is always updating and finding new things and so I said okay, we'll go and we'll learn together.

Q: What do you remember most, what was most memorable?

A: I remember saying to you when I came out [NOTE: Referring to the post-visit interview immediately following the visit] about the babies in the jars. That was very interesting to me.

Q: Why?

A: Because I was really able to see the different stages of the pregnancy, real bodies. That really caught my attention.

Q: Was it a positive experience?

A: You could say that it was, as bad as that may sound, only because it was interesting to me and because I myself have three children. It was interesting to see the process and at the same time kind of, well, it kind of was and it kind of wasn't only because the children in there were no longer alive, but that really stood out in my mind.

Q: Did you see similar things in books?

A: Yes, I had when I was in high school in biology. And then I went to junior college, LA Community College and took psychology, so yeah, they introduced us to pictures like that. Not in reality but in pictures.

Q: But the difference between the picture and the jar?

A: It's realistic when you see them in a jar. In a book, you could see anything in a book, you know but for me it was more fascinating to see the actual things.

Q: What you saw there, did you think about these experiences afterwards?

A: Absolutely, because I mean, I myself have had three children so it was interesting to me the stages that they went through during my pregnancy. I also read up and took up a lot of that. That was just something that was interesting to me.

Q: Did you ever compare what you saw, your mental notes, to what you read in your book?

A: Absolutely, and I think that I unconsciously maybe did that not realizing all the information and the data that I took from when I did all that reading. It kind of made sense [to me] when I saw the actual babies there.

Q: So, you actually read about this beforehand?

A: Oh, absolutely.

Q: And then you went there and the effect was. . .?

A: It made a lot more sense.

Q: Did you continue to read about this afterwards?

A: No, but I probably will. I still have my children's questions, my daughter when she brings home projects or now that she's growing to be a young adult, she'll ask me questions. We have better answers for her or at least I'll know what I'm talking about when I try to describe something to her. I know that what I'm trying to say to her makes sense. It might not make sense to her until she's older. She didn't like going through that [exhibit] because there were dead children and she's too small to comprehend the stages. Being a mother myself, I think it just made a lot more sense and it's much easier for me to explain the different cycles.

[Later in the interview]

Q: When you went inside [the *World of Life* exhibition], do you remember what you did? You said you took a sharp left. Then, where did you go and what did you see?

A: Yeah right, when we went in there we went to the left and then we kind of went around and came back around to I believe the entrance 'cause the first thing I wanted to see was the babies, the stages.

Q: So, you knew about that?

A: Yes. Well, I knew that because, I didn't know that before I went in there [the California Science Center], I knew that when I got there [the *World of Life* exhibition]. I can't remember how I knew when I got there but I knew that it was there. I think it was one of the ladies that was coming out while we were going up the stairs and I overheard her daughter say "Mom, are those real babies?" So, I was eager to get to the top [of the stairs] to see if that was real. . . . Yeah, of all the exhibits the *Human Miracle* was the one that was most interesting to me. Again, this is where they had the samples of the babies throughout the different stages [of fetal development] and I remember this very clearly because there were several chicks that were being hatched right after we came out [NOTE: referring to adjacent exhibit]. . . .Yeah, so there was a lot of questions from my children because I know that the human babies wasn't in a shell but there was something similar to that which was in the uterus so that was pretty interesting. . . . But this was the most fascinating for me.

Q: The reproduction?

A: The reproduction and the genetics.

Q: Would you say it was interesting because of your daughter's interest or are you interested yourself?

A: I'm interested myself. I now have three children, before I had my three children I lost two children at 9 months—they died at birth. So I took up a lot of reading before my very first child. Usually the very first time a woman is pregnant you want to soak yourself with information. After what had happened to me I wanted to know more. And it happened a second time so by the time my third daughter, which is my oldest now, by the time she was born I really soaked myself with information. So this made it even more interesting to me.

Q: I hate to ask, but you had two stillborns?

A: Yes, two stillborns.

Q: Wow, that's tough.

A: That is very tough. Now I'm over that, because I went through a lot of grieving and I went through a lot of counseling but I guess I was just trying to get so much information, being that the doctors weren't able to give me a lot of detailed information that I wanted. They were just, "Well, things happen," and I wanted to know the details which is probably pretty difficult for them to explain to me. I don't know, I'm not a doctor. After going through something so traumatic, you want to know all there is to know about what you're going through and what you have to deal with. So maybe that's the reason why this part for me was so important and attracted my attention.

Q: That would certainly explain quite a bit.

A: And being a woman, I think anybody who has either had an abortion or a miscarriage or a stillbirth, this is probably very attractive to a woman who has gone through that to want to know all that there is about that.

As Sara revealed details of her life history, it became increasingly clear why she was so fascinated with prenatal development. This interview reveals how one particular event, a conversation overheard in a stairway, can dramatically intersect with a person's identity-related needs and interests so as to determine their museum visit experience. Sara did not know about this exhibit before visiting the Science Center, but once she discovered it, her own personal needs and interests caused her to spend considerable time there. She may have stumbled upon it anyway but maybe not, as the exhibit is located in a back corner of the exhibition. Or perhaps, she would have discovered it but only at the point when her children were tired and ready to leave, necessitating a hasty and incomplete exploration of the exhibit. Because of this unanticipated knowledge of the exhibit's existence, the trajectory of her visit was dramatically influenced. Sara made it clear that her reasons for spending time at this exhibit were quite personal, although at some point she indicated that she might want to share this information with others, for example, with her daughter. The details of Sara's experience are not typical; what is typical for many museum visitors is that the topics most vigorously pursued during a visit are usually those about which the visitor already knows something. Many museum professionals assume that visitors will be most attracted to unknown topics. As discussed above, the exhibits most visitors find most appealing are those for which they already possess a strong interest in and knowledge about prior to their visit. As was the case for Sara, despite being well-read on the subject of prenatal development, she felt that her Science Center experience had significantly enhanced her knowledge and understanding of this subject. The authentic objects seemed to help crystallize a synthesizing process of meaning-making and perceived understanding.

As we continued to question Sara about her museum visit, she revealed considerable insights into how identity-related visit motivations drive museum visitor experiences. Although there was clearly some tension between Sara's desire to satisfy her impromptu Professional/Hobbyist motivations (in the *Human Miracle* exhibit) and her Facilitator-like parental obligations to her young children, her answers reveal that these were not the motivations that primarily drove her visit experience. The self-aspects she uses indicate that she perceives herself as a basically curious and interested person, less interested in any one topic or subject, and more interested in learning and discovery in general. Sara expressed self-aspects that typically go along with individuals who assume an Explorer visit-motivation, and overall her in-museum behaviors reflected that motivational bias.

A: I wanted to stay there longer [*Human Miracle* exhibit], but I didn't because my children just thought it was a spooky place to be in. [Note: This part of the exhibition is quite enclosed and dark with the different-aged fetuses arranged sequentially in back-lit cases.]

Q: How did you decide between what you wanted to see and what they wanted to see?

A: If it was pretty interesting I would just stick it out and just tell my children you guys can go in front of me or meet me in the corner and walk real slow and I'd catch up. I just tried to catch on to as much as I could and my children, they pretty much weren't interested in too much. I love to find out about things and always try to stretch my understanding of how stuff works and why things are the way they are.

For many visitors, like Sara, Maria, and Elmira, the museum represents a space for generalized exploration and discovery rather than a place for satisfying a specific outcome. Citing statistics that most visitors only stop at a small percentage of exhibits within an exhibition or museum, Jay Rounds argues that this doesn't represent some kind of deficiency on the part of visitors, but an intelligent and effective strategy for piquing and satisfying curiosity.[19] Using ideas derived from optimal foraging theory in ecology, Rounds hypothesized that curiosity-driven visitors would seek to maximize what he called the "Total Interest Value" of their museum visit—finding and focusing attention only on those exhibit elements they deem to have the highest interest value and the lowest search costs. According to Rounds, this "selective use of exhibit elements results in greater achievement of their own goals than would be gained by using the exhibition comprehensively."[20] Thus, the experience for exploring visitors is generally but not specifically predictable; so much depends upon what the visitor encounters that resonates with his or her various needs and interests. We can characterize these visitors as having "wobble" in their visitor experience trajectory; there's a generalized directionality to their museum experiences but the specifics are likely to be variable and idiosyncratic.

SHIFTING MOTIVATIONS

Given that these entering identity-related motivations are NOT qualities of the individual, but temporary roles that visitors enact to fit the specific needs and leisure realities of the moment, one would expect that many visitors would enter with one set of motivations and exit with another. This certainly would have been my assumption, and in fact, it was when I first began this line of research a decade ago. Much to my surprise, the entering trajectories of most visitors, as defined by their identity-related motivations, seem remarkably stable over the course of a visit. That is not to say that alternative motivations don't intercede as exemplified by Sara's discovery of the human development exhibit. But as demonstrated by Sara, it appears that the motivational goals visitors enter with are also typically the goals they exit with.

As a thought experiment conducted early in my process of creating this model, I attempted to categorize the motivational focus of one of my own museum visits. While in Los Angeles during one of my extended research visits, I visited a museum as part of a family social experience. My brother and sister-in-law live in Los Angeles, and as it happened during this research visit, I often stayed with them to keep down the costs of staying for weeks while conducting my research. On this particular weekend, it was decided that we should do something together and the idea came up to visit a new exhibition that had just opened. It's an important bit of background information to know that my brother rarely goes to museums while my sister-in-law really enjoys visiting museums. This weekend outing, then, was somewhat of a conspiracy between me and my sister-in-law to get my brother to go to a museum. The "bait" was a special exhibition which happened to be on a topic that we both felt my brother would find interesting. We used my presence as an excuse to go (since of course, everyone knew I liked museums). The ploy worked and we went to the museum. Two days later, as I was flying back home to Annapolis, I realized that I could use this family experience as a thought experiment. I wrote down, in approximately one-minute intervals, my entire museum experience as best as I could recall, from the moment we left the house to the moment we got to our next destination. I then attempted to categorize, according to my five identity-related motivations, which identity I was enacting at each moment of my visit. The results were quite revealing. Over the course of the visit, I had actually assumed each of the five motivational types, but overall, my entering motivational type—Explorer—kept resurfacing. Despite slipping into each type occasionally, for example, playing Facilitator to make sure my brother or sister-in-law were happy, or Experience seeker to check out the iconic exhibit at the museum, or Recharger when finding a lovely place to sit and enjoy the space while my brother and sister-in-law investigated the gift shop, or Professional/Hobbyist to admire a design decision, I predominantly stayed in Explorer mode. By my calculation, I spent approximately two-thirds of my time in Explorer mode during that museum visit experience. These surprising results have been borne out time and again as my colleagues and I have talked to other visitors.[21]

Another fact that emerges from my inquiries of visitors is that even when events conspire to undermine a visitor's identity-related goals, they are amazingly persistent and resilient in their efforts to make the space work for them. What follows is an interview with Hanna, a woman in her late 30s who visited the High Desert Museum, a history and nature museum located in Bend, Oregon, with a friend, her friend's son, and her own two children. As will become immediately clear, Hanna entered the Museum with a Facilitator visit motivation. However, based upon past experiences at the Museum, she also likes to see and learn from the exhibitions and programs and because of her background (she's a biologist), she has considerable relevant prior experience and knowledge.

Q: Tell me about your visit in general. What time of year did you go? Do you remember the month?

A: So, I went to the High Desert Museum in Bend and it was probably December of last year. So actually, the weather was good so it must have been earlier. It was probably October. And I went with another woman (Catherine) and her kid. So it was a couple of 7-year-old boys and a baby (Christina). So it was a very child-centric visit. And we just ran around and looked at the animals and played on the paths and stuff.

Q: What if anything motivated you to go on this particular day?

A: I just wanted to take my friend there. She hadn't been there for a couple of years. And I really like the museum. I especially like to go see the birds of prey—the hawks and owls. They have several hawks and they have a nesting pair of spotted owls. And they have done at least one reintroduction, taking the chicks and putting them into foster nests in the wild. And I think they've done it twice, I'm not sure.

Q: Were you able to see them this time?

A: We didn't make it that time. We didn't make it over to the hawks, because the kids were antsy.

Q: To the extent that you can describe a goal for the visit, can you tell me what that was?

A: Oh, I forgot to mention that Alan likes the gift shop. He usually gets a little polished stone or something.

Q: What does he like about the gift shop?

A: He likes people to buy him things. We give him a dollar and he can choose how to spend it. So, no I didn't have many goals. I try to keep my expectations pretty low when I go anywhere with children. I guess my goal was to see the owls and I didn't meet that goal. And my goal was to get through it without any tantrums and I didn't meet that goal either. But at least we got there, we saw it, and we ran around a little bit.

[Later in the interview]

Q: On a scale of 1 to 7, how would you rate your visit? Why?

A: Probably a 4. I was pleased that we made it there and saw some things, and spent a little time outside. And I got to run through this mining frontier exhibit which was cool.

Q: Is Alan ever interested in you reading the signs to him?

A: Well, no not really. He doesn't want to feel like he's being educated in any way. So it wasn't the museum's fault that my visit wasn't rated more highly. It was just the fact of having children and you know . . . I say I try to keep my expectations low, but I still think there are certain things that would be fun if I got to do them.

[Later in the interview]

I probably tried to take them out to the hawk and owl building and got sidetracked. . . . We went inside and went over to the Mining and Frontier Life Exhibit and then Alan wanted to go to the gift shop and I said no, I wasn't going to buy him anything. And he pitched a fit, so Catherine took him in there and she bought him something and bought Tyler [Catherine's son] something. And I probably nursed the baby. Then we probably left. I know that doesn't sound like much but it took a long time. We didn't even get to see the otters. Alan didn't want to see the otters. We spent a lot of time in the play area. It seems like we ran around on the paths a bit. But, I honestly don't remember. But, because I've been there several times, my memory of it is not as linear as if it was the only time I had been there.

Q: Was there a high point of the visit that was particularly enjoyable for you?

A: No. No we just . . . . (laughs and trails off)

Q: Were there any low points?

A: Alan and Tyler got in a couple of spats. So those were the low points. They were in conflict all weekend. It had nothing to do with the museum itself.

Clearly this was a very frustrating experience for Hanna, everything seemed to go wrong—her son misbehaved and didn't seem particularly excited by the visit, and she didn't get a chance to see her favorite exhibits—still she indicates that overall it was a good visit. She primarily attributes the fact that the museum visit didn't totally fulfill her expectations, rating the experience a 4 out of 7, to causes other than the museum itself. The experiences of both Hanna and Sara reveal, despite being different, that even with powerful and unanticipated museum "realities," a visitor's entering identity-related motivational narrative is very difficult to derail. Sara accommodated the realities of the museum she encountered seamlessly into her entering identity-related motivations; the result was a visitor experience that was fundamentally what one would expect from an Explorer—idiosyncratic and exhibit content-driven. Hanna, despite the poor behavior of her son and her friend's son conspiring to undermine a lovely family day at the museum, persisted in interpreting the experience as such; she was a good parent who exposed her children and her friend's child to the benefits of a museum visit. That the behavior of her child created significant dissonance for her and threatened to completely deflect her visit trajectory, did not seem to change her self-concept or sense of satisfaction with the experience—"I try to keep my expectations pretty low when I go anywhere with children." Sara dealt with these challenges by essentially encasing these unexpected events in "lowered expectations" and thus sealing it off from her larger "good parent" narrative. Such are the wonders and complexities of the museum visitor experience!

I have provided just a few examples of the museum visitor experience for which I have demonstrated how it's possible to begin to model the museum visitor experience. However, as noted earlier in the chapter, it will never be possible to completely and specifically model this experience. This is partially due to the stochastic nature of the visitor experience, but more than anything, it is due to the inherently complex and highly personal nature of each human's meaning-making. Still, I would make the case that this view of the museum visitor experience is beginning to provide a degree of understanding that has not been possible. To see how it all becomes a whole and something we can confidently describe and predict, we must again move outside the confines of the museum. To understand the museum visitor experience, we must now move to that abstract realm where the museum and visitor come together over the course of days, weeks, months, and years—the "museum visitor experience" that is constructed within the mind of the visitor and expressed in the form of visitor satisfaction and memories.

CHAPTER 5

Satisfaction

What does not satisfy when we find it was not the thing
we were desiring.

—*C.S. Lewis, 1933*[1]

The following is an excerpt from an interview with Shawn, a 26-year-old white male as he exited the National Museum of Natural History in Washington, DC.

Q: So, tell me about your visit to the Natural History Museum. Did you have a good time?

A: Yes, it was great. My girlfriend and I got see all the things we were hoping to see.

Q: That's great. What were you hoping to see?

A: Oh, you know, the usual. We wanted to see the Hope Diamond, the dinosaurs, all the usual stuff.

Q: So these things, the Hope Diamond and the dinosaurs, were these things you knew about before you visited? Or were they things you found out about once you got here?

A: Oh, definitely knew about before we got here. We'd read the guides and we've been planning this trip to DC for months. All our friends were giving us advice on what to see and do; this museum was a must-see. We needed to see the Hope Diamond, the dinosaurs, we also need to see the big flag and *Wizard of Oz* stuff over at the History Museum and all the air and space stuff like the space capsule and moon rock over at the Air and Space Museum.

Q: Wow, that's a lot to see! Anything else?

A: Sure, we also saw the Capitol yesterday and a couple of the monuments, and tomorrow we've got tickets for the White House. We're only here for a few days [chuckles] but we're going to cram as much as we can into the visit as possible.

Q: Great, so tell me more about this visit to the Natural History Museum. How long have you been here? What did you see first?

A: We spent about an hour or so here. We were just overwhelmed, there's so much to see; it's really mind-blowing. . . . We went first to see the Hope Diamond because [girlfriend] really wanted to see that more than anything. It took us some time to find it, but we went straight there. It was really beautiful. Of course, so were all the other gems there. The whole experience up there just knocked your socks off. While we were up there we wandered a little more around the geology exhibits. Huge meteorites, man! I never knew that so much stuff from outer space hits the Earth every day; it's like several hundred every day.

Q: Wow, I didn't know that! Okay, and then, what did you do?

A: Well, after the gems and geology stuff we made our way down to the dinosaurs. That was really cool, too. I've always loved dinosaurs and it was so neat to see all the dinosaur skeletons and dioramas and stuff.

[Later in the interview]

Q: So, how would you rate your overall visit, from a 1, not satisfied at all to a 7, totally satisfied?

A: Oh, definitely a 7, yeah, definitely a 7. This was really great. We got to see what we came to see here, we had a blast, and it's only our second day in DC. We're really stoked now to see the rest of DC!

Shawn is a wonderful example of a visitor with an Experience seeker visit motivation. Not only was he a tourist in Washington, DC, he was a man on a mission! He and his girlfriend had been planning this visit for months, and between the guides and his friends the two of them had accumulated a visitor's "shopping list" of sights to see and experiences to collect. High on his list were the Smithsonian museums and he was happily ticking them off. He came primarily to see the Hope Diamond and dinosaurs and that's what he did. He actually got more in the bargain than he anticipated, finding out about geology as well as about paleontology. (For the sake of brevity, I eliminated much of that part of the interview, but Shawn talked for quite a while about all the things he saw and re-membered, many of which were tied to his childhood interest in dino-saurs.) He rated his experience a big "7" out of a possible 7 on the scale of satisfaction. And why shouldn't he have?

Shawn had a specific entering identity-related set of needs related to his role as a once-in-a-lifetime visitor to the nation's capital. He was deter-mined to see the important landmarks of Washington, DC—places and things he had long heard and dreamed about, and now he was living that dream. The Natural History Museum played an important role in those dreams and the designers of the Museum did not disappoint Shawn. Al-though way-finding was a small challenge, given that the Hope Diamond is on the top floor of the Museum and some distance from the entrance, Shawn and his girlfriend were undeterred in their search. Fortunately, the designers of the Geology, Gems, and Minerals exhibit made it relatively easy to locate the Hope Diamond once the visitor is in the exhibit area. The design of the dinosaur exhibits also was conducive to this "fast-track" approach. Shawn not only saw and spent time at these iconic exhibits, but for all the reasons outlined in the previous chapter, he spent time at several other exhibits and picked up a variety of personally relevant and interesting facts about geology and paleontology. The sum total of this package of museum experiences was highly enjoyable and fulfilling. In short, Shawn entered the Natural History Museum with a well-defined set of expectations, framed around a "tourist" self-aspect. He hoped to see two of the nation's iconic exhibits that are housed at the Natural History Museum—the Hope Diamond and dinosaurs, and experience the Natu-ral History Museum. In other words, he wanted to be able to say that "he had been there, done that"! Clearly, Shawn exited the Museum feeling fully satisfied that he had accomplished those goals.

Shawn's high rating of the Natural History Museum is not an anomaly as museums rank as highly-satisfying leisure venues. Thousands of cus-tomer satisfaction surveys have been done in museums of all kinds and sizes, and almost without exception, the results are consistently high. Is this because museums are great places? In part, this is true, but the more likely answer is that most people who visit museums already possess some reasonable understanding of what museums afford in the way of leisure benefits. High ratings are the result of a strong match between the entering identity-related visit motivations of visitors and the realities of the actual museum visit they experience.

RESEARCH ON LEISURE SATISFACTION

Most of us have a good sense of what it means to be satisfied. Satisfaction is the neuro-physiological experience of feeling content and at ease with one's situation. Satisfaction is also commonly used as a measure to judge how well an organization's products and services meet or surpass customer's expectations. In a competitive marketplace where many organizations compete for a share of the public's time and money, customer satisfaction is often viewed as a key differentiator because it is a strong predictor of whether people will continue to utilize an organization's products and services. Not surprisingly, many museums have become quite diligent at trying to measure visitor satisfaction. The fact that visitor satisfaction is an ambiguous and abstract concept, and that the actual manifestation of the state of satisfaction will vary from person to person and product/service to product/service, has not prevented institutions from measuring it. Accordingly, the state of a person's satisfaction with any given product or service depends on a number of both psychological and physical variables. Two leading consumer psychologists, Leonard Berry and A. Parasuraman, defined no less than ten dimensions of satisfaction: Quality, Value, Timeliness, Efficiency, Ease of Access, Environment, Inter-departmental Teamwork, Frontline Service Behaviors, Commitment to the Customer, and Innovation.[2] At some level, this research can be applied to the museum visitor experience, but most of the models have been designed for customer purchases of products from for-profit companies.

More directly relevant to our concerns has been the research that has been conducted specifically on the topic of leisure satisfaction using what is called the dynamic model of the leisure experience.[3] Leisure researchers have defined the dynamic leisure experience as a balance between a participant's entering expectations for a leisure experience and the set of interactions that the leisure participant has during a leisure experience, including all the social and physical context interactions in which he or she participates. This is a model quite similar to the one I have been laying out in this book. Since most leisure researchers are quantitatively minded, they tend to couch their models in those terms. Thus, according to the leisure research literature, a leisure participant's overall experience can be conceived as the sum of the experiences that occur during the leisure, with each episode having the potential to confirm or disconfirm the individual's entering expectations. What are these episodes? According to leisure researchers, they include both situational factors such as the presence of litter or crowds, as well as subjective factors such as the perception that things were easy to find, the extent to which goals were met, or the perceived quality of what was seen. Although most leisure researchers, as well as most leisure purveyors (including museum professionals), tend to be overly concerned with situational factors since these are the things they perceive they can control—litter can be picked up and crowds can be managed—they are not necessarily the factors most important to visitors. As leisure researchers Alan Graefe and Anthony Fedler and Steven Whisman and Steven Hollenhorst discovered, leisure satisfaction was most strongly influenced by people's subjective evaluations of the elements of a recreational trip and only indirectly influenced by the situational aspects of the activity.[4] In other words, perceptions of the experience were far more important than were actual conditions.

These ideas were followed up in-depth by leisure researchers Bong-koo Lee, Scott Shafer, and Inho Kang and they confirmed that perceptions were more important than situations. Although all the various episodes and interactions that occurred during a leisure situation were involved to a greater or lesser extent in the algorithm of a visitor's ratings of satisfaction, the most important consideration was how visitors saw themselves within the situation. In particular, visitors' ratings of satisfaction were most strongly associated with the degree to which their self-identity and identity-related needs were satisfied. And these, of course, turned out to be directly related to their entering expectations and motivations for the visit.[5] Quoting from Lee, Shafer, and Kang:

> In conclusion, leisure participants have several expectations or goals when they participate in a leisure activity. Maintaining affective meanings associated with their self-identities (i.e., fundamental sentiments) is one of the expectations or goals. However the expectation may be confirmed at one time during leisure participation, but disconfirmed at a different time depending on episodes (i.e., social interactions between a leisure participant and others). The confirmation/disconfirmation of affective meanings associated with self-identity produces outcomes (i.e., emotions), and, in turn, lead to evaluations on episodes. Evaluations made of episodes determine leisure participants' satisfaction levels (p. 106).

Visit satisfaction was primarily determined by whether or not visitors perceived that their entering identity-related motivations were satisfied. These results have now been confirmed by other studies as well.[6] They are also confirmed by the example of Shawn presented above, as well as for all of the other museum visitors we've met so far in this book— George, Elmira, Maria, Frances, Mara, Sara, and Hanna. And so it is for most people who visit museums.

SELF-FULFILLING PROPHECIES

One other important result emerges from this leisure and tourism research on satisfaction—not only do most people's satisfactions derive from their entering expectations, but these expectations are frequently manipulated by visitors to ensure that they fit. Spanish tourism researchers Ignacio Rodríguez del Bosque and Hector San Martín found that tourists consistently tended to adjust their perceptions to their beliefs in order to minimize cognitive dissonance.[7] The theory of cognitive dissonance holds that inconsistency among beliefs or behaviors will cause an uncomfortable psychological tension. Frequently, this perceived psychological tension leads people to change their beliefs to fit their actual behaviors, but the opposite can also happen.[8] The research of del Bosque and San Martin seems to suggest that in the case of leisure and tourism, people routinely place high importance on achieving satisfaction of their expectations. Thus, even when occasionally something in their experience does not quite match up with their expectations, as for example Shawn's comments about the challenges of finding the Hope Diamond or the behavior of Hanna's son while visiting the High Desert Museum, visitors tend to excuse away these experiences as insignificant in the grand scheme of things. Much of this comes under the topic of self-fulfilling prophesies.

Visitor's identity-related motivations turn out to be classic examples of self-fulfilling prophesies—a situation where a prediction of what's to happen becomes true because of the influence our expectations have on seeing what we want to see. First proposed more than fifty years ago by the sociologist Robert Merton,[9] the effects and impact of self-fulfilling prophecies have been documented across a large number of contexts and situations, ranging from teacher effects on student learning, to selling decisions in real estate, to research scientists reporting of results, and to the impact of mothers on children's underage drinking behaviors.[10] The reason self-fulfilling prophecies occur is because personal expectations are subjective; therefore, the influence of expectations undermines building an objective knowledge base. A self-fulfilling prophecy is simply a cause-and-effect scenario that has been repeatedly proven true—"in the past, I've gone to places like this and this happened so there's no reason to believe it won't happen again. And if it doesn't quite turn out that way, it was probably some quirky event that I can ignore since it was supposed to turn out that way." And so it is for most visitors, most of the time.

WHEN EXPECTATIONS AND EXPERIENCES CLASH

Although satisfaction is the norm, that is not always the case. Felipe is a Latino male in his late 30s who is a social services worker involved with his community, particularly his church. In February 2001, he was one of the individuals we observed visiting the California Science Center. Felipe was visiting the Science Center as part of a large, multi-generational group comprised of at least seven people. These included his two children, his wife, a friend of one of his children, and another family member of this friend. We observed continuous social interaction between and among the group members throughout the visit. Felipe talked to the children, to his wife, and to the others in the group. Over the course of the visit, Felipe was very directive of his children's experiences in particular and constantly telling them what they should look at and what exhibits not to attend to, though they did not always follow his advice. The following excerpt comes from an interview conducted at a local library twenty months later. We categorized Felipe as having a Facilitator motivation during his visit because, as you'll see, Felipe makes it clear that his goal for his visit was to affect a specific learning agenda he had devised for his children.

Q: Why did you go [to the Science Center] that day?

A: I thought it was interesting for [my children] to see nature and it's free and you learn a little bit about being active and the benefit of exercising and keeping your body in motion and that's why I took my kids there.

Q: So, you knew about this exhibition?

A: Yes, when I went with the foster children and I liked it, then I took my children on the weekend.

Q: So, you went back with your children to be exposed to the *World of Life* specifically?

A: Yes.

Q: What in particular motivated you to bring your children to the *World of Life*?

A: I think the big doll.

Q: Do you remember her name?

A: No, I don't.

Q: We call her *Tess*. [*Tess* is part of a theater show on the need for the body to keep in balance featuring a 15-meter/50-foot animatronic female, flashing lights and gauges, and a mixed media presentation on a large screen.] What made her so important for your children?

A: Because it's big and it kind of creates a strong impression in your memory. And then it explains the functions of your body, the blood, circulation and how it works. You hear the heart and see the lungs [move] and it's a movie that's explaining how it works and I think that is all really important to know.

Q: What makes you so interested in these things? What is your interest in having your children learn about it?

A: Well, my kids are a little chubby so that was an encouragement for them to be a part of an exercise [sic], how important it is. And even P.E., if they do it every day at school, to take it seriously during that hour because it's very important for their bodies to maintain the functioning and, you know, so we went over there. I wanted instead of, you know, sometimes we talk to the children but they don't listen. So instead of my talking to them, we [would] go and take them over there and have them sit down and have *Tess* do a little presentation.

Q: An outside source to give the whole thing credibility?

A: Yeah.

Q: Did it work?

A: Yeah, a little. I think more so for my daughter, my son is more active but my daughter wants to be in the house instead of outside.

Q: Do you remember how they responded to the exhibit?

A: They liked it. It also created an impression and it really leaves them thinking, you know, like exercise and the benefits for their body and what we need to do to be healthy.

Felipe was able to identify not only a specific goal for his visit but also what part of the exhibition would be most likely to accomplish this goal. Although Felipe indicated that he thought his goals were at least partially met for the visit, as we talked further it became clear that this physical fitness goal was not the only goal. All of his goals, though, were designed to support specific learning-related outcomes for his children. Felipe saw the Science Center as an educational institution (traditionally defined) and brought his children there so that they could learn specific things.

Q: I'd like to talk to you now about what your expectations were for that visit.

A: To learn about science. To learn about how the body functions and I expected [them] to learn more, like, the kind of ways to prevent destruction of the planet maybe. Forests and kind of things like that.

Q: Were these expectations met?

A: Not really. I think a lot of children go there and it would be a good idea to educate them to take care of their environment and I don't think it's a big issue in the Science Center. I think they do a very good job on how the body functions and how to keep it healthy, the joints and muscles and the heart and how it functions. So there is that part that I was going to find out about, it wasn't there. And another thing that I noticed was that there are too many things when you go there. There's [sic] too many things, you don't know where to start and what you do is you kind of lose interest if there's too many [things to do and see]. If you concentrate on the big ones, the little ones may be important but you don't pay too much attention because there are so many of them.

Q: So, you found the design, the layout of the place confusing?

A: Yes, distracting. I think there should be more things like *Tess*. The place should be redesigned because it confuses you; it really does. Big things like *Tess* create a memory in you and it's short, it's not too long. But all those little machines that are there are confusing. . . . Yeah, you know the kids wanted to go play. And they were looking for games, so I think for the kids the games can be bad. They can spend a lot of time playing games in other places, but games can be good. For example, games like making surgery or I don't know, some kind of other learning game. Like the games that they played and the videos can at the same time make them learn some science; to improve their minds.

[Later in the interview]

Q: You said that you came there to learn. Was that for you? Did you want to learn or did you want your children to learn?

A: I wanted my children to learn. When I went, just *Tess* was worth coming back for and sharing that information with my kids. So I guess my expectations were somewhat met. We wanted to learn more about plants and everything but that place was so confusing. So if you ask me how to improve that place, it would be to create more [exhibits like] *Tess* and games for the kids to play where they can be entertained when playing, but at the same time be educating themselves. I do remember something like, how we live in a, you know, we all live in the same planet, plants, animals, we all share.

Q: You remember that part?

A: Yes. We all share the same environment and we live together, we try to live in harmony and it's like, we can't destroy the plants because that affects us human beings at the same time.

Q: So, you remember that okay?

A: How important the plants are and the animals. Yes, I remember that.

Q: So, did your children benefit from their visit to the Science Center?

A: I don't know if they did, but I think they did. I don't take [them on] a trip like that, that is not beneficial to anybody, whether it's [for the] short or long term, it's there. And you know what you need to do and I think it was beneficial to, like, learn about science. Whether it shows immediately or [takes a] long time, or whatever, but I don't think it's worthless.

Q: But it's hard to pinpoint what the benefits were?

A: For my children, kind of yes, it would be. But I'm hoping that it was the exercise part, how to take care of your body. And also how important plants and animals are. And also to understand the importance of God's creation. . . . And it was my job as a parent to do it. You know, I did ask questions, about what they learned and my expectations were to help them learn, how to keep exercising and how important it is. And so that was my main concern. There may be something else, because one could go there for other reasons, but that was why I went there.

Q: Would you go again?

A: Probably not. I'm not sure it was all that worthwhile anyway. I mean it was okay, but I can think of better things to do.

Q: Like what?

A: Oh, I don't know, like go to Sunday school or something like that.

Q: Why do you go?

A: I go because it's a part of my job, and when I like something I take [my children] to that.

Q: So you mentioned Christianity. Is that a bit of your hobby?

A: Yes. You mean Christianity, church? Yes it is. All my free time that's what I do. I'm very involved with Christian TV and my free time that's what I do. It probably would have been better to have just taken my children to Sunday school. It would have been a better use of their time.

Felipe makes it clear that he was at the Science Center only for his children and not primarily to have a good time as a family, but to support his children's learning. He wanted them to learn specific science content in order to change their behaviors—get more exercise. Felipe was willing to acknowledge that other people might have other motivations for visiting the Science Center, but the only reason for him to go with his children was for them to Learn. [Note: I purposefully use a capital "L" here to emphasize the traditional, narrow definition of the word "learning."] Given that he was unsure of how much they learned, he was only partially satisfied with the experience. In particular, Felipe felt that the design of the Science Center interfered with the learning; it had too many exhibits and not enough focus, particularly on environmental issues. Why Felipe felt that this latter topic was so important for his children was not made explicit in the interview. At the end, he indicated that while he still hoped that the visit was in some way valuable to his children's learning, he believed their time could have been better spent, for example, in learning more about religion.

The Sunday school comment points to a certain perspective on learning in out-of-school settings that Felipe brought to the Science Center. He did not expect his children to learn science as an abstract body of knowledge, but rather as a set of facts with specific outcomes, for example, exercise leads to better health and appreciation of the environment yields an increased appreciation for God's creation. At some level, Felipe seemed to view the Science Center visit as analogous to Sunday school—both help his children make better moral choices. Although being a good parent and doing something about his children's "chubbiness" is clearly important to him, this does not appear to be the manner in which Felipe defines himself. His passion is Christianity which he expresses through his church work. He possesses an 'i' identity to be a good parent; he should help to educate his children. Taking his children to the Science Center was an expression of that identity-related motivation. However, he ended up questioning his decision since he was uncertain if his children achieved the desired learning that his parental motivation dictated they should. Presumably, if his children had demonstrated evidence of the desired changes in knowledge and behavior, he might have felt otherwise. Under the circumstance, it seems unlikely that he will take his children back to the Science Center any time soon, despite the fact that admission is free.

Unlike the other museum visitors we've profiled in the previous chapters, Felipe did not possess a well-honed mental concept of what the Science Center could best offer his children. His prior experiences and understanding of places like the Science Center led him to have a slightly inaccurate model of this experience. The Science Center was an educational institution, but the kinds of learning experiences it supported "looked" and "felt" very different from those Felipe envisioned for his children. His model of learning was more in line with the formality of schooling. The Sunday school classes at his church fit his model, but the more free-wheeling, free-choice nature of the Science Center did not. Felipe's perceptions of the "actual" Science Center experience did not align with his perceptions of the "imagined" Science Center experience. Although he acknowledged that his children probably learned something, and he was aware of the fact that his children seemed to be enjoying themselves, these observations were not consistent with his self-aspect of a "good parent." It is important to note that Felipe's self-identity construct as a good parent was not changed by his museum visitor experience. Two years later, he still could not reconcile the reality of his museum visit experience, in particular the lack of learning he perceived his children experienced, with his expectations for visiting the Museum. The result was dissatisfaction with the overall experience and the likelihood that Felipe will not soon be taking his family to visit another museum.

Felipe was unlike most other museum visitors in the sense that he found the museum visit experience less than totally satisfying. I've tried to suggest that this was primarily because Felipe possessed a deficient understanding of what the Science Center experience offered, relative to his expectations. Not included in the interview excerpts with Felipe was a whole line of questioning about his prior museum experience. He had virtually none, which might explain his difficulties with the exhibits at California Science Center. But his difficulties also point out the issues surrounding the broadening of museum audiences. As I will discuss more fully in Chapter 9 of this book, this model provides important insights as to how to attract new and historically under-represented individuals to museums, but it also suggests what the challenges are. In Felipe's case, we can infer that his misperceptions about what the museum visitor experience should offer were, in part, due to a lack of relevant experience and, in part, cultural. Even if he had a deep knowledge of what learning was like at a place like the California Science Center, Felipe may have opted to invest his leisure time elsewhere because of his culturally informed beliefs of what it means to be a good parent and what "learning" should be like. What was marred by his Science Center experience was not Felipe's self-concept of himself as a good parent, but his concept of what museums offer and how they can be utilized to satisfy important identity-related needs.

CHAPTER 6

Memories

The stream of thought flows on; but most of its segments fall into the bottomless abyss of oblivion. Of some, no memory survives the instant of their passage.

Of others, it is confined to a few moments, hours, or days. Others again, leave vestiges which are indestructible, and by means of which they may be recalled as long as life endures.

Can we explain these differences?

—*William James, 1890*[1]

Frank is an African American in his early 40s. He is college-educated and works as a traffic department scheduler for a large entertainment company in Los Angeles. My colleague Martin Storksdieck and I interviewed Frank in his Anaheim office two years after we first talked with him and observed his visit to the *World of Life* exhibition at the California Science Center. While at the Science Center, Frank spent all his time with his then nine-year-old daughter, allowing her to almost totally dictate the course of the visit. The following are extended excerpts from our follow-up interview.

Q: What did you see or do [at the Science Center] that was memorable?

A: Nothing that stands out. On that particular day, I was more of a follower [laughs], watching my daughter going from exhibit to exhibit. That was her goal, to get all of her stamps. [NOTE: There was a "passport" activity provided by the Science Center designed to encourage children to visit exhibits throughout the museum.] I tried to get her to slow it down a little bit to learn about all of the different things that were going on in the exhibit at that particular time. That was a little difficult, she was just happy to be somewhere. We concentrated on food groups for humans, because to me that's important —making sure she understands a balanced meal and things of that nature. My daughter was also fascinated by *Tess*. [*Tess* is described in the previous chapter.]

Q: So, you saw the show?

A: Yes, but mostly I was just trying to keep up with my daughter.

Q: Do you remember anything about the show?

A: I remember what my daughter's reaction was. She was fascinated with seeing something this large and understanding something about the heartbeat. I think she [a featured girl in the show's movie] was playing soccer.

Q: Did you learn anything from the show?

A: I'm not sure. I was really focused on watching my daughter.

Q: Whose idea was it to go to the Science Center?

A: It was my idea for a family outing. We became members that same day. I've taken my niece and nephew once who are 17 and 14, and they've gone with my daughter on their own.

Q: You said you were a follower that day. What was the purpose of that visit when you were a follower?

A: Having an activity for my daughter to do for a day. My wife had the day off. It's possible that it was a weekday and we both had the day off and we wanted to do something interesting and the museum was one of the first choices.

Q: Do you take your daughter other places to do something interesting?

A: No, she's so involved on the weekends with ice skating, ballet for a while, now volleyball, and in a dance class. She's pretty active on the weekends so we don't have as much time to visit other places.

[Later in the interview]

Q: Can you give me some examples of what you or your daughter saw?

A: We saw the *Human Miracle* and the baby chicks. The first was where the fetuses are. We went in and talked about it. It was fascinating for her and to see the process of being small and growing. She got a kick out of the baby chicks. That part of the exhibition is always fascinating to her even when we've gone back again, she'll stop and look at that exhibit. She loves to see the eggs, some of which are whole, some of which are empty and some of which are in the process of having a chick emerge from them. It makes the process so real.

Q: Is it fascinating for you, too?

A: It's always fascinating, the process of life, even though we've seen it over and over again. I've seen it at the old Science Center, since I was almost her age. Actually, when we were having breakfast one day and opened up an egg and she saw red specks and she asked questions about that, I used the exhibit as a teaching tool. I said that's where chickens come from, remember the Science Center.

Q: So, did you pick up anything? Were there any things that you remembered since your visit?

A: Reproduction, nutrition.

Q: These were things that came up later on?

A: No, not exactly, [there was no] correlation between them. I just thought about them, nothing specific.

Q: What about them? When, while you were watching a TV show or reading something?

A: If anyone would say anything plant life-related or about cells, I'd say, "I saw that at the California Science Center." Clearly, that stuff made an impression on me.

Q: So, did you have a good time?

A: Yes.

Q: How do you know?

A: I bought a membership! [laughs] It wasn't just for the discount in the store! It is a valuable experience to go to the Science Museum at least every 6 months, if not more. If [my daughter] didn't have so many other things going on, I'd probably keep better track of what's going on at the Museum, like seminars, things for kids.

Q: How important is it for you to have a good time? What does that mean to you?

A: I always enjoy going to museums.

Q: For yourself?

A: Yes. I'll go to the LA County Museum of Art just to walk around if I have some time. I used to walk around the Tar Pits, too. I enjoy it.

Q: By yourself?

A: Yes.

Q: When do you do that?

A: Rarely, now that I work so much. Sometimes on the weekends I'm here. But if I have a day off, I'll go there and walk around and I'll see the same exhibits over and over. I just enjoy it.

Q: Did your wife have a good time?

A: I believe she did. [laughs] I think it was just an opportunity for us all to go somewhere together.

Q: How important is it that she had a good time when the three of you go to a museum?

A: It's very important. I hope she's having a good time. Our viewpoints are definitely different in what we concentrate on at the Museum. I look more at the biological makeup of things and she would just say "Okay, there's an ant" and move on. But my Dad was a chemistry professor and he helped develop us; develop a liking for science as we were growing up.

Q: You say "us"?

A: Yes, my brothers and sisters.

Q: Did he take you to museums?

A: Dad was always working so Mom took us.

[Later in the interview]

Q: But this particular Science Center visit was not for you. It was for your daughter.

A: Yes. Definitely for her. . . . As long as she's having a good time, I'm happy. When we go to the movies, she'll take her girlfriend and I take that time to go to sleep. [laughs] As long as she's happy, I'm happy.

Q: Do you ever take her to places that you want to go, or where it's for you?

A: No.

Q: What would you characterize as the single most satisfying characteristic of that visit?

A: That I did something good for my daughter, because she enjoyed it and she took some things with her. If I went by myself, I'd look for a higher level of understanding, but that was not the purpose of this visit. . . . Being exposed to different elements at the museum was a major plus [for my daughter]. It's important to get kids interested [so they can] pursue that which they find interesting.

Over the course of the interview, Frank kept reinforcing that this visit was not for him, despite the fact that when pressed, he admits that he too might have picked up a few ideas about science. Frank describes an almost totally child-focused experience where he sublimates his needs and interests to those of his daughter. Where he does intervene, it's on the behalf of his daughter. His interest in learning, independent of his daughter, was limited. In this regard, Frank is typical of people who visit museums with the suite of visitor motivations I've called Facilitators; they use museums to satisfy a social visit agenda.

Frank was able to share many details with us about what he did and saw during his museum visit, but since the focus of the visit was his daughter, what he remembered best was what his daughter saw and did. In fact, our interview with him two years after his visit lasted twice as long as the time he actually spent in the exhibition with his daughter and was roughly comparable to the total time he spent at the Science Center. How odd! Why, as the William James quote at the beginning of this chapter suggests, would Frank have such strong and indestructible memories of this museum visit, and why these particular memories?

MUSEUM MEMORIES

One of the more striking things I have discovered in more than thirty years of research on museum visitors is how persistent are memories of the museum visitor experience. Beyond all reason, people remember their visits to museums. In study after study, people have been able, and willing to talk to me about their museum visit experiences days, weeks, months, and even years later, often in amazing detail. Why should these experiences be so memorable? In the late 1990s, Lynn Dierking and I did a study of school-children's memories of their school field trips. We interviewed eight year olds about trips they had taken one to two years earlier, thirteen year olds about trips they had taken six to seven years earlier, and young adults about trips they had taken anywhere from twelve to twenty years earlier. Amazingly, nearly 100% of the individuals we talked to were able to remember these trips and describe details from their experience. Even more amazing was the fact that there was no significant difference in the strength or depth of memories across these three groups.[2] In other words, once laid down, museum visitor experiences appear to be strongly held in memory.

In a recent review of the literature on the long-term impact of museum experiences, museum researchers David Anderson, Martin Storksdieck, and Michael Spock similarly emphasized how prevalent it was to find evidence of long-term museum memories. They also made clear that like all memories, museum memories are not a video recording of events. Not all experiences are equally remembered; visitors have been found to be quite selective in what they recall.[3] As we saw above, Frank was very focused on his daughter and thus, the majority of his museum memories were about his daughter rather than the actual contents of the museum. And even those things that Frank "chose" to remember likely changed over time. Some aspects grew stronger in his mind as they were reinforced and consolidated by additional experiences and some memories faded away. Some memories no doubt were embellished and distorted to include some information that "factually" didn't really belong to the visit experience.

This reality was documented by psychologists Maria Medved and Phillip Oatley in a systematic study of museum impact conducted at a Canadian science center.[4] Medved and Oatley studied visitors to the Science Arcade section of the Ontario Science Center, a gallery which contains interactive displays that focus on physical science concepts such as electricity, air pressure, and sound waves. Visitors were interviewed as they left the Science Arcade and by telephone a month later. Overall, there were no significant differences between the amount and type of exhibition-related conceptual understandings recorded immediately after the visit and one month later. The results were presented to a panel of independent raters, blind to whether an explanation was from the initial or follow-up interview. The panel was asked to categorize the conceptual change statements as either "deterioration of conceptual understanding," "no change," or "improved understanding." Results of this analysis revealed that 36% of the responses showed deterioration of conceptual change over the one-month period, 36% showed an increase in understanding over the one-month period, and 28% remained the same. In other words, conceptual understanding was just as likely to improve over time as it was to deteriorate.

In a study conducted by me and other colleagues in Australia, visitors to science-related museums were tested for their memories of the experience immediately following the visit and again several months later. Like in the study above, we were interested to know how stable museum memories were. Our findings revealed that memories remained quite constant for about 25% of visitors, but for the vast majority of visitors, their memories changed over time. In general, what visitors said the impact of their museum experience was as they exited the museum was significantly different from what they believed the impact was four to eight months later. Over time, specific memories tended to disappear and be replaced by more conceptual and "big picture" memories of the experience.[5] This is not surprising, particularly in light of a growing body of research that shows that all memories take time to consolidate and become permanent—in some cases, it takes days and even months for memories to be made "permanent."[6]

Historically, it was assumed that the main thing that contributed to the consolidation of a memory and thus, its persistence over time was rehearsal; ideas are made stronger through continued conversation or thinking. This is a holdover from behaviorist models of learning, stimulus-response-reinforcement, but these days cognitive and neural scientists have come to appreciate that memory is not that simple, nor predictable.[7] A range of factors other than rehearsal likely contribute to making museum memories "stick." Some factors, similar to what was discussed in the previous chapter, represent random events. For example, memory would be encouraged in the situation where the visitor turns on the evening news to see a breaking story that happens to directly relate to what he or she saw or did at the museum the previous day. More typically, a series of less random, but no less unique, events that are collectively assembled by the visitor and result in long-term memories are what support the consolidation of museum visitor experience memories. I use the word "assembled" advisedly since memories, like learning, are constructed realities.

Research in the neurosciences confirms the fundamentally constructive nature of memory. Quite literally, memories are built up and combined as they are created, and over time are reconstructed and recombined.[8] The result is that numerous comparable experiences are combined into a single composite recollection, creating memories that are personal "constructs" of events rather than exact "reproductions."[9] Consequently, the ways in which we develop meaning and build memories is an extraordinarily flexible process. Ideas, images, and even events can be assembled into new and unique configurations. Although the impermanence of memory can sometimes be a liability when trying to remember the name of an acquaintance at a party, it can also be a benefit. The constructive quality of memory enables humans to invent, theorize, and create, and that is exactly what visitors do with regard to their museum experience memories. It appears that the memories people construct about their museum visit, though at some level unique and individualized, seem to share some surprising structural commonalities. It is as if we have stumbled upon some magical housing "subdivision" of museum visitor experience memories. As we travel through this subdivision and view memory after memory, we see that the colors and trim on each are unique, but if we look closely, we can discern that structurally each is built from just a handful of basic designs. Just as the individual's museum visit appears to be shaped by his or her entering identity-related visit motivations so, too, do the individual's long-term memories and meaning making.

IDENTITY-RELATED MOTIVATIONS AS EXPERIENTIAL FILTER

In order to understand how the long-term meanings people make from their museum visit experience can be shaped by an entering identity-related visit motivation we need to begin with a statement of the obvious— memory is always selective. Only a small subset of the things experienced during a visit will be remembered and many, if not most, things will be forgotten. This is obvious, but the question is can we predict which things visitors will selectively remember, and why these things and not others? The key to understanding what is remembered depends upon understanding the highly personalized "experiential filters" every visitor brings with them to museums. These filters create the lens through which memory is formed and recalled.

At the simplest level, visitors only can and do remember things they experience. The memories an individual ends up with must, by necessity, be drawn from the possible wealth of experiences a museum visitor has chosen in the museum. But as stated above, only a small subset of all the things we can and actually do see, hear, taste, smell, touch, and think about at any given moment are encoded into memory. This makes sense since we are constantly bombarded by stimuli; no one could possibly accommodate it all. All of us use filters to determine not only what to attend to, but also what we store in our memory.

In recent years, we have come to equate that which is attended to and remembered with the idea of meaningfulness. By definition, we attend to that we find meaningful and ignore that which we find meaningless. But what is meaning? According to anthropologist Clifford Geertz, meaning is our mind's way of making sense of the world; the translation of existence into conceptual form.[10] Meaning provides a framework for helping us assess what is important and supports our understanding and actions. Humans, in particular, are extremely adept at meaning making—it is arguably one of the things that sets us apart from other life forms. As the pace of cultural evolution has increased, so too have selection pressures for individuals capable of sifting and sorting through greater quantities of information to determine that which is most meaningful. Modern humans are truly experts at making meaning.

Visitors to museums make meaning. Each and every visitor brings to bear their prior knowledge, experience, interests, and values in order to actively, though not necessarily consciously, determine which parts of the museum are worth focusing on. Museum visitors only attend to those aspects of their visitor experience that at the moment are most meaningful to *them*. Let me make this point very clear. As we suggested in the previous chapter, the realities of the museum—for example, the content and design of exhibitions and labels—are important. But exactly which elements of a museum visit experience a visitor will actually attend to is only somewhat predictable based upon the contents of the museum. On any given day, two visitors will walk through the exact same space, at the exact same time, and come away having seen and thought about entirely different things. And for each of these two visitors, *reality* is what they paid attention to, not what was there. The museum visitor experience is always a personally-constructed reality; it is not tied to any fixed entity, space, or event. Not only can two visitors have a different visitor experience standing in front of the same exhibit, but the same individual on two different days will almost certainly have a different visitor experience because he or she is not the same person those two days.

So who was Frank, the subject of our chapter interview, on the day of his visit? As I mentioned previously, Frank was enacting a Facilitator role on that day; the reality of the California Science Center that Frank experienced was filtered through the lens of how he perceived his daughter's interests and activities, not his own.

Q: Do you remember anything about the [*Tess*] show?

A: I remember what my daughter's reaction was. She was fascinated with seeing something this large and understanding something about the heartbeat. I think she [a featured girl in the show's movie] was playing soccer.

Q: Did you learn anything from the show?

A: I'm not sure. I was really focused on watching my daughter.

Although meaning-making has become highly evolved in modern humans, it is a process that has its roots deep in our evolutionary history. Meaning-making evolved long before there was language, in fact, before there were humans, primates, or other mammals at all. No matter how eloquent the theory of meaning-making or poetic the description, ultimately it is a process/product of a complex series of electro-chemical interactions in the brain and body that have evolved over many hundreds of millions of years. (For reference, human-like creatures have been on this planet for less than 10 million years and modern humans for much less than a hundred thousand years.[11]) The process of making meaning, even as practiced by twenty-first century humans, is constructed upon a very ancient, whole body, biological base. It is profoundly important to appreciate the long evolutionary history of meaning-making; it is not just a recent cultural overlay unique to modern humans.

Meaning, and for that matter, memories, are never constructed *de novo*; visitor meaning is always constructed from a foundation of fundamental personal needs, prior experiences, and interests. Over the past decades, hundreds of people have shared their museum memories with me and my colleagues, and in virtually all cases these individuals' entering needs, experiences, and interests have figured prominently in their recollections. Their entering "frames" helped shape both the broad narrative of their recollections as well as the specifics of their narratives.

With Frank's memories as an example, he kept reinforcing that this visit was not for him in the interview, despite the fact that when pressed, he admitted that he too might have picked up some information from the exhibits. Frank talked about growing up in a family that valued learning and intimated that he's trying to be more involved with his daughter's upbringing than his father was with his upbringing. Still, he's obviously proud of his father; the fact that Frank's father instilled a love of science in him and his siblings is clearly important to him. Going to museums thus emerged as something deeply rooted in his sense of self. Frank explained to us that there was little time for additional experiences in his daughter's busy life and in his life, as well. Choices had to be made, and the choice to specifically visit a science education venue might have had much to do with Frank's own family history. Visiting the Science Center appeared to satisfy several of his important identity-related needs, all of which were bound up with Frank's multi-dimensional concept of what being a "good father" meant to him. Unlike his own father, taking his daughter to the Science Center meant not being so preoccupied with his work that he neglected doing enjoyable things with his daughter. It also meant that, like his father, he was providing a positive role-model, in particular valuing science and learning. We can infer that this was a major motivation behind Frank's purchase of a Science Center membership, which as he quickly pointed out, was not in order to save money at the gift shop, or on future admissions since admission to the Science Center is free. It was clear that this visit to the Science Center was extremely important to Frank for a lot of reasons, many of which represented deeply-felt needs; it was also clear that Frank felt a great sense of personal satisfaction about his visit. As I will discuss more fully, this visit resulted in changes to Frank's own sense of self, particularly his sense of being a good father and uncle, as well as an enhanced perception of the benefits a setting like the California Science Center afforded. And unlike Felipe, who we discussed in the previous chapter, Frank's opinion of the Science Center as a valuable educational institution was positively reinforced.

These deeply held identity-related needs and visit motivations—Frank's desire to be a good father and support his daughter's science learning—form a large-scale prism through which virtually the entire visit experience is viewed. For Frank, his visit to the Science Center was remembered through the Facilitator self-aspect lens of "good father"—every memory began and/or ended with this perspective. This self-aspect helped to create the main architecture of Frank's memories. However, the details were framed by the specifics and realities of his experiences, only some of which involved the actual visit itself.

For example, when Frank talked about seeing the chicks in the exhibition his memories were a mixture of his prior museum experiences, his actual visit on that day, and his subsequent experiences with his daughter:

> It's always fascinating, the process of life, even though we've seen it over and over again. I've seen it at the old Science Center, since I was almost her age.

Actually, when we were having breakfast one day and opened up an egg and she saw red specks and she asked questions about that, I used the exhibit as a teaching tool. I said that's where chickens come from, remember the Science Center.

As we can see, prior experiences and interests, through the lens of identity-related motivations, frame what is attended to and what is remembered. Consistent with brain research, psychological studies have found that prior knowledge and experience directly influences how people perceive an event or what part of a situation is attended to in the first place.[12] People pay attention to and remember only what they are predisposed to attend to and remember; people predisposed to an action are most likely to perform that action.

This is why an understanding of the entering identity-related motivations of visitors represents such an important predictor of what people will attend to and remember. The power of the relationship between intention and action has long been understood. Nearly a half century ago, psychologist Victor Vroom formulated a model of action which he called expectancy theory. Expectancy theory states that an individual will act in a certain way based on the expectation that the act will be followed by a given outcome and on the attractiveness of that outcome to the individual.[13] Vroom's motivational model was later modified and elaborated on by several people,[14] but the basics of the model remain—what a person expects to find in an environment also affects how an individual responds to it.[15] Recent leisure and tourism research now indicates that not only do these expectations strongly influence what experiences an individual will have, but they also represent, as seemingly occurred with Frank, the best predictors of experience satisfaction and memory.[16]

Further evidence of just how powerful this relationship is between expectations, behaviors, and satisfaction comes from an unlikely place— medical research on drugs. A common phenomenon among medical researchers is what is known as the "placebo effect."[17] A placebo is usually a "control" used by researchers to mimic the "intervention" but is designed to be something that actually has no "real" value. For example, an experimental drug might be injected or given as a pill to a group of patients while another group of patients is given a placebo of a sugar water injection or a similar-sized and -colored sugar pill. If the treatment group has any positive or negative effects relative to the control group, those effects can be assumed to be caused by the "real" drug rather than just the process of receiving medical intervention. The reason scientists feel the need to invest so much energy in this charade is that in most studies of this sort, a large number of people have positive effects just by being part of the study. It is not uncommon for as many as half of all participants receiving the placebo treatment to show the same improvements as those being treated with the actual medicine.[18] The expectation of receiving benefit seems sufficient enough to cause benefit.

Evidence for the benefits engendered by placebo effects go beyond just self-reports and can include actual changes in patients' physiological condition. For example, in one set of studies involving antidepressant medications, brain scans of patients who were benefited by the medication showed significant changes in a particular area of the brain. Approximately half of all patients receiving placebo medications also showed changes in activity in these exact same areas of the brain.[19] Further, there is additional evidence that the placebo effect is not just a "psychological" phenomenon, as it has been shown to occur in experiments with laboratory animals like rats. In other words, the placebo effect appears to have some basis in neurochemistry, not just in conscious expectation. The implications of this phenomenon should be clear—whether people remember their museum visit experiences because their entering identity-related expectations actually shaped their visit or because they perceived that it shaped their experiences is immaterial. What is important is that the expectations created by a visitor's entering identity-related motivations represent powerful shapers of memory construction. Thus even though our harried Facilitator Hanna's actual museum experience sounds as if it were hellish, her memories of the experience are much more benign.

Returning to our example in this chapter, Frank believed that going to the Science Center would be an opportunity for him to enact his role as a "good father"—a father who cares about his daughter and wants to ensure she has quality learning opportunities. During the visit we actually observed Frank trying to enact this fatherly role. We observed him staying with his daughter, even though she was running all over the museum. Importantly, we also observed him trying to talk with his daughter about what she was seeing and trying to help her think about the meaning of some of these exhibits. Two years later, not only were his memories of the experience quite positive, they also tended to follow this same basic narrative. He talked about trying to slow down his daughter so that she'd be able to understand important things. He specifically remembered attempting to focus her attention on certain subjects and specific exhibits, "We concentrated on food groups for humans, because to me that's important—making sure she understands a balanced meal and things of that nature." Frank's expectations for his visit helped to create a self-fulfilling prophecy. He came to accomplish something, he used the museum to accomplish that goal, and his memories of the experience were built around the accomplishment of his initial goals. All of which led him to conclude that the visit was a great success. The success of this initial visit prompted him to repeat the experience of visiting the Science Center with his daughter; we can assume that his perceptions of the "correctness" of his initial expectations have now been reinforced by subsequent visits.

Whereas Frank's entering identity-related motivations helped to create the basic architecture of his memories, several other important factors also directly contributed to the specific details of his memories. These three factors were *choice and control*, *emotion*, and *context and appropriate challenge*. Not only do these three groups of factors contribute to the details of memory, they are also the factors which I believe are instrumental in making museum memories so enduring.

CHOICE AND CONTROL

Museum experiences are wonderful examples of free-choice learning; I have come to believe that it is because they are so quintessentially free-choice that they are so memorable. Humans, and quite likely other organisms as well, actively seek to have control over events in their lives. This, according to leisure expert John Kelly, is why people so highly value leisure time—it's often the only time in our lives where we can exercise considerable choice and control over what we do.[20] It is also why learning experiences that incorporate choice and control are among the most powerful and memorable. Museums are settings in which visitors have the opportunity to exercise considerable choice over what things to look at, and what ideas to think about it. Or framed in another way, visitors have the opportunity to control their own meaning-making. Choice and control are fundamental, but understudied variables in both the wider world of memory and learning as well as the world of museums. A whole range of important variables play a role in visitor choice and control including interest, motivation, self-concept, attribution, and locus of control. Most of the research on these variables has been conducted in laboratory or school settings—situations in which individual meaning-making is severely constrained and goals are externally imposed. So, perhaps not surprisingly, most traditional studies of memory have discovered that forgetting, rather than remembering, is the norm.[21] One could hypothesize that when meaning-making occurs in a free-choice setting like a museum, a setting in which learners have significant choice and control over their decision-making and experiences, they should exhibit greater interest, motivation, self-esteem, attribution, and locus of control. In sum, when all of these things are positive the result should be enhanced memory formation. In the few cases where this has been investigated, this is exactly what has been found.[22]

A recent *Scientific American* article highlighted the importance of both studying more natural experiences and the important role that choice and control play in thinking and remembering. Science writers John Pearson and Michael Platt begin their article by pointing out that although a major insight of recent neuroscience research has been the discovery of key areas of the brain where specific neurological functions like speech, vision, and hearing tend to be localized, less often discussed is the companion notion that the power of the brain, the key to its flexibility and coordination, lies also in the connections between these dedicated processing centers. "For modern neuroscientists, the whole story must lie not just in the brain's *compartmentalization*, but in its *communication*."[23]

Pearson and Platt describe a breakthrough research study that attempted to overcome the challenges of investigating how different parts of the brain communicate. Bijan Pesaran of New York University and collaborators at the California Institute of Technology recently managed to "eavesdrop" on sets of neurons in an experiment designed to catch the cross-talk between two specialized regions of the brain during decision making. The experiment was set up so that monkeys were monitored under two conditions, one where they were given a rote choice of tasks and the second where they got to execute free-choice; both resulted in a reward. The researchers found that when the monkeys were freely searching for a reward, the firings in the two distinct parts of the brain were significantly more coordinated than they were when the monkeys were following the fixed search pattern. The researchers concluded that the two brain regions shared more information under the free-choice than the mandated-order condition. What's more, analysis of the relative timing of activity in the two areas seemed to suggest that firing in each region was influenced by activity in the other and this resulted in an increase in the overall robustness of the neural network under the free-choice condition. In other words, with choice and control the strength of neural pathways, which is neuroscience talk for "memories," were enhanced.

One of the few museum-based studies on the importance of choice and control was conducted by museum visitor researcher Deborah Perry as part of her doctoral work at Indiana University. Perry found that the confidence that came along with free-choice learning, coupled with the motivation to control one's environment, were among the most important variables determining successful learning from a children's museum exhibit.[24] Perry discovered that six motivational variables played major roles in museum learning. Although it was not surprising that factors such as curiosity, challenge, and play had a role in children's museum learning, the need for children to feel in control and confident about their environment was surprising. Perhaps, one of the reasons so little attention has been focused on choice and control in museum learning is because it is almost too obvious. Since these variables tend to be intrinsic to the museum experience, it is all too easy to overlook how important a contribution they make to most museum-based learning. Investigations by Finnish museum researcher Hannu Salmi confirmed that the motivating effects of freedom and control over the environment can be used by museums to enhance student learning.[25] In fact, these motivational attributes of museums have been observed by a wide range of investigators and are frequently used as a justification for why schools should take children on field trips to museums.[26]

Perhaps the best evidence for how important central choice and control is to the visitor experience comes from the handful of studies that have attempted to understand what happens when free-choice is denied to museum visitors. It turns out there are natural experiments for this—they are called overly-structured school field trips. Comparisons between groups of schoolchildren whose visit experiences were tightly prescribed and groups of schoolchildren who had opportunities to self-direct their experiences have yielded very provocative findings. Australian museum researcher Janette Griffin investigated matched groups of schoolchildren in museums under two conditions. The first condition was an organized, traditional, teacher-directed school field trip, and in the second condition, students were freed from the typical constraints and structures imposed by teachers and allowed to freely define their own learning agenda in the museum. The second condition was not only perceived by the students as more enjoyable, but learning was actually facilitated.[27] Interestingly, students in this second situation were observed to behave and learn in ways similar to children in family groups.[28] Griffin identified three variables important to students in these learning situations: choice, purpose, and ownership. Given ownership of learning, learning and enjoyment became intertwined, and according to Griffin ultimately, inseparable in the minds of the children.[29]

So, why was the visit experience of our Facilitator Frank so memorable? I would postulate that it was partly because Frank was the person who picked the Science Center to visit. Although he did not select the pathway through the museum—his daughter did that—he did help to influence that pathway and felt very much involved with the visit. We know from our research data that Frank did not remember all the exhibits he and his daughter stopped at that day; why did he remember some but not others? He remembered the *Human Miracle* exhibit and the chick exhibit, also the exhibit about food groups. Arguably, all of these were salient for Frank because they were exhibits where he felt he was able to specifically interact with his daughter, and by extension as a Facilitator, exercise some control over the experience. An interesting outlier to this pattern was the *Tess* exhibit, which is salient in and of itself—90% of all visitors to the Science Center see this show and 90% of those are able to talk about what they've learned from it.[30] Interestingly, Frank claimed not to remember much about the *Tess* exhibit, except some specifics directly related to his daughter's interest.

Finally, it is quite likely that the visit was much more memorable for Frank than it was for his daughter, since the visit was his choice not hers.[31] Frank chose to be a facilitator of his daughter's experience and he clearly felt good about having made that decision. The fact that the visit was his decision and he got to actively participate in the experience, as opposed to a movie where he might go with his daughter but fall asleep, almost certainly helped to make it memorable for him. Due to the high degree of choice and control, another important reason contributing to Frank's strong memories of his visit was the fact that it made him feel good.

EMOTION

The fact that Frank had an emotional involvement with his daughter's Science Center experience is non-trivial. Emotion is the second important contributor to memorable museum visit experiences. Although Frank was not so moved by his Science Center visit that he broke down and wept when we talked to him, it was clear that Frank's visit experience and his subsequent memories involved not just descriptions of what he saw and did, but expressions of feelings, attitudes, and beliefs.

One of the most startling findings of the last quarter century of brain research has been the critical role played in all memory by the area known as the limbic system. The limbic system is evolutionarily one of the oldest parts of our brain. Located in the middle of the brain and made up of a number of discrete structures (for example, the amygdala, hippocampus, and thalamus), the limbic system probably first evolved among reptiles, but it is well-developed in all mammals. Appropriate to its ancient lineage, the limbic area was recognized as the major brain center for emotional and geographical memory.[32] However, as mentioned earlier in this chapter, the brain is increasingly being appreciated for how highly integrated and interconnected its various structures are.[33] The limbic system structures have been found to be extensively connected in looped circuits to all parts of the brain, as well as to all of the body's organs and systems, responding to the needs and demands of various body functions and cycles.[34] This system not only helps regulate emotions and geography; it has emerged as the focal point for regulating memory.[35]

Before any perception begins the process of being permanently stored in memory, it must first pass through at least two appraisal stages involving the limbic system.[36] All incoming sensory information is given an initial screening for meaningfulness and personal relevance by structures in this system. It is also filtered for its relationship to our internal physical state (for example, "I'm hungry, so I guess I'll focus on things related to food rather than Shakespeare"). This filtering and interpretation of incoming sensory information is centered in the limbic system but it involves virtually every part of the brain, and the body.[37] In essence, this process both determines *what* is worth attending to and remembering (for example, "Will this be important information in the future? Does it relate to something I already know, feel, or believe?") and *how* something is remembered (for example, "That object reminds me of an interesting experience I once had. I saw that beautiful painting at the same time I was having a good time with my spouse."). In this way, in fractions of a second, our mind separates, sorts, combines, and judges perceptions occurring both inside and outside of us. The key role of the limbic system in this process has made cognitive scientists come to more fully appreciate just how important emotion is in the entire meaning-making process.

Current neuroscience research has shown that learning cannot be separated in the Cartesian sense between rational thought and emotion, nor neatly divided into cognitive (facts and concepts), affective (feelings, attitudes, and emotions), and psychomotor (skills and behaviors) functions as many psychologists and educators have attempted to do for nearly a half century. All meaning-making, even of the most logical topic, involves emotion, just as emotions virtually always involve cognition.[38] By virtue of its journey through the limbic system, it seems that every memory comes with an emotional "stamp" attached to it.[39] The stronger the emotional "value," the more likely sensory information is to pass this initial inspection and be admitted into memory; and interestingly, pleasant experiences are strongly favored over unpleasant ones.[40] Evolution has thus insured a dependency between learning, memory, and survival by making the process of acquiring and storing information both very thorough and, by virtue of its relationship to the limbic system, an intrinsically pleasurable and rewarding experience.[41]

Historically, emotions were thought to be a set of stereotyped and automatic expressive behaviors. Now it is understood how nuanced and variable emotions are and that emotions are an integral part of brain functioning. In one of the most widely accepted theories of emotion, psychologist Richard Lazarus explained that

> emotion recruits cognitive and affective components in order to assess the import of events in the environment for a person's key goals, such as a key relationship, survival, identity, or avoiding moral offence. The brain makes an initial judgment of whether the information it has received bodes 'good' or 'bad' for such goals. The characteristic feeling of the particular emotion (fear, love, anger etc.) is then felt at some level of intensity. This is the 'primary appraisal' process. It shows that emotion is intrinsically cognitive, although the thinking may be more or less rapid and unconscious.
>
> Beyond the evaluation of the event as good or bad, the person may also cognitively generate a plan (the 'secondary appraisal'), giving emotion a

directive quality; we usually are inclined to act in some way when we have a strong feeling about one of our key goals.[42]

As the quality of brain research has increased, these ideas have been confirmed and a more elaborated picture of emotion has emerged. As neuroscientist Jonathon Turner explains, "Emotions give each alternative a value and, thereby, provide a yardstick to judge and to select alternatives. This process need not be conscious; and indeed, for all animals including humans, it rarely is. . . . One can't sustain cognitions beyond working [i.e., short-term] memory without tagging them with emotion."[43] Thus, we can see that our brains store memories in networks of meaning and that emotions play a big role in whether an event is experienced as meaningful and whether and how it is remembered. If an emotion is engaged, the brain marks the experience as meaningful, and stores memory of it in the networks activated by the emotion and similar experiences. What a person remembers is thus largely determined by previous emotional arousal, and vice versa. Emotionally rich memories are particularly memorable because they involve the limbic system in memory formation; some involvement is a good thing, and a lot of involvement is even better.[44] The fact that virtually every study ever conducted on museum visitors has found that visitors find the experience highly enjoyable and satisfying should help to explain, at least in part, why museum memories are so long-lasting. Enjoyable experiences are memorable! But visitors typically only remember selected parts of the visitor experience; what makes some parts of an overall enjoyable experience particularly memorable, and not others?

In 2008, one of my graduate students, Katie Gillespie, and I attempted to directly test the assumption that emotion influences visitor learning and memory. We tested these ideas using a new traveling exhibition developed by the California Science Center called *Goose Bumps: The Science of Fear*. This exhibition was designed to help visitors not only learn about fear, but to experience fear in a safe environment through an interactive fear "Challenge Course." The challenges allowed visitors to experience several common fears: fear of animals, fear of electric shock, fear of loud noises, and the fear of falling. It was assumed that these challenges would elicit visitors' emotions, more so than the more traditional Science Center exhibits. This made the exhibit an ideal setting in which to investigate the role of emotion on cognition.

We compared a random sample of visitors who visited this traveling exhibition with a random sample of Science Center visitors who did not see the exhibition. [45] We measured visitors' pre- and post-emotions using a technique called Russell's Grid. [46] According to Russell's circumplex model, emotion can be measured along two dimensions: arousal (alertness) and valence (pleasure). [47] As predicted, *Goose Bumps* visitors reported significantly higher emotional arousal levels than did the control group of visitors, but there was no significant difference in the emotional valence scores of the two groups of visitors. The interpretation of these results suggests that the "challenges" in the *Goose Bumps* exhibition had their intended effect of making visitors more aroused/excited, but all visitors to the Science Center found the experience equally pleasurable. Three to four months after their visit, we interviewed members of each group by telephone. As expected, all visitors were able to recall their visit and could describe their experiences and provide examples of what they saw, did, and felt. However, the *Goose Bumps* visitors had more salient memories of their visit than did visitors from the control group. When asked to describe a Science Center exhibit of their choice, *Goose Bumps* exhibition visitors provided responses of significantly greater breadth and depth than did control group visitors. [48] Overall, when asked to describe something they had learned during their initial visit, *Goose Bumps* exhibition visitors provided significantly higher quality responses than did control group visitors. *Goose Bumps* exhibition visitors were also significantly more likely than control group visitors to have reflected on their Science Center visit and to have shared their reflections with others. In summary, the Science Center visitor experience was more salient and memorable for *Goose Bumps* visitors than it was for visitors in the control group. This research provided direct evidence that, as predicted, an emotional experience, in particular an emotionally arousing visitor experience, resulted in strong and lasting memories. In this case, these memories were even above and beyond those created by a normally stimulating and pleasurable Science Center visit.

A careful reading of the interview transcript at the beginning of this chapter reveals that emotion also played a role in Frank's Science Center visit and likely figured prominently into the particular aspects of the visit that were remembered. For example, "I tried to get her to slow it down a little bit to learn about all of the different things that were going on in the exhibit at that particular time. That was a little difficult, she was just happy to be somewhere." In another passage, Frank says, "She got a kick out of the baby chicks." The joy that Frank derived from this visit was clear throughout our interview with him; his daughter's joy was his joy— "I remember what my daughter's reaction was. She was fascinated with seeing something this large and understanding something about the heartbeat. . . . That part of the exhibition is always fascinating to her even when we've gone back again, she'll stop and look at that exhibit." For Frank, and other visitors, choice and control and emotion appear to be important contributors to memories of the museum visit experience but there needs to be more. After all, on the grand scale of emotionality, museums are unlikely to be a "10." There are many other life events that are likely to be equally, if not more, emotion-laden. What else is likely important?

CONTEXT AND APPROPRIATE CHALLENGE

The third critical piece of the puzzle is the importance of context and appropriate challenge. The interview with Frank revealed that the *World of Life* exhibition provided a context for him to help his daughter understand something about human development as well as the development of chickens. Because the experience was so concrete, it allowed Frank to help his daughter make the connections between the eggs at the kitchen table and the birth of chicks in an incubator. It is examples like these that make the museum so memorable; museums provide tangible building blocks for the making of memories. Museums are very contextually relevant and rich places; they are full of real things, situated within relevant contexts. Because of this, museums are places that make it easy to form memories. This contextualization of the world enables visitors to make "real" that which was previously only "sort of real."

We can better understand how this happens if we know a little more about the process by which memories are formed. Memory-making is always a continuous, constructive process, both literally and figuratively. Although the total picture is yet to be understood, one theory of the brain holds that all of our memories are stored as pieces of images.[49] Different parts of the brain may actually store different pieces. When we attempt to "remember" something, we literally reassemble the pieces of our memory as best we can into a single whole. We perceive our memories as perceptual wholes even if some of the details are fuzzy or glossed over;

this is in spite of the fact that, more often than not, our memories are almost always actually less than "whole cloth."[50]

Not only does memory retrieval require the reconstruction of bits and pieces of images through mental action, it also requires an appropriate context within which to express itself. In the absence of contextual cues from the outside world, the patterns and associations stored within each person's brain would remain dormant or have no meaning.[51] As we talked to Frank about his Science Center visit, he constantly framed his recollections within the context of the actual exhibits seen by him and his daughter. For example, "I remember what my daughter's reaction was. She was fascinated with seeing something this large and understanding something about the heartbeat. I think she [a featured girl in the show's movie] was playing soccer." And, "She got a kick out of the baby chicks. That part of the exhibition is always fascinating to her even when we've gone back again, she'll stop and look at that exhibit. She loves to see the eggs, some of which are whole, some of which are empty and some of which are in the process of having a chick emerge from them. It makes the process so real."

Not only do museums create contextually relevant experiences, they have a knack for creating experiences that are appropriately scaled to visitors' interests and abilities. As originally investigated and described by psychologist Mihalyi Csikzentmihalyi, and confirmed by a wide range of other investigators, people appear to exhibit a common set of behaviors and outcomes when engaged in tasks which they find intrinsically rewarding.[52] Csikzentmihalyi found that chess players, rock climbers, dancers, painters, and musicians all used similar explanations when describing the attraction of the activities they enjoy doing. Csikzentmihalyi called this common experiential quality the *flow experience*, because it is generally described as a state of mind that is spontaneous, almost automatic, like the flow of a strong current.[53] Three general characteristics of activities that produce flow are that they have clear goals, continuous feedback, and the tasks demanded of the participant are in balance with the person's abilities. In a game of bridge or of chess, one knows every second what one would like to accomplish. Musicians find out immediately if they hit a wrong note; tennis players find out if they hit the ball badly and if they're competitively matched or over-matched by their opponent. According to Csikzentmihalyi, this constant accountability and feedback is a major reason one gets so completely immersed in a flow activity. If the challenges are greater than the skill levels, anxiety results; if skills are greater than challenges, the result is boredom.[54] This phenomenon appears to hold across a wide array of skills including physical, mental, artistic, and musical talents. The more one does an activity, the greater one's skill. The greater one's skill, the greater the challenges are required in order to continue enjoying the activity and remaining in a state of flow.

Most successful museum exhibitions and programs possess these qualities. They permit the participant to seek the level of engagement and understanding appropriate for the individual, across a broad range of visitor identity-related motivations. By allowing understanding to occur at many different levels and from many different perspectives, good exhibitions and programs simultaneously define the boundaries of experience and allow the visitor to intellectually navigate the experience in a way that makes sense for them. Thus engagement, a flow experience, can result because there is sufficient depth to permit appropriate levels of challenge for a wide range of users.

Apropos to the immediately previous section of this chapter, flow learning experiences are not just mental experiences, they are also emotional experiences. As Csikzentmihalyi states, "when goals are clear, feedback is unambiguous, challenges and skills are well matched, then all of one's mind and body become completely involved in the activity."[55] In this state, the person becomes unaware of fatigue or the passing of time. It is truly an exhilarating experience—physically, emotionally, and cognitively. Accordingly, it is also extremely pleasurable. People who experience something even approaching flow, desire to do it over and over again. At some level, most frequent museum-goers can be characterized as having something akin to a flow experience. If they did not derive deep intrinsic rewards from going to museums, they would not keep going to them again and again. Above all, flow experiences are memorable experiences. Although there's no way to retroactively test this, it is a fair assumption that the specific experiences Frank found most memorable were the ones that came closest to approximating a flow experience. What was a flow experience for Frank likely to look like? As Frank was seeking to be a supportive parent of an active nine-year-old girl in a science center, the answer would be that he would be feeling flow at those times when he felt that the museum setting afforded him an intellectually and emotionally satisfying connection between himself and his daughter.

THE CONSTRUCTION OF MEANING

Thus, we can conclude that the things people see and do in museums are memorable because museums are places that allow people to build tangible memories based on seeing real things in appropriate contexts. The things people see and do in museums are memorable because they occur during emotionally positive and rich times in people's lives which makes them highly salient and perceived as important. The museum experiences that are most memorable are highly likely to be those that allow visitors to become engaged at intellectually and emotionally appropriate levels. The fact that visitors can exercise considerable choice and control over what they see and do significantly increases the likelihood that a visitor will find exhibitions and programs that are intellectually and emotionally appropriate for them. Collectively, these qualities make visitor experiences extraordinarily memorable. These factors help to explain much of *why* museum experiences are so memorable; they also begin to help us understand *which* memories in particular are likely to stick. We can see that the specifics of Frank's recollections were strongly influenced by his ability to choose and to a degree, control his daughter's activities. For example, both he and his daughter enjoyed the chick exhibit and he was able to reinforce this experience for his daughter when at home. The fact that design of the exhibit enabled him to use the conceptual ideas behind the exhibit in a way that was appropriate to the needs and interests of his daughter was critical; the very concrete nature of this experience also helped make it memorable. And nothing could have been more concrete and "real" than a 50-foot, animatronic woman with flashing lights! Finally, Frank particularly seemed to remember the times his daughter was excited by the museum and appeared to be really enjoying herself. Also highly salient were the times he perceived that not just his daughter, but the two of them, were enjoying themselves. This emotional component reinforced his overarching "good father" self-aspect and provided a strong memory marker. What held all these factors together for Frank, as they do for nearly all visitors, was his entering identity-related visit motivation.

Frank came away from his visit with a range of specific memories about the California Science Center and his and his daughter's interactions at that museum. Equally notable, though, was what impact the whole experience seemed to have on him. As we talked with Frank, he was continually laughing and smiling. No doubt he is a happy person, but clearly the recollections of this experience were a source of great joy and satisfaction for him. As mentioned several times, Frank used this experience to strengthen and build his own set of identity-related needs, in particular the desire to be a good father to his daughter. He perceived that not only did the experience support this self-aspect, but by purchasing a membership he could extend this identity-related need beyond fatherhood and his daughter to include "unclehood" and his niece and nephew. He was carrying on his family's tradition of building respect and appreciation for learning in general and his father's commitment to science in particular. It was Frank's way of "passing forward" to the next generation the advantages he perceived that his parents had given him and his siblings when they were growing up. It does not seem like much of a stretch to assert that a major outcome of Frank's museum visit experience was identity-building.

As pointed out by Jay Rounds, a large part of how we come to understand who we are—our identity—comes through the *post hoc* process of interpreting what we've done. This is a looking-backward process; "We understand backwards by looking at what we did, and considering how we felt about doing it, and asking what sort of person it is who acts and feels that way. We explain ourselves to ourselves, using our actions as evidence. You can't know who you are until you see what you do."[56] Although the California Science Center aspires to "stimulate curiosity and inspire science learning in everyone by creating fun, memorable experiences . . .", the primary outcome for Frank of his museum visitor experience did not directly relate to science learning or even curiosity, though certainly something related to science learning and stimulating curiosity were achieved. For Frank, the primary benefit of the experience was his ability to build and strengthen his self-perception of himself as a good father and uncle, and perhaps most importantly, it also allowed himself and others such as his wife, his siblings, and parents (if they are still alive), and as it turned out Martin Storksdieck and me, to see tangible evidence of this identity. Not a bad day's work, though as also pointed out by Rounds, identity-work is an on-going, never-ending process, not a one-time product.[57] Frank will need to continue working at this self-aspect of being a good father and uncle. But now, he has added to his mental repertoire that visiting the Science Center is a good way to accomplish this good father/uncle role. We know he's already acted upon that perception and we can safely assume he's also told others, friends and family, about this.

In this way, the other outcome of Frank's museum visit experience is a small, but significant increase in his and the broader community's sense of how a science center can support a person's leisure experiences. Frank was happy to share his positive feelings about the Science Center and describe how it was a good place for supporting the kind of facilitating role that he played with his daughter. Every museum visitor does this, to greater or lesser extent, whether their perceptions of the museum were positive as was the case for most of the visitors described in this book, or negative as Felipe felt his were. All visitors come away from their museum visit experience with a better understanding of what these institutions called museums afford. Predictably, the perceptions a person has about a museum he or she has visited are framed by the lens of their entering identity-related visit motivations. For Frank, visiting the California Science Center as a Facilitator reinforced for him that science centers are great places to take children. While for Frances, visiting the Berkeley Botanical Gardens as a Recharger reinforced for her that botanical gardens are great places to find peace and tranquility and a release from the stresses of everyday life. As we learned from Frank's interview, he clearly has knowledge of other museums as well, for example the Los Angeles Museum of Art and the La Brea Tar Pits; he has a sense of what these places might afford as well. However, since these are places he described visiting by himself and thus, were almost certainly satisfying different types of identity-related needs than those enacted at the California Science Center, we can predict that Frank's perceptions of what these museums afford is quite different than his perceptions of what the Science Center affords. What the museum visitor experience model predicts are different entering motivations result in different exiting understandings.

What the museum visitor experience model also predicts is that through the process of Frank sharing his experiences and perceptions of his Science Center visit with others, he is, in a small way helping to shape the larger community's perceptions of the Science Center in particular, and museums in general. Museums invest considerable resources in communicating to the world who they are and what they do (e.g., brochures, banners, media placements), but most of the publics' knowledge and perceptions derive from word-of-mouth descriptions and recommendations by former visitors. Individually these conversations between friends and family have a modest impact, but collectively they have a huge effect. Person-to-person communications about their museum visitor experiences largely shape and define how society views individual museums as well as museums collectively. These background perceptions of what museums afford form the context for leisure decision making that all of the Franks of the world draw upon when trying to decide what to do in their leisure time.

The museum visitor experience model predicts that, as was the case for Frank, the basic structure and functioning of a museum visitor experience—from behaviors to long-term memories—will largely be determined by an individual's entering identity-related motivations. If we could have known something about why Frank was visiting the Science Center prior to his visit, and if we could have known a few salient facts about his prior knowledge and experience, we would have been able to make some educated guesses about what his visit that day would have been like. We also could have made some educated guesses about what the general nature of his visit memories would have been. Although, of course, the specifics of Frank's museum visit experience could not have been predicted in detail beforehand, the general outline of his experience could have been. Frank's entering identity-related Facilitator motivation created a basic structure and trajectory for his visit. We also could predict that the salience of Frank's memories would be influenced by his ability to exercise some measure of choice and control over what he and his daughter saw and did (influenced by Frank's prior knowledge, interests and experience); by the times when his daughter's interactions with him and the Science Center evoked positive emotions (influenced by verbal and non-verbal communication with his daughter); and by situations when he encountered specific exhibits that allowed him, by virtue of their context and appropriateness, to actualize his identity-related visit goals (influenced by the quality of those exhibits and their spatial arrangement, as well as personal and socio-cultural context variables as well). All of this is by necessity quite complex, but it is not so complex as to prevent us from generically describing and predicting the kinds of Science Center experiences Frank would ultimately find memorable. This, then, is why these ideas are so valuable. Although the museum visit experience model will not allow us to predict with certainty what every visitor will do and remember all of the time, I do believe it allows us to describe and predict the basic shape and trajectory of a large percentage of museum visitor experiences.

The Museum Visitor Experience Model

We have inherited from our forefathers the keen longing for unified, all embracing knowledge . . . But the spread, both in width and depth, of the multifarious branches of knowledge during the last hundred odd years has confronted us with a queer dilemma. We feel clearly that we are only now beginning to acquire reliable material for welding together the sum total of all that is known into a whole; but, on the other hand, it has become next to impossible for a single mind fully to command more than a small specialized portion of it. I see no other escape from this dilemma (lest our true aim be lost forever) than that some of us should venture to embark on a synthesis of facts and theories, albeit with second hand and incomplete knowledge of some of them—and at the risk of making fools of ourselves.

—E. Schrodinger, 1944

In the previous chapters, I have laid the foundations of a model that describes the museum visitor experience. It is a model that begins with the first conceptualization of the idea that visiting a museum in one's leisure time could help to satisfy an identity-related need and concludes long after the museum visit ends through the individual's development and enrichment of personal identity. In between, the individual's identity-related visit motivation propels the experience, shaping not only the reason for visiting but also the actual visit and even, the laying down of long-term memories. It is a model that is based upon strong theoretical foundations and which is supported by considerable research collected both inside and outside of museums. In the final chapter of this theory section, I will summarize again the basic outline of the model as presented so far. I will illustrate how the model works using a detailed example, once again, using data from my research at the California Science Center. Finally, before moving into the practitioner section of the book, I will provide a big-picture overview of what this model can and cannot tell us about museums and their visitors.

OUTLINE OF THE MUSEUM VISITOR EXPERIENCE MODEL

- We cannot understand the museum visitor experience by looking exclusively at the museum (e.g., content of the museum or its exhibits and programs), or at the visitor (e.g., demographic characteristics of the visitor like age, income, or race/ethnicity), or even at easily observable and measurable attributes of museum visits (e.g., frequency of visits or the social arrangements of visitors as they arrive at the museum). The museum visitor experience is not something tangible and immutable; it is an ephemeral and constructed relationship that uniquely occurs each time a visitor interacts with a museum.

- Understanding the museum visitor experience requires appreciating that it actually begins before anyone ever sets foot in a museum. It begins with the confluence of two streams of thought on the part of the prospective visitor.
  - An individual who wishes to satisfy one or more identity-related needs and decides to satisfy one or more of these needs through some kind of leisure time activity.
  - The individual possesses a set of generic as well as specific mental models of various leisure settings, including museums, that individually and collectively support various leisure-related activities.

- These two streams of thought come together when an individual makes a decision that visiting a specific museum will be a good thing to do in his or her leisure time. That decision is generally justified by the prospective visitor believing that a good match exists between his or her perceptions of what a particular museum affords in terms of leisure-related opportunities and the specific leisure-related needs and desires that he or she possesses at that particular time and place. This decision-making process results in the formation of an identity-related visit motivation.

- Most identity-related museum motivations fall into one of five categories:
  - Explorer
  - Facilitator
  - Experience seeker
  - Professional/Hobbyist
  - Recharger

NOTE: Although this entire process actually happens and is thus "observable," typically the most "visible" piece of the process is the individual's identity-related visit motivations. These represent the tangible and mostly conscious manifestations of the process and take the form of the self-aspects people use to describe their reasons/goals for visiting the museum to themselves. Other parts of the process are typically more deeply submerged in the person's mind/unconscious and thus, are much more challenging to "see."

- The actual museum visit experience is strongly shaped by the needs of the visitor's identity-related visit motivations. The individual's entering motivations creates a basic trajectory for the visit, though the specifics of what the visitor actually sees and does are strongly influenced by the factors described by the Contextual Model of Learning:
  — *Personal Context:* The visitor's prior knowledge, experience, and interest.
  — *Physical Context:* The specifics of the exhibitions, programs, objects, and labels they encounter.
  — *Socio-cultural Context:* The within- and between-group interactions that occur while in the museum and the visitor's cultural experiences and values.

- The visitor perceives his or her museum experience to be satisfying if this marriage of perceived identity-related needs and museum affordances proves to be well-matched—in other words, visitors achieve what they expected. If expectations are not met, the visitor perceives that his or her museum visitor experience was less-than-satisfying. Currently, the overwhelming majority of museum visitors find their museum visit experiences very satisfying. This is in part because the public has a fairly accurate "take" on museums and thus possesses relatively accurate expectations. It is also in part due to human nature; we have a propensity to want our expectations to be met and work hard, often unconsciously, to fulfill them, even if it means modifying our observations of reality to match our expectations. Occasionally, however, bad experiences can and do happen.

- During and immediately after the visit the visitor begins to construct meaning from the experience. The specifics of the meaning a visitor makes of the museum experience is largely shaped by his or her identity-related motivation and the realities of the museum (under the influence of the factors highlighted in the Contextual Model of Learning). The following factors make certain experiences and memories more salient and thus, memorable than others:
  — The choice and control visitors exercise over the experience.
  — The emotional nature of the experience.

— The context and appropriateness of what visitors encounter in the museum.

• The resulting meanings that the visitor constructs of the museum visitor experience fall into two general categories. Since people visit museums primarily to satisfy one or more identity-related needs, it is not surprising that the major outcomes most visitors derive from their museum visit experience relate to identity-building. The sense of self that the individual projects on the visit, typically expressed as self-aspects, is strengthened, modified, and/or extended by the museum visit experience. Given the very diversity of identity-related needs that motivate people to visit museums, the range of identity-related outcomes is also diverse—ranging from increased understandings of art, history, science, and the environment to enhanced feelings of mental well-being. A secondary outcome is that the individual also enhances his or her understanding of museums. By virtue of direct experience in the museum, the individual's working perceptions of what one does in a museum in general and this museum in particular are reinforced and/or reshaped. Through communications with others the individual helps to influence not only his or her own understanding of museums, but the broader community's perceptions as well. These two types of meanings and understanding flow back into the basic model described above. Past museum visit experiences shape the individual's future museum visits as well as contributing to other potential visitors' future visits through input into the broader publics' understanding of what museums afford.

Although the general patterns of a visit are predictable as outlined above, the details of each visitor's experience is highly personalized and unique. A graphic representation of this model is depicted on the facing page.

THE MODEL AT WORK

We can see how this basic model plays out by dissecting the experience of another visitor to the California Science Center, a 40-year-old college educated (history degree) white woman who we'll call Susan. On the particular day we observed Susan, it was a weekday and she was in town

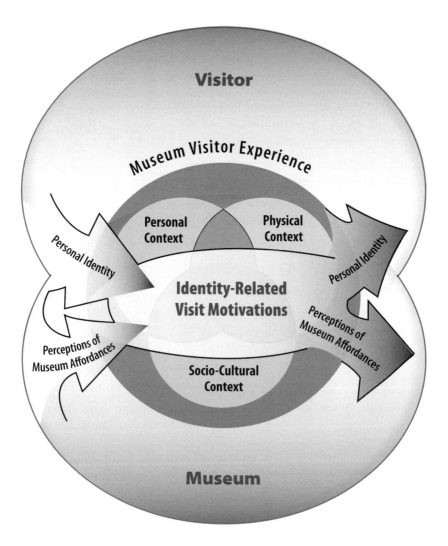

The Museum Visitor Experience and the
Role of Identity-Related Visit Motivations.

visiting her parents along with her three children. The excerpts below
are from a series of interviews and observations with Susan that occurred
both at the time of her visit (the initial interview occurred at the threshold
of the *World of Life* permanent exhibition) and again, eighteen months
after her visit.

PRIOR TO THE VISIT

Q: Tell me about why you decided to visit the Science Center today. Whose idea was it to visit today?

A: I did [*decide*]. My parents like to do things with the family, so we were spending the week with them so we sort of decided this week to go [to the Science Center]. My kids are out of school and we are spending the week with [my parents] and my husband is traveling so we thought it would be a good time to go.

Q: Why the California Science Center? Have you been here before?

A: Because I've taken my kids before and they loved it.

Q: What about your parents?

A: They haven't been in a long time and I thought it would be fun for them to see it and they showed interest in going.

Q: Since you have been here before and it was your idea to come today, what are you hoping will happen? What's your goal for the visit?

A: Well, I guess I just want to have fun with my kids and parents, but I also want them to learn something.

Q: Sure, that makes sense. But tell me more about what would be fun for you and what kinds of things do you think you want your children to learn.

A: What will be fun for me is if my children enjoy themselves and enjoy being with their grandparents. I also want the kids to learn something, that they'll see some things that will help them in school and generally in their life.

Q: Great, tell me more about what you want your children to see and do.

A: I want them to see the chicks, and the smoking and hand-washing exhibits [all in the *World of Life* exhibition].

Q: Well, that's interesting. Why those exhibits?

A: The chicks will help them learn about birth and development and caring for life. The smoking and hand-washing exhibits will help them learn important things for staying healthy. But speaking of that, I've got to ask if I can go now. I've got to catch up with my kids and make sure my parents are okay.

We can see that already when Susan entered the exhibition she had a strong sense of purpose for her visit. She describes a situation that includes time away from her husband but in the presence of her parents and her two children. Since her children are out of school and her parents are retired, she perceives her situation as a leisure problem related to finding something that will be suitable to the needs of all parties. Based upon prior experience, Susan realizes that a visit to the California Science Center could satisfy her needs. It is close-by, the children enjoy it and can learn there, and her parents will enjoy watching the children and might also enjoy the content of the museum. She decides that it will be the perfect solution, and we can infer that she successfully "sold" the idea to her children and parents. We can also infer that her children probably did enjoy themselves on their previous visit so were easily persuaded to revisit.

Although Susan made the decision to visit the Science Center, she reveals that her decision was aimed almost entirely at supporting and facilitating others—her children and her parents—rather than some personal learning goal or desire. She saw herself acting as the social glue that held this multi-generational group together and the supporter of both her children and her parents. Susan envisioned herself acting as both a good parent and a good child. Susan also makes clear that in addition to her desire to have a fun, social-bonding outing with her children and parents, she also has a general and a specific learning agenda for her children. She has a self-concept of what it means to be a good parent—good parents support their children's learning, in particular learning things that will be important to them in the future. Using her prior knowledge of the museum, Susan has formed a visit goal that includes interacting with three specific exhibits; each has an educational message she hopes her children will learn. She enters the Science Center with a suite of identity-related motivations characteristic of Facilitators.

In the *World of Life* Exhibition

The Visit After the entry interview, Susan catches up with her parents and children who have stayed together at the urging of Susan's mother. They have not proceeded too far into the exhibition, drifting off towards the right side of the space. With Susan back "in charge" the group loosens up. "In charge" is actually not an apt description of how Susan allowed this visit to unfold. She basically held back and chatted with her parents while her children moved from one exhibit to another. Only occasionally and superficially did Susan actually engage with an exhibit. Every now and then she suggested a direction to the children or answered a child's question. Sometimes, she posed questions herself, but this was not the norm. Most of the time she was content to follow the children around to wherever and whatever attracted their interest.

There were a few exhibits that Susan became engaged with, most notably the *Surgery Theater* exhibit and the *Washing Hands* exhibits. The latter she specifically directs her children to view. At these two exhibits Susan actively is involved with her children in viewing, talking, and reading labels. Her parents also become involved with these exhibits offering their comments and thoughts. The children needed no encouragement to stop and watch the chicks hatching; in fact, Susan doesn't approach the exhibit while the children are there. She hangs back and continues to talk with her parents. Susan also actively directs the children to the *Smoking* exhibit, although she doesn't say much while they are there.

As it is a weekday morning, the *World of Life* exhibition is quite crowded and noisy, primarily because of school fieldtrip groups. On several occasions, the path of Susan and the children through the exhibition seems to be diverted by groups of schoolchildren and their chaperones. On at least two occasions, it appears as if they purposefully change their route in an attempt to avoid crowds of students.

Analysis Overall, Susan and her group spend a little more than 30 minutes in the *World of Life* exhibition. During the visit the group covers slightly more than half (57%) of the exhibition area. However, Susan is only observed interacting with 12 exhibits—13% of the total exhibits in the exhibition; as noted above, most of these exhibits she interacts with only superficially. By contrast, Susan's children interact with more than three times the number of exhibits. As is typical of a child-driven visit, Susan's pathway through the exhibition is not orderly as the children dart from one exhibit to the next.

Susan's museum behavior follows the pattern of many parents with a Facilitator motivation. Her pathway through the exhibition is child-driven and outwardly random; more of Susan's time is devoted to social interaction than in looking at and interacting with exhibits. Since Susan had two groups she was trying to facilitate, her children and her parents, she divided her time between them. Her social interactions are mostly directed towards her parents rather than her children. However, at a few exhibits she becomes quite engaged with her children and enters into significant learning-focused social interactions. And at the *Surgery Theater*, her engagement with the exhibit appeared to be at least equally motivated by her own personal curiosity. There did not appear to be any particular exhibit that Susan stopped at specifically because of her parents. Her parents occasionally also looked at the exhibits in which the children showed interest, but they usually hung back and seemed content to watch the children and now and then, talk with Susan. Overall, Susan appeared quite amenable to allowing her children to enjoy the museum on their own terms. Occasionally, she imposed her own agenda on the group, but mostly she allowed the children to select what they wanted to see and do. It is notable that in important ways, Susan's museum experience is influenced and shaped by visitors outside her family group; the noise makes it difficult to talk and the crowds force changes in what and how long she and her children can interact with certain exhibits.

Eighteen Months Later

Q: Do you remember why you went to the California Science Center?

A: Absolutely. I remember that my kids were out of school and we were visiting my parents while my husband was away. We went to the Science Center because we thought it would be a good time to go. My parents live not too far from the Science Center and we all agreed that it would be fun.

Q: Tell me about why you decided to visit the Science Center that day. Whose idea was it to visit?

A: Mine. My parents like to do things with the family so we were spending the week with them so we sort of decided that week to go [to the Science Center]. My kids were out of school so it seemed like a great thing to do with them. It's fun and educational.

Q: Now having gone there, you said your children loved it and your parents hadn't been in a while and might like it. Going there, did that have anything to do with the fact that it was a Science Center, that it presented science, or was it just that it was a place to go and do stuff as a family?

A: The fact that it was a science center was good. The fact that it was educational and interactive was really important.

Q: Right. I'd like to go back to the point when you actually went there. I'd like to talk on multiple levels about the expectations you may have had and if they were met.

A: My expectations would have been that my kids showed interest in science that they got some information at the same time as being entertained. That it opened some dialogue for us to talk about things we might not talk about normally. That it's interesting so when I go back and do homework with my kids, I can know how to talk with them and get them to learn things. So, I guess creating the dialogue is what I look for, too.

Q: Right. And did that happen?

A: Oh, yeah.

Q: Excellent and did that happen with your kids or also with your parents?

A: Both.

Q: Excellent. So, I'll take it your expectations were met?

A: Absolutely, yeah and it was met long-term.

Q: What do you mean by that?

A: Just that it opened up a frame of reference that we talk about.

Q: In what ways do you talk about this?

A: Well, you know the germs and the cigarettes and the chicks and the, I don't know what you call it, the physics part with the sailboats in the other part of the Science Center. I mean all that stuff. The kids have a broader frame of reference.

Q: I might sound stupid, but what do you mean by frame of reference?

A: They have something to hold on [to], when they go to school and they learn in their science class about something they have another frame of reference to plug and place in their brains.

Q: Oh, alright.

A: Another tree of references that is sprouting.

Q: So, they can place whatever they learn into another experience that they had before, maybe?

A: Yeah, so the sum of all their experiences becomes bigger.

Q: Did you learn anything?

A: I'm happy to get what I get, because it's mostly for them. I'm happy to pick up something now and then; that's one of the fun things of being a parent, you get to do these things.

Q: Okay. I'd like to dwell on that for a moment if I may. You say it's fun to be a parent because you get to do these things.

A: I probably wouldn't [have gone] to the Science Center that day if it weren't for my kids.

Q: But going there you actually realized it is fun, is that what you're saying? So would you say that those who don't go, who don't have children are probably making a mistake? Or is it only fun because you are there with your children?

A: No, it's not something I would probably do if I didn't have children because I wouldn't think of doing it and I would choose to do something else, but it's so fun to do those things.

Q: Very good. How do you think your children and your parents benefited from this visit?

A: Well, my kids, like I said benefited just by having that multi-dimensional reference frame from the tactile and the visuals and the exhibits and they get to touch things and not get yelled at. And just opening the dialogue and just talking about things and I figure we'll go again and that just reinforces what they've already seen.

Q: How about your parents, how do they benefit from being there?

A: Well, they're interested in it because they probably didn't have as much science as we had in school and so it's interesting to them to see it in such a simplistic form. Then, they can apply what they've learned in their life to that, I guess. They're just that kind of people that continually learn.

Q: Is that why you brought them to a place like this?

A: Yes. Because it's fun for adults to get to do things that kids get to do. And they're retired, they like to go out and do things and they like to learn. And they like to see the kids have fun and they like to read about stuff and see the exhibits. They just kind of enjoy that sort of thing.

Q: And you like to be there when they do that?

A: Oh, yeah.

Q: What I was trying to get at is how does that make you feel doing that with your children and your parents?

A: Oh it's fun, you look for things to do that are memorable and sort of different and that's a great day, a great thing to do . . . the Science Center or Sea World . . . You feel like you're getting it all in one. You're getting education, you get a fun outing, you get together as a family. The kids have a day they remember specifically as opposed to just another day at the park or something. It's very interactive, the kids can get involved, the interactive characteristic of it helps them remember, recall. My kids always talk about certain aspects of that biology part with the chickens and the all that. The surgery—do you want me to go on with the specifics?

Q: No, that's quite alright. I'm actually going to go there in a moment. But first, I want to follow up with your comment about biology. Would you say this exhibition is about biology?

A: Yeah. Biology and science. Science in general.

Q: Okay, so tell me what did you find particularly memorable in the *World of Life*?

A: Well, the germ exhibit, with the hand-washing. We talk about that a lot at our house. We talk about the cigarettes a lot, too. I think I mentioned that to you on that day, too. We talk about the surgery video, and [the] human body. We talk about the chick from the incubator. Those are the ones that stand out. I mean I can think of others but those are the ones that stand out.

Q: Right and I would like to ask you why do they stand out? Let's start with the germ exhibit. What about the germ exhibit? You said you talked with your children about this.

A: Yeah, because they don't understand why you ask them to wash their hands. So, that is just such a great visual of why and they understand it and all my kids are great hand-washers now.

Q: Are you concerned about cleanliness, washing, germs?

A: Well, yeah. I'd like them to own it and me not have to tell them every time after the bathroom and before a meal and I think it helps keep our family pretty healthy.

Q: Since you have been to the Science Center with your kids and they have seen what happens when you have your hands not washed for a few days, do you think you're more successful in conveying that than other parents you know?

A: Oh, yeah.

Q: You do? Really?

A: Oh, yeah.

Q: I'm glad we are achieving something here.

A: Oh, yeah—that's huge.

Q: Wonderful. The other thing you mentioned is the cigarette exhibit. Why is that so powerful?

A: Well, we talk about smoking a lot and you know we talk about that to our kids and they in school they get talked to so just the effect of it—negative effect of it. It's a nice visual for them to realize.

Q: It seems another thing you are concerned about that your children might be smoking or do you know anyone who smokes?

A: Yeah. We don't know that many people that smoke but yeah, it's just we talked to them about all that stuff.

Q: What makes the surgery exhibit so memorable?

A: It was just sort of a different way, a different visual. It was so dimensional and I guess it helped the kids to kind of see. It was kind of gross to them but at the same time they loved it. It was the same for the adults I think.

Q: So, you found this particular exhibit interesting?

A: Oh, yeah. I was really intrigued by the visual nature of it, that it looked like you were actually right there at a surgery and you look inside the body cavity and see the heart and organs and everything. That was really neat.

Q: And the last one you were mentioning was the chicks.

A: Yeah, we always like to see that. That's fun.

Q: Is it because it's fun or because you use the chick-hatching to explain something to your children?

A: Definitely it creates dialogue about animals and different species and yeah, it opens dialogue that way but it's just so fun for them to watch it, too.

Q: Okay, let's switch gears a little. Let's talk about your actual visit. After you finished talking with me and left to go inside, what did you do, what did you see?

A: I would guess that I went to where my family was which was to the right. Which was, I'm not sure, there was a heart exhibit over there. Is that right?

Q: Yes, there were hearts when you looked straight ahead.

A: Well, they were either there or at the chicks. I can't remember where they were but I went to meet my family.

Q: And do you remember after you met your family, what you did after that?

A: In that specific area?

Q: Yes.

A: No.

Q: What about in the rest of the exhibition?

A: Well, I know we wandered around. We obviously saw the surgery exhibit and the chicks and smoking and hand-washing exhibits. I think we may have also looked at an exhibit on bat vision and something about digestion. But honestly, I can't really remember much about what we did or saw. I was just following along, trying to keep my parents happy and trying to be helpful to my kids if they needed me.

Several things stand out in this visitor recollection. The first is that Susan clearly recalls this visit and in particular, remembers that everyone enjoyed themselves. She makes it clear that she thought this was an important experience for her children and it helped them in their intellectual development. She also indicates that her parents enjoyed the experience and makes the projection that they too learned from the experience. In this way, Susan reveals the strength of her identity-related self-aspects for that day—being a good parent, as well as being a good child herself. Her strongest goal though was helping her children grow and become healthier and happier. She makes a point of stating that the museum visit was not like taking your children to the park; this kind of experience has greater value. Overall, she expresses great satisfaction with her visit to the Science Center.

Her memories of the day support her good-parent narrative as she recalls how her children have a greater appreciation for the dangers of smoking and the importance of hand-washing. In fact, Susan offers evidence that her children not only have a greater appreciation for the importance of hand-washing, but that this appreciation is over and above that of other children. Although she did not actively interact with, or even spend much time watching the chick-hatching exhibit herself, the fact that her children really enjoyed this particular exhibit has great salience for her. Susan was able to share her children's delight with the exhibit which, in turn, reinforced her self-aspect that she was being a good parent.

Exactly what Susan remembers about the day is also very revealing. She finds it easy to talk about what her children did and what kinds of things they might have learned. When pressed, she indicates that she too enjoyed picking up some information, but she's quick to point out that this was not really the purpose of the visit. The one exhibit that stood out for Susan in this regard was the surgery exhibit; otherwise she dwells on the exhibits that she particularly wanted the children to see and learn from. In contrast with the depth of her social memories, Susan has few memories of the actual exhibition itself. She is hard-pressed to remember any details of what she specifically saw and did that day at the museum. Also absent from Susan's recollections are any negative memories such as the noise and crowds of the Science Center; these memories have been swept away by her Facilitator narrative. Again, her interest and needs entering, while in the museum, and then again after the visit, were focused primarily on her children and secondarily on her parents. Because of her Facilitator agenda, Susan was only minimally concerned with her own personal curiosity and interests or even comfort. Her entering Facilitator identity-related motivations created the framework for both her actual visit experiences and her memories of those experiences, and thus formed an overall trajectory for her visit. In sum, Susan had a working model of what the Science Center would afford her and her family—an enjoyable, educational experience—and then ascribed a series of self-aspects to her visit that were consistent with this model—"I'm a good parent who helps my children learn the things they need to live a healthy and successful life." Susan "enacted" these identity-related self-aspects during her visit to the Science Center. She was rewarded later by feedback from her family that suggested that everyone enjoyed themselves and even learned some things she had hoped they would.

We can see from Susan's interview after the visit that not only did she have long-term memories of the experience, but that she also used the experience to enhance her self-concept as a good parent:

> My expectations would have been that my kids showed interest in science, that they got some information at the same time as being entertained. That

it opened some dialogue for us to talk about things we might not talk about normally. That it's interesting so when I go back and do homework with my kids I can know how to talk with them and get them to learn things. So I guess creating the dialogue is what I look for, too.

Susan believes that good parents encourage interest in subjects like science and they encourage their children's intellectual growth and curiosity. She also indicates that she believes that good parents are active participants in their children's learning process; this is not just the role of the schools. These were beliefs Susan likely had prior to her visit to the Science Center, but it's clear that all of these beliefs were reinforced by her museum visit.

We can also see how Susan's own adult self-identity was shaped by the visit in her projections about the benefits she believed her parents received from the visit:

Well, they're interested in it because they probably didn't have as much science as we had in school and so it's interesting to them to see it in such a simplistic form. Then they can apply what they've learned in their life to that, I guess. They're just that kind of people that continually learn. . . . Because it's fun for adults to get to do things that kids get to do. And they're retired, they like to go out and do things and they like to learn. And they like to see the kids have fun and they like to read about stuff and see the exhibits. They just kind of enjoy that sort of thing.

Although we didn't focus our observations on Susan's parents, the data does not suggest that they actually spent much time looking at and learning from exhibits. However, this perception of her parents was reflected in both her pre-visit expectations and persisted in Susan's long-term recollections of the experience. For Susan, this view of her parents was reality.

Finally, we can believe that Susan's prior understanding of what a science center in particular, and museums in general afford family visitors was strengthened by her experiences at the California Science Center. We would not be surprised (though she didn't offer this information to us) that she communicated to others, both friends and family, about how wonderful the California Science Center is for a family visit. As we can see from this example, visitors do use their identity-related visit motivations to justify their museum visit in advance, to guide their behavior during their museum visit, and to make sense of their museum visit retrospectively.

TRAJECTORIES AND STOCHASTIC MODELS

As described in Chapter 4, I would propose that a model of the museum visitor experience is basically a stochastic model. A stochastic model assumes that "initial states," for example, a parent's desire to support their children's meaningful learning-related experiences and one's prior knowledge and interest in particular topics, are extremely important. These initial states are then influenced by other factors, for example, the exhibits and objects an individual encounters while visiting a museum and the conversations one has with one's family group while in the museum, and so on. The basic trajectory of the individual changes over time through interactions with both predictable and unpredictable events. The collective interactions, rather than just the initial state, determine the outcomes. In addition, random events, such as Susan's misfortune of visiting the Science Center on a busy day, potentially influence and modulate the relative amplitude of impact that the various contextual factors have on the museum visitor experience. This is what is meant by a stochastic model ("stochastic" being a fancy way to say "random" and "unpredictable"); stochastic factors influence both the quality and quantity of experiences that result.

The model postulates that virtually all people who visit museums begin from a relatively common, culturally-shared frame of reference—museums are leisure educational institutions that afford a suite of possible benefits. Depending upon the needs an individual has and his or her perceptions of what a particular museum is likely to afford, the visitor "launches" his or her museum visitor experience following a generalized museum visit "trajectory." Currently, museums seem to afford five basic types of visit trajectories—Explorer trajectory, Facilitator trajectory, Experience seeker trajectory, Professional/Hobbyist trajectory, and a Recharger trajectory. Although many visitors arrive with some combination of these basic motivational trajectories and some visitors arrive with no strongly-held entering motivations and thus no obvious trajectory, the current evidence would suggest that a majority of visitors enter the museum with a single, dominant visitor motivational trajectory.

Each of the five basic trajectories is, within the limits of our current knowledge, generally predictable. Rechargers and Professional/Hobbyists probably have the "straightest" trajectories. These visitors typically enter with a fairly specific goal in mind, a relatively sophisticated understanding of the physical layout and design of the museum, and a fairly clear sense of how to accomplish their goals. For example, "I came to take pictures of the big cats" or "I'm looking for neat exhibit design ideas that I can use in my own museum." They can and occasionally do get sidetracked by experiences outside of their initial intentions, but for these two groups, this is the exception rather than the rule. More often than not these visitors make a beeline to the exhibits or spaces they are interested in, spend whatever time it takes to accomplish their goal(s), and then depart. Although they may "graze" upon exiting, this is primarily to take stock of things for their next visit.

By contrast, the trajectories of Explorers and Facilitators are much more generalized and less laser-like. The Explorer is seeking "interesting things" while the Facilitator is seeking "interesting things for others." What guides the Explorer in this quest is their own inner compass which is "magnetized" by the visitor's unique prior knowledge, experience, and interests. They can't tell you what will pique their curiosity before they get there, but once inside the museum, they will know immediately what interests them! At exhibits that strike their fancy, they will spend considerable time and perhaps, even discussing it with their social group, though many Explorers prefer to go alone once in the museum. They're happy to share what they've found but they fear being distracted by someone else's interests. An Explorer's journey through the museum is likely to be somewhat wandering, punctuated by periods of intensive looking and pointing at objects, labels and exhibits, as well as times of concentrated conversing with others.

The general approach to the museum is much different for the Facilitator. They, too, have only the most general of goals—to satisfy the needs of someone else and to help maximize the quality of that other person's experience. Whereas individuals with an Explorer motivation are focused on the physical aspects of the museum, individuals with a Facilitator motivation are primarily attuned to the social aspects of the visit; they are focused on what their significant other finds interesting and enjoyable. Facilitators, like Susan, tend to sublimate their own interests and curiosities unless they feel that by sharing these, they might be helpful in satisfying the needs and interests of others. Return visitors, like Susan, are likely to have some ideas going into the visit about what might be worth seeing and doing, but they are also usually happy to let other members of their social group define for themselves what is worth attending to. Facilitators engage in considerable social interaction within their own social group; visitors like Susan in this chapter and George and Frank in earlier chapters may spend a disproportionate amount of their visit attending to their companions and chatting with them rather than focusing intently on the exhibits. This works just fine for them since this kind of social interaction is why they came in the first place—the museum is a stage setting for this social play to be enacted and the exhibits are mere props. Thus, a Facilitator's track through the physical space will appear somewhat haphazard, despite being quite purposeful.

Finally, the trajectory of individuals with an Experience-seeker motivation is a blend of the Explorer and the Facilitator. They, too, have a generalized goal for their visit, but rather than satisfying their personal curiosity or the specific intellectual needs of their companions (though both of these are very likely to be strong secondary motivations), the Experience seeking visitor is in search of what is most famous and important in the museum. They have come to see the Hope Diamond or the *Mona Lisa,* or whatever the museum is most famous for. Most Experience seekers are first-time visitors to the museum and many are relatively infrequent museum visitors. Thus these visitors, unless they receive guidance from the museum, often believe that the best way to see the museum is to start in the first gallery and read every label they encounter. After a while, they realize this strategy is not going to meet their needs so they start picking up the pace and skimming through the museum in an effort to see every exhibit. Those with more savvy will go straight to the icon and then skim through the rest of the institution. Either way, the basic pathway of an Experience seeker is likely to be fairly direct at the beginning of the visit and quite "wobbly" towards the end, as they start walking quickly through halls in an effort to see everything. To date, research seems to suggest that most Experience seekers have multiple motivations—Experience Seeking Facilitators or Experience Seeking Explorers—and thus, tend to enact a "blended" trajectory characteristic of both entering motivations.

As discussed previously, the specifics of what any given visitor is likely to attend to in the museum will depend upon what's available for them to view, but also it will be based upon the visitor's own personal interests and understandings and those of their companions. Overall, people tend to use museums to build on and reinforce their own prior knowledge and interests rather than as a vehicle for generating "new" knowledge and interests. The visitors most likely to break out of this mold are individuals with an Explorer motivation, but even these visitors will primarily focus on things that resonate with their pre-existing understanding of the world.

All visitors will be particularly prone to remember those things that struck an emotionally positive chord for them. What's emotionally positive will of course vary between visitors, but more often than not it will be consistent with their entering identity-related motivations. Explorers will find that ideas and objects that pique their curiosity generate high affect. Facilitators will be looking for their social group to be enjoying themselves; what excites a child or significant other will be highly salient and be remembered. Experience seekers will be attuned to seeing what they were "meant" to see—if they came to see the giant T-Rex, than this will be a real high for them and quite memorable. Professional/Hobbyists will find accomplishment of their personal goals quite satisfying—"I was looking for new ideas and saw a really fabulous use of lighting and scrim which I know I can use back home." Finally, the Recharger is in search of peace and psychological uplift; if they find this, it will create a sensation of great pleasure and this feeling will remain in memory. Most people's memories of their museum visitor experience will be framed through the lens of their entering identity-related motivations and the self-aspects they formed to understand personal needs and interests. The details of what the visitor remembers will vary but the basic form and structure of his or her memories is likely to be quite predictable.

In general, we can see that a visitor's entering identity-related motivation predisposes the visitor to interact with the setting in predictable ways. Once in the setting, the visitor is affected by a whole series of additional factors, some of which are under the control of the institution (e.g., mediation provided by trained staff, orientation brochures and signage, good and bad exhibits, and the nature of interpretation tools such as labels and audio guides). But much of what affects the course of the visitor experience is not directly under the control of the museum such as the prior experience, knowledge, and interests of the visitor and his or her social group. Although these factors are not directly "controlled" by the museum, they can be understood and, at least to a degree, predicted by the museum. Thus, these very critical factors are within the realm of the museum to affect. That's not to say that there aren't also unpredictable, often random events that influence the visitor experience over which the museum has less control. These events, such as a crowd standing in front of an important explanatory label that causes the visitor to avoid it, or an accompanying child who suddenly needs to go to the toilet may or may not occur, but when they do, they can strongly influence a visitor's experience and significantly diminish the predictability of any museum visitor experience outcome. In other words, the basic course of the visitor experience depends in large part on things the museum can predict and thus, plan for and design around. However, there will always be some aspects of the museum visitor experience that are unpredictable and beyond the control of the museum.

Using this model and returning once again to our chapter example of Susan, we can see that once we had a sense of her entering identity-related motivations for visiting the Science Center and knew a few of the details about her prior experiences, interests, and background, we could predict with reasonable accuracy the basic shape and form of her museum visit experience. We could also make some predictions as to what she would likely remember from her visit and even, in general, the meanings she was likely to make from the experience. That's a lot of useful information to have up front!

This is the basic framework of the model—it suggests that much of the visitor experience is actually knowable and predictable. Accordingly, it is a model that could allow museums to become markedly better at the services they provide to visitors, if we knew what to look for and how to appropriately respond. In the next section of the book, I will introduce some thoughts and suggestions on how these ideas can be applied in practice—ideas for attracting, engaging, and retaining visitors as well as suggestions as to how these ideas could better define and measure the impact of the museum visitor experience.

PART II

Practice

CHAPTER 8

Theory to Practice

There is nothing so practical as a good theory.

—*Kurt Lewin, 1951*[1]

As I have argued for years, despite existing and competing in a twenty-first century Knowledge Age, most museums still operate with a twentieth-century industrial age business model.[2] The hallmark of the Industrial Age was an abundance of standardized ("one-size-fits-all") inexpensive goods and services. Although mass production allowed for the unprecedented availability of goods and services, it depersonalized both the production and delivery process. By contrast, the trends in the Knowledge Age are for an increasing desire on the part of consumers not just for quantity of choice but also for quality, not just for reasonable prices but for real value. Most significantly, consumers today are growing to expect that goods and services be designed to specifically meet their own personal needs and interests. They are much more discriminating, in part because they can afford to be given the glut of available products and services. It is a rare product or service that cannot be had in myriad shapes, sizes, and price-ranges and that includes museum-related experiences. Above all else, consumers today are seeking to forge long-standing relationships with the people they "trade" with; they do not want to be just another nameless, faceless consumer. Collectively, these trends represent a sea-change in the marketplace and a radical departure from the norms of doing business of even a decade ago.

It is against this background that we can see how out of step most museums are with these trends. The world has and continues to change rapidly; gone are the simple "truths" of previous times. No longer can a museum survive merely by collecting important objects and presenting them with commendable scholarship in an orderly fashion. Gone is the wonderfully naïve idea that the museum can accommodate the needs of all people by aiming at some non-existent "typical visitor." Most in the business world have been struggling for years to adapt to the reality that trying to satisfy a diverse range of people with a single generic approach is no longer a viable strategy in today's complex and highly competitive marketplace.[3] Although museums still attempt to hang their financial success on blockbuster exhibitions created using a "one-size-fits-all" approach, it should be clear that this strategy is rapidly becoming unsustainable for most institutions. If the preceding chapters have attempted to make any point, it is that all museum visitors are not alike; different groups of visitors have very different needs and interests. Eventually, if museums cannot adapt to the changing times, large segments of the public that currently utilize museums will find alternative ways to satisfy their leisure needs.

Despite all these dire predictions, a skeptical reader might well point out that the museum industry is doing relatively well and that most individual museums continue to be amazingly popular and successful in their respective marketplaces. What explains this paradox? Maybe museums do not need to change what they do as visitors will figure out how to make museums work for them in the future just as they have in the past.

As outlined in earlier chapters, museums have had the good fortune to be on the correct side of history—sometimes it's better to be lucky than good! Society has undergone unprecedented shifts in leisure patterns commensurate with the transition to a Knowledge Age at the end of the twentieth and beginning of the twenty-first century. Foremost among these shifts has been a significant rise in demand for meaningful leisure experiences, particularly those associated with identity-building through experiences like free-choice learning. Museums were "pre-adapted" for these major societal changes—in the right place, at the right time, with the right mix of offerings. As a consequence, most museums have flourished. Whereas in the 1980s, approximately 40% of Americans visited some kind of museum at least once a year, by 2000 that number had risen to over 60%—a 50% increase in one generation.[4] But looking ahead, it is quite possible that the successes museums enjoyed these past few decades could be ephemeral. The world is full of smart people and the recent success of museums has not gone unnoticed. Every year, more and more competitors have begun to emulate the museum model. Libraries and corporations are putting exhibits in their buildings, developers are anchoring shopping malls with museum-like entities, corporations like Disney are trying (historically with limited success) to make their attractions more museum-like, and even ultra-religious groups are promoting their views through museum-like venues. Despite the fact that collectively museums have had an amazing run of success in years past, it is inevitable that increasing competition will eventually erode that success—initially through a process of dilution of the "brand" and eventually through replacement by some other, better adapted, and more compelling model. That is, of course, unless museums can make the necessary changes to keep ahead of the curve and remain competitive.

Evidence of the impact of increasing competition and dilution of the museum brand is evident to anyone who cares to look objectively. During the first decade of the twenty-first century, attendance at museums leveled off following two decades of exponential growth. Over these past several years, most individual museums have felt fortunate if their attendance has merely leveled off; many witnessed declining attendance. On the up side, the museum brand is still strong and thus, theoretically the ability and opportunities for change will never be better—it is much easier to make changes when times are good than when things are in wholesale decline. On the down side, we seem to be entering a period of significant economic challenge when change will be required by all, but meaningful change will be difficult because of worldwide financial stresses.

The museum visitor experience model I have developed in this book provides a roadmap for how museums can begin to make some of the changes required in order to be more in step with the needs of consumers in the Knowledge Age. Over the next three chapters, I will lay out some suggestions for how museum professionals can use the model proposed in this book to customize the museum visitor experience so that it delivers the type of personalized, high-quality value and meaning sought by today's visitors. I will also suggest how the museum visitor experience model can lead to a rethinking of how to define and measure the value museums deliver to society.

RE-ENVISIONING THE MUSEUM VISITOR EXPERIENCE

Let's begin with some basic information. To be successful in the Knowledge Age every museum must be able to answer the following questions:

- Do you really know why people come to your museum and what it takes to get people to visit?
- Do you know how to attract new and different audiences to your museum?
- Do you know what your visitors actually do in your museum and why they do these things?
- What is the one thing you are not providing your various publics today that they are secretly longing for?
- Do you know what impact your museum has on the public, in particular what meanings visitors derive from their experience?
- Do you know what would make a visitor come again and again to your museum?
- Do you know how a new, or existing, competitor could take away your audience?

I believe the museum visitor experience model outlined in this book could enable museum professionals to begin to more honestly and accurately answer these questions. This, then, is the goal of these final chapters, to begin to clarify some answers to these questions by applying what we now know about museums and visitors. The implications of this new model do not suggest that we can continue doing business as usual. If taken seriously, it will lead museums down a very different pathway than what they have historically followed. In particular, the next three chapters will lay out some bold and new ways to think about museums and their audiences. First, by suggesting ways that museums can begin to revise how they attract and build audiences. Second, by reframing how museums can best satisfy the fundamental needs and interests of the people who utilize their exhibitions and programs. And finally, by suggesting that in light of this new model of museums and their visitors, museum professionals may need to fundamentally rethink how they define their purpose and measure success.

Attracting and Building Audiences

The secret to attracting and building audiences is helping potential visitors understand that the museum can meet and satisfy their individual identity-related needs.

The heart of the modern museum is its visitors. Logically then, the first questions every museum wants to ask is how can we best attract audiences? How can we keep past visitors coming as well as how can we build new audiences? In response to these audience-related concerns, museums over the last twenty-five years have become increasingly market-driven. Marketing budgets have swelled (though nowhere near as fast as those in the private sector) and every museum of any size has added full-time marketing staff. Commensurate with perceived importance, the top marketing person in larger museums is usually ranked just below the Director/President with the title of Vice President. Museums appreciate that they operate within a crowded marketplace and considerable energies are invested in trying to attract and retain audiences. At the expense of over-generalizing, I will assert that the vast majority of museums are not investing their limited marketing dollars as wisely as they should. Despite the sincere intentions of museum marketers, they are operating from a frame of reference that handicaps their capacity to make a difference. This is because of a combination of factors. Clearly problematic are the continued use of questionable strategies and beliefs about the nature of the museum visitor experience such as a continued over-reliance on demographic segmentation of visitors, a tendency to cling to the historical content-first view of what makes museums attractive places to visit, and a dependence on the audience focus group as the primary mechanism for collecting visitor input. All of these factors show a lack of institutional awareness of the larger framework in which the public's museum-going decisions are made.

What are the major factors that contribute to whether someone opts to visit a museum? Historically, the answer would be framed in terms of the great objects and exhibitions on display and the ability of the museum to communicate about both to the public. As discussed in the first section of this book, the assumption is that the factors that most significantly influence museum-going are events within the museum—the creation of great exhibits and the successful marketing of those exhibits. I have tried to make the case that the factors that most influence someone to visit a museum primarily originate outside of the museum; ideas, experiences, and events that have only a tangential relationship to what is currently happening within the museum. Although we'd like to believe that the museum has a significant amount of control over who visits our premises, it's sobering to discover just how limited is our actual direct influence. Is the public really visiting because of the "cool stuff" on display and the great advertising of that stuff? Why is it that most first-time museum visitors report they are not exactly sure what is on display at the museum? The public's visit decisions are influenced by perceptions of the institution, but these perceptions are typically general in nature and are only slightly based upon a detailed reckoning of what is currently on exhibit.

Museums are jostling with many other organizations and institutions for a piece of the public's leisure time. Currently, an overwhelming percentage of the public has been to a museum within the past year; 80% claim to use such sites on a regular basis.[1] In other words, people know about museums and have a general sense of what kind of leisure experiences they afford. Most leisure experiences are initiated not by a desire to see or do something specific, but as outlined in the museum visitor experience model, as a desire to fulfill one of many highly need-specific, identity-related motivations. The decision to visit a museum is normally a group decision, but almost always it is initiated and promoted by a single individual. If that individual's identity-related motivations align with his or her perceptions of what a museum is like, then he or she will decide that a museum might be a good venue for a leisure experience. If the museum visit idea progresses this far, then the visit decision will need to be run through the person's mental accounting system for price, convenience, and perceived value, as well as through a process of approval from others in his or her family or social group. The order of these two steps may vary, but again typically one individual is leading the decision-making process and after arriving at a solution, attempts to "sell" it to the others in his or her social group. All the other members of the social group will have their own decision-making process about the museum visit; each will weigh their own understanding of what the museum affords against their own personal set of identity-related needs. To the extent the museum visit emerges as a good idea, each visitor will create their own set of identity-related museum visit motivations. Then, and only then, the decision to visit a museum will begin to be actualized.

That's all true, you might think, but isn't the visit decision still basically determined by the content of the museum, in particular the promotion and advertising of what is currently on display? Years of museum market research consistently tells us the answer is "no"! As outlined in the first chapter, a majority of museum-goers report that the primary thing that influenced them to visit was a word-of-mouth recommendation from friends and/or family.[2] Not surprisingly then, the more friends and family one has who are museum-goers, the more likely it is that you will also go to museums. Not only do people hear about the institution through word-of-mouth, it also was the single most important factor in influencing them to actually visit. For all museums, advertising and publicity programs account for less than 20% of visitors. The previous visitor who made the word-of-mouth recommendation may have seen the same current exhibits and may have seen and heard the same current museum promotions, but just as likely the recommendation is based upon outdated informaton. Thus, the primary catalyst for causing an individual to visit a museum in the present, are events that happened in the past, including exhibits and marketing. It is not that the museum's content and promotions are unimportant, it is just that they are rarely as central and important as most museums have thought them to be.

As outlined in the first section of this book, the impetus for someone to promote a museum visit to a friend, family member, or colleague is their own successful visit experience; by definition, it is one that has fulfilled a person's entering identity-related motivation for visiting. The most productive way to influence future museum visits is to ensure that current visitors have a great experience. This, of course, becomes somewhat circular—in order for there to be successful word-of-mouth promotion, people have to go the museum in the first place, for people to go to the museum in the first place, they need to be encouraged by someone else who had a successful museum experience. The key message here is that museums need to think very differently about their institutions. They need to see them as part of a much larger whole than they have historically done; museums are part of a much larger leisure system. They are one of many possible venues that create high value free-choice learning experiences. Deriving from a combination of an individual's own prior museum experiences; the museum's reputation, advertising, and word-of-mouth recommendations from friends and family; museums are currently perceived as supporting one of five general types of leisure time identity-related outcomes. Most of these outcomes have some kind of free-choice learning leitmotif. The most effective things museums can do to influence who and how many people visit are to understand the nature of the different identity-related needs the public perceives they afford and then, help to distinguish for the public how they best support these needs. It also matters whether or not the museum actually fulfills these identity-related needs when someone does visit. Let's take a look at what some of these needs might look like for each of these different types of identity-related visitor motivations.

MARKETING FOR IDENTITY-RELATED NEEDS

Research to date seems to suggest that virtually all visitors arrive at museums hoping to satisfy one or more identity-related motivations; the majority arrive with a single dominant visit motivation. Although it is possible that the same individual can possess a different visit motivation on different days and that an individual can and occasionally does switch his or her motivation during a single visit, research suggests that most visitors will arrive at *your* museum with a single dominant identity-related visit motivation. This visit motivation will persist throughout the visit and drive much of what transpires during the visit. The entering identity-related visit motivation will also shape much of what is recalled about the museum experience long after the visit has ended and will thus, influence future visits.

Research also suggests that although most museums attract visitors possessing all five of these types of identity-related visit motivations, the public tends to pigeon-hole individual museums as disproportionately affording certain kinds of experiences. For example, the majority of the public perceives that science centers and children's museums are great places for adults to visit with children and they are particularly well-suited as places for adults to enact their role as parental facilitators. They are not widely perceived as settings where adults could or should visit by themselves, particularly if they have a Recharger motivation. Meanwhile, art museums are generally perceived by large sectors of the public as settings well-suited to adult exploration of high culture; they are generally not perceived as places that optimally support family experience-seeking. The result is that most visitors arrive at a particular museum with both a specific, pre-determined concept of what that museum is capable of affording them in the way of a leisure experience, and a preconceived concept, almost a "plan" for what they personally hope to get out of that experience. All of this suggests that museums can, and should work to influence the public's museum visit experience expectations. The broad term under which this kind of influence falls is marketing.

One of the key insights the museum visitor experience model suggests is that marketing is important but only if it is the right kind of marketing. Marketing will be successful to the extent that it supports the expectations and needs of each of the major kinds of audiences the museum is likely to attract. The expectations and identity-related needs of individuals with an Explorer motivation are not the same as those who plan on using the museum to satisfy a Facilitator or Recharger motivation; appealing to these different types of visitor motivations requires very different types of messages. Most museums don't just attract visitors with a single type of identity-related motivation; some percentage of visitors is likely to expect each of the five basic kinds of experience. Hence, a typical museum needs to communicate multiple messages, each appealing to a different subset of the visiting public. However, it is quite likely that every museum currently attracts a very specific profile of visitors. This profile has been determined in part by the past actions and activities of that particular institution, but it has also been determined by the perceptions within the larger society of that type of museum. If you have the word "museum" or "center" in your name, and if you modify that name with words like "children," "history," "art," "science," or "nature," then you can safely assume that the majority of the public already thinks they know what they can expect from your institution. Accordingly, each institution can decide whether it wants to market to all the possible audiences that might be attracted to their institution, or whether they want to put all or most of their marketing "eggs" into a single identity-related motivational "basket." Whichever decision a museum makes, what follows are some thoughts on how they might approach marketing to these different motivational segments.

Attracting Explorers

Explorers are individuals who say they are visiting the museum because of curiosity or a general interest in discovering more about the topic or subject matter of the institution. Large numbers of these visitors self-describe themselves as curious people who enjoy learning new things. Explorers believe that visiting museums reinforces who they perceive themselves to be; museum visits confirm their self-image. The typical Explorer visitor perceives that learning is fun![3] This is indicated by comments like, "If you don't try to revisit your knowledge in some way by reading or watching TV or [visiting] museums like this I think you forget a little bit on the educational part and these things are very important." And "I think about the same things all the time on my job, I don't get to think about different things. Not many things I do allow me to be on a steep learning curve. When I'm on a steep learning curve, it's fun. It's a brain vacation when I'm on a steep learning curve."[4]

Explorers may or may not be well-educated in a traditional sense with a college degree, but, as a group, they are individuals who highly value learning. They are inclined to read newspapers, listen to news programs, enjoy watching educational television, and love to discover new and interesting facts about their world. The typical Explorer is likely to possess only a slightly better than average knowledge of the subject matter of the museum they are visiting. Although not particularly knowledgeable, they are likely to be highly interested and eager to learn about the content. Typical are the comments made to me by the same Explorer visitor quoted at the end of the last paragraph when talking about her recent visit to an art museum, "Actually I hoped I'd learn a little about art. In particular, learn a little bit about [the artist on exhibition]'s art. I've had no art education. I stopped doing art after I was allowed to in the 9th grade. I'm on a steep learning curve. I wanted to go learn about this artist, become more literate. I wanted to be able to look at pictures in a different way."[5]

Explorers are visitors who actually care about the content of the museum, but they care in generic not in specific terms. Although an Explorer might say they are an art, science, or history lover, that doesn't mean they are an expert. They are the group most likely to be attracted to visit because of a new exhibition, primarily because it appeals to their desire to expand their horizons rather than dwell upon the details of the exhibition. Quoting another Explorer, "The more you are exposed to [the content of the museum], the more you are going to want to learn and you know hopefully want to strive for more."[6] Explorers are mostly visiting museums so they can "expand their horizons" but not in order to learn anything in particular.

As a generalization, individuals who seek to satisfy an Explorer visit motivation tend to be the kind of people who regularly visit museums. They not only regularly visit museums that support their specific interests; for example, if they like art, they will regularly visit all of the art museums in their region as well as any art museum they might encounter while traveling, but they are also likely to visit any and all museums. After all, their goal is to satisfy their curiosity, which is as likely to be generic as specific. As one woman said to me, "Of course I visit art museums, actually I visit all museums. It doesn't really matter what's going on, I just like to see what's there."[7] Consequently, people with an Explorer motivation are likely to be relatively frequent visitors to their local museums and first-time visitors at museums when they are traveling. They are museum-savvy and begin with a well-formed concept of what a museum is likely to afford.

How would you attract someone seeking to satisfy an Explorer visit motivation? Given their interest in museums in general and their desire to expand their intellectual horizons, it makes sense that promotions that emphasize opportunities for seeing new exhibitions displaying rare and/or unusual things would be appealing to them. In part, this is why Explorers are often attracted to blockbuster and special exhibitions—the once-in-a-lifetime opportunity to see the artifacts from King Tut's tomb, all of Vermeer's art, or the recovered contents of the Titanic. Things like this are grist for the Explorer's intellectual mill. Given that this is typically how most museums market their institutions these days, it is not surprising that most museums currently attract many Explorers, particularly larger art museums who have lived off the blockbuster exhibition for years, but increasingly science centers, zoos, and aquariums which have also migrated to this mode of running their institutions.

Promotional materials should feature the most compelling images—the unusual, the rare, and the intriguing. Since Explorers are motivated by the desire to push their own intellectual boundaries, they'll be attracted by marketing that suggests there's much to see and investigate, things that few have seen before, and vast depths of material ideally suited to the intrepid visitor. Hence, multiple images are likely to work best, particularly if they imply depth and variety. Since individuals with an Explorer motivation are attracted by the opportunity to learn new things, promotions that emphasize conceptual themes and describe the opportunities for multiple sources of inquiry may also be appealing.

Explorers are influenced by word-of-mouth recommendations as much as any visitor, but they are particularly influenced by others who share their interests and curiosity. A good "buzz" about a new exhibition or program will be highly motivating for them, but it needs to be a buzz that is consistent with their desires and interests. It needs to communicate opportunities to see and do new things; particularly appealing is the allure of seeing and doing things that most people rarely get to see and do. Remember, these are intellectually adventurous folks, looking to broaden and expand their intellectual horizons. They don't want to become experts, but they do want to be challenged. In framing promotions, it's important to strike that fine line between the lowest and highest intellectual common denominator.

Attracting Facilitators

In contrast to Explorers, Facilitators are visiting in order to satisfy the needs and desires of someone they care about rather than just themselves. Facilitators tend to come in two broad sub-groupings, Facilitating Parents and Facilitating Socializers. Facilitating Parents are commonly parents or grandparents who visit in order to accommodate the needs and interests of their (grand)children. Facilitating Socializers are adults visiting to satisfy the needs of another adult, for example, a spouse, friend, or boyfriend/girlfriend. Sometimes the goal is to "host" a visiting relative, or sometimes it is just to spend quality time in a convenient and attractive space with an adult the Facilitator cares about. When asked why they came to the museum, a Facilitator will say things like "Science is important for the children." "It's a fun place for kids to run around and interact with the native habitat of [area] and maybe get some nature learning in. Sneak it in there." "We both enjoy these kinds of places and it's fun to do this together" or "I knew Mary would enjoy visiting."[8] In all cases, the primary objective of a person with a Facilitator motivation is to ensure that their companion is satisfied.

Facilitators are truly altruistic; they regularly defer their own intellectual interests to those of their companions. Make no mistake, though, Facilitators are just as invested as any other visitor in satisfying their own personal identity-related needs. It is just that their identity-related goals for a visit are defined as being a good parent or a good social companion; it is not being a curious knowledge-seeker.

A large percentage of Facilitators fall into the category of committed parents—individuals who say they like to visit museums because they are places that present information on art, history, nature, or science in an enjoyable and interactive way for children to learn. As Frank from Chapter 6 said, "[I] wanted [my daughter] to pick a few things, not many things because she's so young, just focus on a couple of things that we could talk about later." While another father said, "We can enjoy it together, and learn something whilst we're there."[9] Like Explorers, most Facilitators not only perceive that learning is fun, they do not discriminate between learning and fun.[10] Facilitating Parents are motivated to visit a museum because they believe that the visit will be a valuable experience for their children; the fun and learning are aimed at their children, not themselves. In fact, a number of these individuals are quick to say, "I wouldn't be here without children" or "I personally would rather go elsewhere."[11] They see museums as fun, educational places where *others* will be the beneficiary.

In a parallel way, the visit goal for Facilitating Socializers is social and other-directed. Although there are quite a few Facilitating Socializers who visit museums in order to support the needs of a loved one, the object of attention for the vast majority of Facilitating Socializers are not spouses or relatives. Most Facilitating Socializers are individuals who have discovered that museums are great places to meet and hang-out with friends. They'll regularly meet at the museum for lunch or a quiet stroll through the galleries, happily chatting away, occasionally glancing at exhibits or labels. Although they are likely to become members (for economic and perhaps, status reasons), their primary objective is to gain access to what the museum affords socially rather than what it offers intellectually.

Facilitators may or may not be particularly knowledgeable about the content area of the museum. When asked, they will be quick to say that they think that the content of the museum is significant, but they will also point out that their own personal knowledge and interest are of little or no particular importance. Since this visit is for someone else, what's important is that the other person finds this place interesting and educational. Facilitators say things like, "Billy loves animals; that's why I come here." "I want Francine to have an opportunity to see more art; she's very talented and this is important." "I'm somewhat lukewarm about the place, but my friend really loves the place and I find it to be one of the nicest places to meet people in the city."[12] However, when asked the open-ended question, "What other things like this do you do with your child/friend?", individuals with a facilitating motivation are likely to say that they like to go to the movies, shopping, or visiting a park as they are to suggest that they go to another museum. Facilitators view these museum visits as opportunities to exercise their social role as providers of fun, positive experiences for their children in the case of Facilitating Parents and great places to gather and bond in the case of Facilitating Socializers. Neither type of Facilitator sees the museum primarily as a place for extensive personal learning and growth. It is quite common for Facilitating Parents to adamantly assert that a museum visit was a great learning experience for their child but when pressed, be totally incapable of specifically stating what it was that their child learned. This apparent paradox can be easily explained when it's appreciated that for the parent, what the child actually learned was not really that important. The goal was satisfying their identity-related need to be perceived by themselves, their children, and others as being a good parent.

By and large, Facilitators are regular museum-goers. Often, they'll visit many different museums—the children's museum this week, the science center next week, and the zoo the following week. Facilitating Socializers may visit a given museum weekly in order to gather with friends. Those who take relatives to visit are infrequent visitors; maybe visiting only once every few years. If Facilitating Parents are inclined towards becoming members, they are often quite pragmatic about membership. For example, they might be members of the children's museum this year, the science center next year, and the zoo the following year so that their children are exposed to many different types of settings and experiences; they are also likely to be quite price-conscious. Facilitating Parents will make a cost-benefit decision on whether the price of the membership today will pay off over time if they make repeated visits. When they travel with their children, Facilitating Parents are likely to visit appropriate museums in the new city they are visiting; that tends not to be the case for Facilitating

Socializers. Facilitating Parents are also highly likely to sign their children up for afterschool, weekend, and/or summer programs at the museum.

The Facilitator's reward for a good visit is the happiness of their companion or child. A Facilitator is attentive to the child who demonstrates that they are having fun and says they want to come back again. They are also attentive to verbal and nonverbal behavior of a companion who gets excited about what they are seeing and doing. These are the kinds of feedback a Facilitator is seeking from their visit, and when they receive this feedback they deem it to have been a good visit.

What does it take to attract a Facilitator? Given that their interest is generally not the topic(s) of the museum, but their wish for a positive social experience, promotions that emphasize people doing fun and engaging things will be most appealing. Traditional marketing that features some compelling image of a rare object or striking exhibit is not what is going to push their buttons. Instead, particularly for Facilitating Parents, images of adults with children, where the adult is shown helping a child learn, will be highly salient. Images of just children will be sufficient but not as engaging as an image of a parent and child interacting together. Given that the Facilitator wants to feel good about their decision, anything that reinforces that this is a place that good parents bring their children to or that good partners bring their significant others to will be successful. Individuals wishing to enact a Facilitating Socializer agenda will be attracted by a picture of two adults talking over a cup of coffee or perhaps, strolling through a garden deeply engaged in conversation. This is not how the museum typically sees itself, but this is how a Facilitating Socializer is likely to see the museum.

Facilitators are highly susceptible to word-of-mouth recommendations from others like them. Since the goal of a Facilitator, particularly a Facilitating Parent, is to be seen as a good parent, and currently museums are widely viewed as excellent educational experiences for children, having other parents know that they take their child to a museum is an important thing for them to talk about. Facilitating Parents like to "brag" about having taken their children to the museum, and about all the things their children learned. They find that encouraging others to do so also helps to solidify and reinforce their self-perception that they are good parents. If someone else praises your decision, or even better yet, takes your advice and goes to the museum, then clearly it confirms the value of having done it yourself. So, promoting museum visits through organizations like the PTA, church, reading groups, or other types of social networks where parents, particularly mothers, are likely to share parenting ideas, makes great sense. Advertising in parenting magazines or on the education page of the local newspaper are also excellent places to reach Facilitators. Remember, the motivations for these visitors are their children, so describing how a visit to the museum will do wonders for their child is what's important. The specifics of an exhibit or even what someone might learn is less important than the fact that these experiences are what will help ensure a child's later success in life.

As mentioned above, more than most visitors, Facilitating Parents are likely to be quite price-conscious. On average, the adults accompanying children are younger than the adults accompanying other adults. Many are at a stage of life where there are numerous expenses associated with raising children and although they are eager to provide the kinds of experiences represented by museums, museum-going can become quite expensive, particularly since the typical museum visit experience involves more than just admission. Museum marketers need to be very aware that the trip to the museum equally involves food and a stop at the gift shop; supporting this experience for 3 or more people is costly. By contrast, individuals motivated by a Facilitating Socializer goal are likely to be price-conscious in the opposite direction since hanging out at the museum is likely to be a less expensive way to spend time with their friends than are many other options, such as going to a spa or going shopping. Often, Facilitating Socializers will only spend time in the free parts of the museum, the café or entry areas, or purposefully select museums that have free admission; either way these venues represent a marketing opportunity.

Facilitators are also likely to be very mindful of the biggest variable limiting museum-going—time. Facilitators are often the self-appointed time-keepers during a visit. The Facilitator in a group will be the one who knows when the parking meter is running out or when they promised to be home so Aunt Martha can drop by. When trying to attract Facilitators, it is important to frame the experience within a time context—a great way to spend a couple of hours or a full day's enjoyment at a half-day's price.

Attracting Experience Seekers

This group of museum visitors, often tourists, are typically motivated to visit primarily in order to "collect" an experience, so that they can feel like they've "been there, done that." When questioned, many of these individuals indicated that they came in order to fulfill the expectations of others—"My brother-in-law was on my case because I hadn't taken the kids here yet," or driven by recommendations or opinions of others— "We were on vacation and looking for things to do and the guy at the hotel said, you should go to the Getty Museum."[13] This category also includes a variety of different types of specific self-aspects. One visitor self-described her motivation by saying she was "a tourist," and another person said he is the kind of person who likes "fun and exciting" things to do on the weekend. There was also the individual who was satisfying his girlfriend's directive and described himself as wanting to spend his weekends more productively instead of just watching football games on TV. When questioned further about the use of the word "productively," he said, "like making sure we see the new movies when they come out, going to a concert at least once a year, maybe going to a nice restaurant once in awhile, you know, things like that."[14] The primary goal of Experience seekers is to see the destination, building, and what's iconic or important on display. There is a temptation among museum professionals to denigrate the Experience seeker motivation, and to view this need as somehow more trivial or less important than others. This would be a mistake;after all, who among us has not felt compelled to visit some shrine or icon in order to have the experience of being in the presence of greatness or uniqueness? Experience seeking is as pure and appropriate a motivation for visiting a museum as any other.

Most Experience seeking visitors are also socially motivated visitors; a large part of their visit motivation relates to having a good day out with friends and/or relatives. They are generally not strongly motivated by the specific topic of the museum, regardless of whether it is art, history, natural history, science, or animals; they are motivated by the idea of being in a culturally important place. Experience seekers are quite mindful that they are in an educational setting. Despite visiting the museum for primarily recreational reasons, they are well-aware that they have not come to a theme park. Consequently, they are likely to value that the setting affords "learning" but they are unlikely to rate "learning" as their highest visit priority. For example, one Experience seeking-motivated individual said in recalling her science center visit, "I remember having a great time. For example, there were things they [children] thought [were] pretty funny. The burping of the body and where it makes sounds as the food goes up and down and stuff like that, all the little gross sounds, they loved that."[15]

Visitors with Experience seeking motivations are, as a group, less likely to be regular visitors to a single institution or even regular visitors to museums in general. They are unlikely to have visited museums as children. Large numbers of visitors with this visit motivation are inclined to visit museums now because museum-going has become increasingly viewed as a "good" and "in" thing to do. Except for the large iconic institutions like the Metropolitan Museum of Art, Smithsonian museums, Guggenheim Museum Bilbao, J. Paul Getty Museum, or the British Museum, most museums do not attract large numbers of pure Experience seeker-motivated visitors; most are hybrids such as Experience Seeking Facilitators or Experience Seeking Explorers. These hybrids are likely to be attracted by a mix of messages characteristic of both modalities.

Individuals with an Experience seeker motivation are looking to visit the "must-see" destinations within a community. This is a status that relatively few museums attain; as much as it seems like every museum in the last twenty years has strived to convince their boards, donors, and local politicians that they are! A museum like the Smithsonian Institution's National Museum of Natural History can expect to attract five million visitors per year, approximately half of whom will be Experience seekers, without investing in marketing and promotion. But they have been in this situation for more than 100 years. Trying to achieve this kind of iconic status if starting from an unknown status is not easy; but it's not impossible either. The following example of the Washington, DC-based International Spy Museum provides a compelling case study of how it is possible.

This relatively small, privately funded and operated Museum has been able, almost overnight, since its opening in 2002 to position itself as a must-see, tourist attraction for anyone traveling to Washington, DC. To accomplish this, the International Spy Museum invested heavily in marketing and was able to generate amazing buzz. Even though it was competing with many of the world's most visited museums, most of which were free, the International Spy Museum was able to generate tremendous pre- and post-opening press. The Museum worked on getting its name mentioned on virtually every travel brochure and included in most packaged tours. The International Spy Museum staff made a point of meeting with local concierges, taxi drivers, and tour coordinators and they focused on paid ad placements in tourist publications. They also flooded the local news media with press releases and invited press to pre-opening tours. All of this special attention paid off as these folks now regularly recommend the International Spy Museum as a "must see" visit while in Washington, DC.

Of course, success breeds success. The millions of visitors since the 2002 opening go home and tell their friends and relatives that they had a great time in DC, and to prove it they show them pictures and relate stories of having gone to the International Spy Museum which, of course, proves they're hip and on the cutting edge of what there is to see and do in DC.[16] This inspires the next round of Experience seekers to visit the International Spy Museum when they come to visit.

Attracting Experience seekers requires convincing potential visitors that this is a one-of-a-kind experience—something that they cannot afford to miss if they want to feel like they've had a complete visit to Washington, DC, or wherever. This is well-illustrated by what Amanda Abrell, Media Relations Manager for the International Spy Museum has to say about her museum, "The International Spy Museum is the only public museum in the United States solely dedicated to espionage and the only one in the world to provide a global perspective on an all-but-invisible profession that has shaped history and continues to have a significant impact on world events." If your museum has a rare or one-of-a-kind object that everyone should see during their lifetime, that is what you want to feature in your promotional material aimed at Experience seekers. Alternatively, as does the International Spy Museum, try to make the whole visitor experience seem rare and unique. Although one would think that Experience seekers are attracted by blockbuster and special exhibitions, they generally are not. They are actually more interested in the permanent collections and are disinclined to spend the extra money that usually accompanies temporary exhibitions.

If you wish to attract Experience seekers, don't forget that these visitors are looking for the whole package—exhibits, food, gifts, and a good time. Marketing materials for this group should prominently feature the food services–great food at a moderate price, the gift shop–great values and unusual gifts for the entire family, and generally emphasize how much fun will be had by all while participating in a once-in-a-lifetime experience.

Attracting Professional/Hobbyists

Typically, individuals with a Professional/Hobbyists motivation represent the smallest category of visitors to most institutions, but they are often disproportionately influential. Given that these individuals often possess strong ties to the people who work in the museum, because of their content and/or professional knowledge, their satisfaction is often deemed extremely important. Subject matter curators want to make sure that people with content expertise will judge the content to be accurate. Designers want to make sure that others with knowledge of design will find the exhibits innovative and creative. Educators will want to be sure that other educators will find the exhibitions and programs engaging and educational. Everyone wants their peers to come and see what they've created, and at the same time worry about if they will be harshly judged.

And judge they do! Professional/Hobbyists are often the most critical visitors, since unlike Experience seekers or Explorers, their primary motivation in visiting is not some generalized goal but typically something quite specific. Although occasionally a Professional/Hobbyist could visit just to wander around and discover whatever attracts them, that is not the norm. These visitors are typically on a mission. Classic examples of Professional/Hobbyists are museum professionals themselves. When a museum professional visits a new museum they tend to view the museum through very different eyes than the typical visitor. We are extremely savvy about museums, and our visit agenda significantly differs from that of most visitors. The typical museum professional is looking critically at how an exhibition is put together, how labels are written, whether certain objects are on display or not, what the front of house services are like, and all of the details that any professional would be concerned about when viewing a competitor's work. If queried after a visit about what really stood out, a museum professional is most likely to talk about a specific nuance of design or museum practice, rather than the content of the museum; that's an appropriate response for a Professional/Hobbyist.

Museum professionals are not the only visitors who are more interested in learning about how the information in a museum is conveyed rather than the information as such. For example, in interviewing science center visitors, I have had individuals say, "I'm in the medical field and [the science center] does an extremely good job in describing to nonmedical people how our body works and how we process food and turn it into energy [which I use when talking with others]." Another spoke of the desire to learn some specific nuance of the content, "We home-school our children and we were studying human development at that time. We came so we could use the chick and frog hatching exhibit as part of our lesson for that day. . . . I explained to [the] kids about how the chicks hatched and which eggs would work and which did not."[17] At a history museum I had someone say, "I'm a history teacher and I always get ideas for how to convey tough concepts by when I visit history museums." And a glass artist once told me about her visits to art museums, "I guess for me specifically, I'm always looking for ideas for my work. I always like looking at shapes and forms for my work, giving me ideas for different patterns and colors that I might be able to use."[18] The latter comment is typical of a relatively small, but not insignificant number of all art museum visitors who are art students, artists, or academics visiting in order to aid their studies, to critically engage with the art, to get ideas for teaching, or perhaps, to just inspire them or stimulate their creativity. The Professional/Hobbyist's motivations are NOT your typical visit motivations.

While interviewing zoo and aquarium visitors about their reasons for visiting, individuals with a Professional/Hobbyist motivation jumped out of the crowd by virtue of the very conscious, specific, and frequently narrow purpose they ascribed to their visit. One zoo visitor said he was a professional photographer who used the zoo to capture great close-up images of wildlife as such candid pictures in the wild were difficult to get. Another individual described his visit to the aquarium as primarily for the purpose of going to the gift shop. He had just started a saltwater aquarium and was hoping to find some good books on the topic in the store. One living history museum visitor told me that he was an amateur blacksmith and he regularly visited the museum in order to swap ideas with the blacksmith, as well as just generally learn from this older, more experienced craftsman. And one of my graduate students described talking to a marine science center visitor she had intercepted in order to ascertain his reasons for visiting that day who was trying to find out information on good places to go crabbing. After completing the interview, the student helpfully pointed the man in the direction of a local volunteer who could answer that question. The visitor walked over to the volunteer, asked him about crabbing locations, got the information he was looking for, and promptly left the science center to go crabbing! In short, there are thousands of possible reasons someone could find for using a museum to support one's profession or hobby, but what all visitors with this motivation have in common is the desire to use the museum setting as a vehicle for achieving usually one narrow, personally-important task. Although the museum clearly affords these opportunities, few museum professionals think of their institutions as settings primarily designed to support these purposes; but why not?

Professional/Hobbyists are generally not visiting in order to see a new exhibition, in fact if they can, they may avoid visiting during these periods or going into these spaces because of the crowds. Or, if like Mara in an earlier chapter, their day job prevents them from visiting during quiet times, they grudgingly accept others in their space. Because of this, Professional/Hobbyists are among the least likely individuals to visit the museum as part of a social group. Social interaction is not what motivates them to visit. Perhaps more than any other group of visitors, individuals who are Professionals and Hobbyists have the clearest, least ambiguous, and most conscious motivations for their visit. They can tell you without hesitation why they are at the museum, how they plan to achieve their goal, and by the end of the visit, whether or not that goal was achieved. In many ways, attracting individuals with a Professional/Hobbyists motivation should be easy.

At the most basic level, you do not need to find Professional/Hobbyists, they'll find you. They know you exist, know what you have to offer, and know how to use your resources to best meet their needs. Professional/Hobbyists are the ultimate insiders; in some ways they are already us. As compared to most other visitors, individuals with these motivations are in temperament and knowledge the visitors that most closely mirror those who work in museums. Given their interest in the topics of the museum and their desire to use its resources to extend their professional or avocational goals, what these visitors need from the museum is an invitation to visit.

You don't effectively reach Professional/Hobbyists through mass marketing strategies; these are the ultimate micro-niche audience. They are unlikely to be lured in with typical brochures or billboards; they need to be reached where "they live." Fortunately, technology is making it ever easier to reach out to these widely scattered—geographically, demographically, and socially—individuals. Using Internet tools, it should be possible to identify and directly market to specialist groups—hobbyist sites of every possible kind, support groups surrounding a specific hobby or profession, suppliers of specialist tools or materials, professional schools—whomever you can imagine might find the specific setting, objects, programs, and experiences of your museum of interest.

An entirely different approach to reaching these audiences is to make space available to any and all hobby groups working in topic areas related to your museum. Making space available for meetings and social gatherings, at a reasonable price, is a great way to forge long-term relationships with individuals who could prove to be important supporters and benefactors of the museum. These small groups, only some of whom are officially organized, are usually operating with limited funding and almost always under the management of volunteers. Having an established organization like a museum provide direct services such as space for meetings, photocopying support, or even minimal administrative support can represent the difference between viability and not. These small gestures can generate huge dividends in loyalty and even financial support from the organizations and their individual members.

Another strategy that has proven to work wonders is to run annual "collector" or "hobbyist" fairs. Museums are typically perceived to be the local "authority" in a particular topic area such as natural history, art, or animal husbandry. By inviting all of the amateurs in the community with these interests to gather on one particular day, to share their collections, to get advice from the experts, or just to have an opportunity to meet with others with similar interests, has the potential to generate tremendous amounts of good will towards the museum and help open doors for future visits by Professional/Hobbyists who may not see the museum as a resource. For example, the Florida Museum of Natural History inaugurated their annual Collectors' Day event more than a quarter century ago with very modest expectations. They initially envisioned it as a relatively small event that would serve a small, but important group of museum users, but it has proven to be among the most successful and popular days of the whole year. Not only did collectors from all over Florida converge on the museum to display their collections, so too did all the future Professional/Hobbyists in the general public; the former to share with their peers and the latter eager to see what these "real" collectors had to offer and to be able to talk with them about their particular interests. What began as a "small gesture" towards the collecting community ended up being the biggest visitor attraction of the year and one of the greatest win-win decisions this museum ever made.

Marketing to Rechargers

Although comprising a modest percentage of visitors at most museums, individuals with a Recharger motivation represent a discrete and important visitor population. These are individuals who visit in order to reflect, rejuvenate, or generally just bask in the wonder of the place. Some kinds of museums, for example, art museums and aquariums, and many botanical gardens and natural area parks, may well have a large percentage of their visitors falling into this category.[19] These individuals express an awe or reverence for the subject matter or setting. They say things like, "This is such a beautiful building, I often come here just to look at the space." "I always enjoy the quiet and tranquility of this place." "The Science Center is a place for introspection, a place to be surrounded by science." Or occasionally, "This place reveals the wonders of God's creation."[20]

The vast majority of Rechargers see museums as places that afford them an opportunity to avoid, if only briefly, the noisiness, clutter, and ugliness of the outside world. They see the museum as a respite from the world and often think of the institution's spaces, collections or scenery as sources of inspiration. Most Rechargers are seeking opportunities to become rejuvenated, what Steven Kaplan and Jan Packer have described as restorative experiences.[21] To be restorative, experiences need to be effortless and physically or mentally removed from one's everyday environment.

The kind of person who would feel that they should visit a museum in order to recharge their life would typically be one with a strong sensual aesthetic, not just while at the museum but across their whole lives. They would be the kind of person who would consciously seek to fill their daily life with good food, drink, travel, music, art, and literature. Visiting a museum for this reason is rarely "by accident." Although most museum visitors would agree with "visiting the museum is an enjoyable break from my daily life," relatively few would offer this as their primary visit motivation upon entering the museum. However, if the question is framed properly, Rechargers will say that this is the reason why they come to visit. Although mindful of the educational opportunities afforded by the museum, most Rechargers would not suggest that learning is a high priority for their visit. Although they are as likely relatively well-versed in the content of the museum, it is not what primarily drives their visit. For the individual with a strong Recharger motivation, rest and relief from the stresses of everyday life predominate as reasons for visiting. They see mental and physical rejuvenation as important uses of leisure time, and museums as excellent venues in which to accomplish this goal. Although they are willing to get their rejuvenation wherever they can find it, generally, if they like art, they frequent art museums; if they like history, they frequent history museums; if they like nature, they frequent outdoor sites.

Given their interests, attracting Rechargers requires selling the museum as a place of wonderful beauty and/or tranquility. For some institutions, this is an easy sell as they already have a reputation within the broader community as being places that possess these attributes. National Parks, most botanical gardens and arboretums, most art museums, and many aquariums are widely perceived to be such places. By contrast, most science centers, children's museums, history museums, and zoos are perceived to have many attributes, but peace and tranquility are unlikely to be at the top of the list. For those institutions that are already perceived by the public as possessing the qualities a Recharger is seeking, they need only emphasize those attributes in their promotions. By contrast, if your museum is a place that defies this stereotype, then you will need to work hard at convincing individuals with this motivation to visit. To accomplish this, you'll have to generate marketing materials that reinforce the attributes a Recharger is seeking.

Images of beautiful, deserted spaces would be a big draw. Objects will be less of a concern for the committed Recharger; the objects are just part of the scenery. If a grizzly bear wanders across the horizon while an individual with a strong Recharger motivation is perched on a high vista at sunset, all the better, as long as it doesn't attract a crowd. The Recharger didn't travel to this distant spot in order to see bears, they came to get away from people! Consequently, Rechargers will rarely be attracted to blockbuster and special exhibitions—the only thing these promotions will communicate to the erstwhile Recharger is CROWDS! Given that these are niche visitors, it's best to approach marketing to this group as a niche group. Although potentially pricey, ad placements in culinary magazines or high-end travel magazines are likely to reach these very discriminating and cultured visitors.

Rechargers are not immune to good word-of-mouth recommendations from others like themselves. If you can encourage your Recharger visitors to communicate to their friends that the museum is one of the great, little known secrets—a refuge of quiet and tranquility right in the middle of the busy city—you might just discover that you attract a whole new cadre of visitors. But like any buzz, it needs to be consistent with the desires and interests of the user group. The Recharger buzz needs to communicate that the museum affords fabulous opportunities to become refreshed and rejuvenated, to get a new lease on life. Remember, these are sophisticated visitors and they can afford to go virtually anywhere and partake in virtually any leisure opportunity the community has to offer. You need to make sure your marketing efforts are as specific to the needs of this audience as you can possibly make them. This is definitely a time when one size does not fit all!

BUILDING AUDIENCES

As should be clear by now, the marketing goal of the museum should be to escape the idea that a single promotional strategy or approach will suffice. We can't create a single message, a single set of images, or utilize a single type of media outlet such as print ads in the local newspaper, and expect these to work. We also need to leave behind any notion that segmenting visitors using traditional demographic or even social grouping categories will ever buy us much. The museum visitor experience model suggests that we should try and segment audiences as a function of their identity-related motivations, beginning with the five basic motivational categories: Explorers, Facilitators, Experience seekers, Professional/ Hobbyists, and Rechargers. One cautionary note as we proceed—all of these five categories include not just a single type of visitor motivation but are a cluster of several closely-related types of visitor motivations, each with their own unique identity-related needs. Research to date seems to suggest that these five basic categories are sufficiently robust to allow important generalizations and predictions to be made that will help us move down the road towards greater specialization and customization. However, we should never deviate from the longer term objective of getting better at making fine distinctions among and between visitors. For the moment, the approach I have described promises to give us the basic tools to begin to more effectively customize marketing efforts and to better appeal to the underlying motivations that drive people to visit museums.

In the previous section, I outlined some ideas about how a museum might selectively think about attracting individuals with each of these five motivations with the goal of focusing on how they develop audiences within each individual segment. This is clearly the most straightforward approach to the issue, but, to date, efforts are insufficiently advanced to know just how it will work. To illustrate these ideas, I will return to an audience development effort I have previously described.[22] This effort was made long before the ideas described in this book were formulated. Still, the results of that audience broadening effort can be reinterpreted using the framework I have presented here. I believe the results actually make more sense now in light of these new ideas than they did at the time Lynn Dierking and I were first describing them.

In the early 1990s, the Virginia Museum of Fine Arts (VMFA), with support from the Lila Wallace Foundation, committed to making a sincere effort to be more inclusive to a group of visitors that had historically been seriously underserved by the museum—the African American community of Richmond. The VMFA's concept for how to accomplish this task was to reinstall their vast African art collection. The assumption was that emphasizing this focus on Africa would be a natural way to appeal to the African American community. In so doing, more African Americans would visit the museum and their goal of broadening their audience would be accomplished. It probably does not surprise anyone that the museum believed that it could achieve its goal by primarily focusing on its collections (and there are still many museum professionals who believe this strategy should work, after all there are testimonials to the effectiveness of this approach presented at virtually every museum conference). And it would also not surprise anyone if I told you that the marketing approach the VMFA initially launched to support this initiative featured beautiful images of some of the fabulous African art objects in the collection. These images were utilized in all the normal ways—stunning, glossy brochures in print ads placed in the major Richmond daily newspaper and on the banners the museum hung on the outside of its building. Despite all this effort, the number of African American visitors to the VMFA hardly changed.

Conversations with members of the African American community revealed that most thought that the objects shown in the brochures and banners were truly lovely, but neither these particular objects nor the marketing strategy seemed sufficient to change the attitudes among Richmond's African Americans towards visiting VMFA.[23] In fact, the VMFA was discovering, whether they fully realized it or not at the time, that their basic assumptions about how to effectively attract underserved audiences was seriously flawed. To the credit of the Director and her staff, they did not just throw up their hands and say, "Oh well, we tried." In the absence of a good working model for how the museum visitor experience works, the VMFA was left with the old tried and true method—try a number of different approaches and through the process of trial and error see if we can figure out how to make this work. They were also aided by a very hard-working and creative African American woman with considerable marketing experience who spear-headed new efforts to reach the African American community. In the end, they were successful and in the process they discovered some very interesting things about audience-building, all of which accord very nicely with the model presented here.

With the help of their new audience development leadership, the first thing the VMFA "discovered" was that the African American community was not monolithic. There were large differences in the interests, experiences, and receptiveness of this community relative to the idea of visiting the VMFA; there were also huge cultural impediments to overcome from years of overt, as well as covert, racism. Interestingly, as the museum tried to figure out how to break down historical barriers and become truly supportive of increased visitation by African Americans, they discovered that they needed different message content and delivery for different groups within the African American community. For example, there was a group of African Americans who really enjoyed art, and who already were regular visitors to art museums. Although many of these individuals did not regularly visit the VMFA because of perceptions of current and past racism, they were open to reconsidering their relationship with the museum. When the VMFA engaged these African American art lovers in conversation, they were told that the museum's emphasis on African art was interesting but unmoving. For most of them, their motivation for going to art museums was to see art, broadly defined; they were as interested in exhibitions on Baroque and Impressionist art as they were in African art. If and when they went to the VMFA, they were interested in exploring all kinds of art and discovering new things, whatever the origin or media. In other words, these individuals were operating from an Explorer or even a Professional/Hobbyist motivational perspective. As a consequence, the marketing approach the museum used, in particular emphasizing just African art images, was insufficient to overcome the other more social and cultural impediments to visiting. What it took to move these individuals to become more frequent visitors to VMFA was not the reinstallation of the African art collection, but a change in the attitudes of the institution towards black visitors, starting with the guards and other service personnel, but including the creation of special events and other promotions that made them feel welcome.

Another group of African Americans, though, was highly interested in the new African Art Hall and a small percentage of these individuals actually did show up to see the reinstalled exhibition; but most only came once. They did feel a deep sense of identity with African culture and were interested in the expansion and reinstallation of the VMFA's collection. Some of these individuals possessed expertise in African art that exceeded that of the museum's curators. Once these individuals were identified, the museum was able to invite these Professional/Hobbyists to become more involved with the museum and the collections. However, the challenge was the identification of these individuals. It turned out that there were many more individuals within the Richmond African American commu-nity who possessed a strong knowledge and interest in African art and culture than there were those who were aware of the new reinstallation at VMFA. Working primarily through black churches, the museum was able to begin to reach these individuals. Some of the churches already had African culture interest groups, but even those without such a spe-cific program were able to find ways to reach those in their congrega-tions who possessed such interests. Through the churches, the museum organized a series of special tours of the exhibition, lectures, and even behind-the-scenes discussions with the curators. Some who participated in these events became so excited by the exhibition that they volunteered to become docents and in the process, became long-term "visitors" to the museum. For this relatively small group of individuals, the content of the original images worked well, but the placement of these images did not. They came from all strata of the African American community, but few regularly read the major Richmond newspaper and fewer still drove by the highly segregated area of town in which the VMFA was located. By working with the black churches in town, as well as promoting the exhibition through the local black newspaper that most Richmond Af-rican Americans read, the museum was able to reach this population of potential visitors.

Finally, there was a third group of African Americans in Richmond who potentially were amenable to visiting the VMFA, but who never felt welcome or thought of it as a place that would fulfill their specific leisure identity-related needs. These were African American parents. When the VMFA began to create advertising materials that showed African Ameri-can parents doing things with their children in the galleries, large groups of African American parents began, many for the first time, to envision the VMFA as a possible place to visit. When the VMFA first distributed literature through black beauty salons and barber shops and advertised on the sides of buses and through the local black newspaper, these same African American parents became aware that the VMFA was not only a possible leisure site, but a potentially good one. Thus for Facilitators, the key was highlighting this social facilitator role. The fact that the advertised content related to African art was a nicety for these black parents—they were happy to share this particular experience with their children, but it was not a sufficiency—content alone was not an adequately compelling reason for visiting.

But the real coup in convincing African American parents to visit the VMFA was a museum supported school-based program of African music featuring a world-renowned African musician who taught African drumming and dancing to the children. The live performance was held at the museum, which reinforced that this was a great place for families. However, arguably the event would have been just as effective if it had focused on early twentieth-century art and involved children in learning about jazz or mid-century modern art and involved children in learning about the roots of rock-and-roll and rhythm and blues. The key was that the museum emphasized that it was a great place for parents and children to do things together; it was this focus on facilitation that ultimately helped to significantly increase the number of African Americans visiting the VMFA.[24]

In the end, the conventional wisdom prevailed that what worked was reaching out to the black community using methods and messages that related to this community and their interests. A reinterpretation of the marketing effort reveals that the VMFA was discovering that "one size does not fit all." It also suggests that defining the problem primarily as a race/ethnicity issue was not a useful framework for changing visitation patterns. And finally, reinterpreting the results through the perspective of the museum visitor experience model suggests that different segments of visitors, as defined by their identity-related needs, require different messages and different delivery mechanisms.

Up to now, I have suggested that the way to approach the problem of attracting audiences is by creating different messages for different people. This, however, is not the only way to accommodate the ideas represented by my museum visitor experience model. An interesting alternative was developed by the Tyne & Wear Museums of northeastern England. Their marketing strategy was designed to help potential visitors self-select which museum in their community might best fit their specific leisure and identity-related needs. Rather than trying to convince the public that each individual museum could meet any and all of their needs, the museums in the community worked collaboratively to divide the different visitor identity-related niches that offered options to the public. The museums devised a scheme that helped drive visitors with specific motivations to the appropriate venue for satisfying that motivation. This strategy was made somewhat easier because the regional government in northeast England oversees 11 different institutions as part of the Tyne & Wear Museums. However, there's no reason why all of the museums and cultural organizations within a community could not do something similar if they were willing to work in a collaborative manner.

The Tyne & Wear Museums include archaeology, history, natural science, and art institutions. Using the museum visitor experience idea as a departure point, these museums experimented with promoting different lifestyle and identity-related motivational leisure interests and needs using the Web as a delivery mechanism. Their website (www.ilikemuseums. com) features more than 80 different visitor experience "trails," each beginning with the phrase "I like . . . ." Some examples are: I like. . . a challenge, I like. . . architecture, I like. . . celebrities, I like. . . dressing up, I like. . . monsters, I like. . . Romans, I like . . . scary things, I like. . . science, etc. When you click on any one of these museum-related self-aspects, the web site will help you plan a personalized Tyne & Wear museum experience that meets your specific interests. For example, if you click on "I like. . . a challenge," the web site encourages you to "Exercise your grey matter at this selection of museums" and then gives you a list of eight different institutions where you can be intellectually challenged with directions and specific information about each institution. In this way, the Tyne & Wear museums have allowed the visitor to actively self-select an experience that is customized to meet their specific identity-related needs. Through this process the likelihood that the loop between needs, expectations, and experiences will be closed has been significantly increased.

Reaching New Audiences

Finally, I would like to directly address the vital question of how insights contained in the museum visitor experience can be used to attract audiences who have not historically visited museums. How can we use these ideas to reach new audiences? When museums such as the VMFA have attempted to broaden their audiences, they approached the problem by doing basically the same thing they've always done—create new exhibitions and invest in more marketing. The fact is that such "more of the same" approaches rarely work. The museum visitor experience model provides some interesting insights into how to attract new audiences. What the model suggests is that the reason most people do not attend a museum has everything to do with the fact that they do not perceive that the museum will adequately satisfy their leisure, identity-related needs. Rarely are issues of race, gender, age, ethnicity, education, or even economics (except in the extreme), the *primary* reason individuals opt not to visit a museum. The primary reason for not visiting is invariably a lack of perceived value which often correlates with some of these demographic characteristics; it is descriptive of underlying realities but not predictive. People who perceive no relationship between what they think museums afford and what they see as their identity-related needs will not have any desire to visit a museum. Those that do perceive that such a relationship exists, or could exist will be at least inclined to visit. Although the VMFA defined their problem as an African American problem, the problem really was not about African Americans, it was about individuals feeling like the museum did not meet their needs.

Every person has identity-related needs and interests. The need to express one's curiosity, to support being a good parent, or to provide relief from the stresses of daily life is not unique to people who visit museums. These and other similar identity-related needs are common to virtually all people in the twenty-first century, at least to those who have obtained some measure of economic, political, and social security. What separates those who visit museums from those who do not is the perception that a museum is a good and reasonable place for satisfying those needs. Thus, the key to broadening audiences is communicating (and delivering) on this promise. That is what the VMFA was able to do, for example, with African American parents in Richmond. The fact that the topic related to the big 'I' or "African" identity of the audience undoubtedly played a role, but more importantly, the museum was able to appeal to the little 'i' identity needs of these Richmond mothers and fathers and reinforce that the VMFA would be a good place for fulfilling their parental identity-related needs. Arguably, the key ingredient was communicating that this is a good place for Richmond parents to help their children be successful in life and that it was a comfortable and welcoming place in which to accomplish this. In a similar way, it required that the VMFA staff understand the needs of potential visitors with Explorer and Professional/Hobbyist motivations and communicate to them that the museum could be a suitable and welcoming environment for satisfying their needs.

Thus, we can observe that whether attempting to entice those who are already inclined to visit the museum or encouraging those who have never visited the museum to come for the first time, the tasks are similar. Building and sustaining audiences requires an understanding of the real needs and interests of the public. It requires a commitment to communicate to prospective audiences that your institution has the capability to satisfy every individual's personal identity-related needs and interests. And finally, building and sustaining audiences requires a willingness and the means to actually deliver on this promise if and when the public actually shows up, so that these individuals will leave as satisfied customers who will in turn encourage others like themselves to visit. It is to this latter challenge—supporting the visitor experience itself—that we now turn.

Making Museums Work for Visitors

Creating museums that work for visitors requires changing how
we think about visitors and museum exhibits and programs.
We need to stop seeing these as parts of a whole and start seeing
them as a single complex, integrated system. Specifically, we
need to move away from thinking about types of visitors to types
of visits (which vary by identity-related motivations), and from
exhibits and programs with specific, singular outcomes to ways
of experiencing and using exhibits and programs that allow
visitors to achieve multiple, personally relevant goals.

The key to ensuring that visitors leave our museums as satisfied customers, eager to return as well as give positive word-of-mouth recommendations, is to provide high-quality, personally engaging museum
visit experiences. What makes a museum visitor experience high-quality and personally engaging is that it fully satisfies the visitor's entering
identity-related museum motivations. As museum researcher Zahava
Doering wrote,

> Rather than communicating new information, the primary impact of
> visiting a museum exhibition is to confirm, reinforce, and extend the
> visitor's existing beliefs . . . . [the] most satisfying exhibition[s] for visitors
> are those that resonate with their experience and provide new information
> in ways that confirm and enrich their [own] view of the world.[1]

Museum experiences like these help visitors feel competent and satisfied so that they will repeat the activity. This process of feeling competent
and successful is referred to in the psychology literature as self-efficacy.[2]
Self-efficacy beliefs play a strong role in mediating between prior experiences and future decision making, essentially serving as a filter to determine what is worth engaging in again.[3] In other words, people are much
more likely to re-engage in activities about which they feel competent
and good. Within the context of the museum visitor experience, this appears to be continually anchored in the visitor's entering identity-related

visit motivations, particularly, in the visitor's mental articulation and satisfaction of their self-aspects.

For example, individuals with an Explorer motivation are more likely to feel a sense of self-efficacy after having museum visitor experiences
that reinforced their self-perception as curious individuals who like to
see and learn about new and interesting things. Facilitators are most
likely to feel self-efficacious if they perceived that their museum visitor
experience supported their self-perception as supportive people who
provide a positive experience for a significant other. Helping visitors
satisfy their entering identity-related visit motivations turns out to be
fundamental to the long-term success of a museum. So many visitors,
so many self-aspects, so many diverse visitor needs!

If there is a single theme in this book, it is that the museum visitor
experience is neither about visitors nor about museum exhibitions and
programs; it is about the dynamic interaction of these as they briefly
come together in space and time. Despite the uniqueness and diversity
of visitors and their needs and the wide range of museum topics and
ways to present content, much of this complex phenomenon can be
organized and dealt with by viewing the museum visitor experience
through the lens of the public's entering identity-related needs. The
five categories of visit identity-related motivations I have defined earlier provide a useful filter for understanding and predicting much of
the museum visitor experience. However, as I have pointed out, reality
is more complex than just these five motivations. Knowing a person's
entering identity-related motivation provides only part of what is required to meet his or her museum visitor experience needs, but it is an
important place to start. As outlined in Chapter 4, a person's visit motivations, shaped by their identity-related needs and their perceptions of
what the museum affords, create a basic trajectory for a visit, but that
trajectory is shaped by a range of other factors, most of which can be
understood through the framework provided by the Contextual Model
of Learning. The number of factors that could potentially directly or
indirectly influence a visitor's in-museum experience probably number
in the hundreds, if not thousands. However, after considering the data
from hundreds of research studies, Lynn Dierking and I concluded that
in addition to a visitor's entering motivations and expectations and subsequent reinforcing experiences, ten factors, or more accurately suites
of factors, are particularly influential.[4] These ten factors are:

Personal Context

1. Prior knowledge
2. Prior experiences
3. Prior interests
4. Choice and control

Socio-cultural Context

5. Within group social mediation
6. Mediation by others outside the immediate social group

Physical Context

7. Advance organizers
8. Orientation to the physical space
9. Architecture and large-scale environment
10. Design and exposure to exhibits and programs

An in-depth investigation by my colleague Martin Storksdieck and me confirmed that all of these factors do influence the museum visitor experience, but that not all factors equally influence all visitors.[5] For some visitors, factors such as social interaction or exhibit quality seemed to dramatically affect their experience and learning, for other visitors these same factors assumed little or no obvious significance. Understanding why this was true and for whom emerged as critical to making progress towards better meeting visitor needs. This is where understanding something about a visitor's entering identity-related motivations provides us with some guidance. A visitor's entering identity-related motivation provides a reasonable way to know which factors are likely to be important for which visitors—not all of the time, but frequently enough to be a useful planning tool. What follows are my informed, and at times, educated guesses as to which factors are most likely to be most important for fulfilling the needs of visitors with different entering visit motivations.

ACCOMMODATING THE NEEDS OF VISITORS

Needs of Explorers

As often described in this book, individuals with an Explorer visitor motivation are seeking to satisfy their personal interests and curiosities. Since Explorers often comprise a large percentage of a museum's visiting population, figuring out how to meet this group of visitors' needs should be a high priority for most museums. In many ways, Explorers are like serious shoppers or habitués of flea markets; they love to browse and bump into intellectual "bargains." Like any serious shopper, they begin with a generalized rather than a specific sense of what they're looking for as some things are more likely to catch their eye and be more attractive than others. Their visit pathway is unlikely to be fully linear, and to the outside observer it might even appear "illogical." However, there's nothing illogical about how Explorers utilize museums; their pathway and behavior makes perfect sense if we are mindful of what they're trying to accomplish. If you know something about an Explorer's personal context variables such as their prior experience, knowledge, and interest, their pathways through the museum makes perfect sense.

Given our current capabilities, it might seem a daunting task to try and customize the museum visitor experience based upon knowing the prior knowledge, experience, and interest of each individual visitor. However, we can make great progress by realizing that for this group of visitors these factors are important and that they will strongly shape their experience. Our goal should be to design exhibitions, programs, and interpretive tools that make it easy for the Explorer to explore. Let's take, for example, the interpretive tools of guided tours and audio guides. Although Explorers are likely to value the information contained in these interpretive tools, most currently shy away from them because they believe that these tools will be too structured and will actually prevent, rather than assist, their curiosity-driven exploration. However, if these tools can be designed to be flexible and responsive to the individual's specific needs and interests, then they might be very satisfying to this type of visitor. It may require, for example, creating several different versions of a tour, but in all instances it will require a change in the way these tools are promoted to visitors. Visitors with different needs should realize that the museum has taken these traditional tools and redesigned them to accommodate their needs. This is an important first step towards customizing the museum visitor experience.

Similarly, exhibitions need to be designed in ways that support different types of visitors. Good design matters, but what is good exhibit design for an Explorer? Visitors with an exploring motivation are typically experienced museum visitors, so they understand the language of exhibitions. Explorers expect museum exhibitions to support choice and control, but what they do not appreciate are exhibitions that are too linear or prescribed. For example, as happens in some popular blockbuster exhibitions, if Explorer visitors are forced to shuffle along with the crowd, from one station to the next, they will hate the experience. Although they may be initially thrilled to see what's on display, they will end up expressing great dissatisfaction with their visitor experience. The Explorer visitor is looking for exhibitions that support browsing, and that are rich in detail and information which allow them to exercise their minds. Explorers are looking to not only satisfy their curiosity, but to also engage in a process of discovery. The typical Explorer visitor does not want to be spoon-fed information; they need to have visual and intellectual clarity, so they can quickly determine if this is something that they might find interesting.

This brings us back to the importance of the personal context variables. Given the important role played by prior knowledge, experience, and interest for Explorers, exhibition designers would be well-served by conducting front-end evaluations to help determine some key "hooks" for this group of visitors. The caveat is that these front-end information collection efforts cannot be successful only by talking to a random sampling of visitors, but should be targeted specifically at Explorers. This will help to ensure that the Explorer visitor can find what he or she is looking for; it will also help the museum achieve its educational goals by helping them know how to frame and present arguments and conceptual themes.

The Explorer visitor population is the most likely to read labels, brochures, and guides and to achieve the kinds of learning outcomes museums tend to claim for their visitors. Of course, they'll be selective in which sections they engage in. Explorers know that they can't read everything, so they'll be judicious but thorough in what they do read. As suggested above, predicting what an Explorer will find interesting is challenging because so much of their curiosity is driven by their own personal prior experience and knowledge. However, they are not disinterested in what the museum professionals think is important. If exhibitions and programs are mindful of the Explorer visitors' interests and prior knowledge, museums can create experiences that meet them halfway and help move this group of visitors towards satisfactory learning outcomes.

New technologies also offer museums unprecedented opportunities to meet the needs and interests of visitors with an Exploring motivation. These technologies allow for greater flexibility in what and when information is presented and offer the visitor significantly more choice and control over content than a typical silk-screened label on the wall. The "kiss of death" for an Explorer is to encounter text and labels that they find too simple or basic. The label that works great for a Facilitator or Experience seeker is likely not to work for an Explorer. Again, this emphasizes the current challenges of trying to be "all things for all people" with a medium that has limited flexibility. Given the rigidity of wall text, one strategy that has proven effective is the creative use of layered labels, with a simple, large-print sentence followed by more in-depth information designed for Explorers. Ideally, this information could be supported by touch-screen computers rather than cluttering up walls or text panels.

Since Explorers are typically repeat-visitors to their local museum, they require very little orientation support or guidance when visiting. However, when visiting a museum for the first time while traveling, they will likely be very demanding and in need of good maps, orientation signage, and knowledgeable and responsive floor staff. When visiting a new museum, Explorers are not likely to start at the "beginning" and proceed in an orderly fashion, but they are likely to have a general sense of their area(s) of interest and know that they can go directly to this area. Consequently, they want to get there as quickly and efficiently as possible and their expectation is that the museum will, and *should* support them in this effort.

Most museum visitors learn as much from their social group as they do from the exhibitions and programs; this is also somewhat true of Explorers. As the previous examples in this book illustrate, many individuals with an Explorer motivation are as likely to navigate through the museum by themselves as they are with others, but almost all arrive with a social group and will want to spend some of their time interacting with others. Compared to other groups of visitors, supporting in-exhibition social facilitation is less important with this group. Whereas many visitors are likely to interact with museum staff primarily for directions to the restrooms or café, Explorers are thrilled when they encounter a knowledgeable staff person with whom they can interact and ask questions about the content of the exhibition. A museum that is mindful and attentive to the needs of Explorers will try to proactively help facilitate these kinds of interactions. Every museum's goal should be to learn the name and interests of their regular Explorer visitors and enter into a personalized relationship with them so that each visit can be designed to appropriately challenge and continually push their understanding. I had this model in mind while writing the introduction to *Thriving in the Knowledge Age*, where an entire family, with the help of technology, could be encouraged to come back week after week to build upon their own individual interests and knowledge.[6] With museum encouragement and support, the Explorers could be transformed into Professional/Hobbyists.

Individuals with Explorer-style motivations are also likely to be among the most regular patrons of the non-exhibit aspects of the museum. Not only will they attend lectures and programs, but they will typically visit the café. This is a group who will need to be recharged during their visit. Whereas many visitors will use the café as a final stop before departing, Explorers are likely to use the café as a mid-point, resting up and refueling before heading back into the galleries for more viewing. Since these individuals tend to be regular and sophisticated visitors, they want good value for their money—the McDonald's experience is not what they had in mind!

Explorers will also be regular users of the gift shop. They won't be looking for trinkets and souvenirs but books on the topic of the museum's exhibits or something more substantial. They, like all visitors, see the gift shop as an integral part of their visit experience. Explorers, in particular, will be seeking to find something that will extend their visit and their new-found interests. If an Explorer discovered something interesting about nineteenth-century life while "cruising through" an exhibition, he or she will now want to read more and expect to be able to find an appropriate book in the gift shop. If unsuccessful in the gift shop, he or she will be frustrated and disappointed. A good gift shop manager thus will anticipate these needs and go out of his or her way to accommodate the interests of this group of visitors, even perhaps offering to order books to help satisfy the needs and curiosity of the intellectually-intrepid Explorer.

It is not unusual for Explorers to use the end of one visit to scout out possible topics and exhibits to see on their next visit. They assume that they're coming back and appreciate that their in-museum time and attention are finite, so they will take advantage of their current visit to store up ideas for the next visit. If the museum is aware, the staff could help the Explorer by interacting with them towards the end of their visit in order to let them know what might be interesting to see on their next visit; "Did you happen to see the X? We just got that in. You'll definitely want to see that next time you come."

Needs of Facilitators

Facilitators are visitors who arrive at the museum with a strong desire to support what's best for their loved one or companion. The museum that helps ensure a positive experience for this loved one or companion helps ensure that the Facilitator's experience will also be positive.

As mentioned in the previous chapter, it's best to think of Facilitators as two variations—Facilitating Parents and Facilitating Socializers. Let's start with Facilitating Parents; what are the needs of parents and how can museums best support their needs? To have a successful visit, the parental Facilitator needs to occupy, stimulate, and engage their children. As for Explorers, prior knowledge, experience, and interest are important to them, but in the Facilitating Parent's situation, the prior knowledge and interests of their children, rather than their own, are most important. The typical Facilitating parent uses their understanding of their children to help guide the museum visit experience and support their children's learning and enjoyment.

It would serve the museum staff well to also know something about the Facilitating adult's prior knowledge and experience, although their knowledge and experience in using museums to support learning are more critical than their knowledge and experience with the content of the museum. The average Facilitating Parent can benefit from some guidance about how best to support their children's museum visitor experience. Many museums have created family guides or backpacks designed to provide this kind of support. These are certainly an excellent strategy, particularly if the entering parent is made aware that such services are available. It's also worth noting that not every parent who enters the museum is there primarily to be a Facilitator. Thus, the museum needs to create opportunity for parents to self-select interpretive support, but not assume that such support will or should be utilized.

Once in the museum, Facilitating Parents will typically rush into the visit since they're usually trying to keep up with their children, who naturally are quite excited about being there. Thus, any signage or orientation materials need to be designed to be seen and internalized quickly, literally "on the fly." After all, who has time to ask for directions or suggestions when they are trying to keep up with their children who are sprinting ahead? Since Facilitating Parents may not know which of the exhibits on display would be ideal for their children, signage that indicates those which are "child-friendly" would make great sense, particularly in a museum that isn't overtly child-friendly. Of course, the parent facilitating the experience needs to know that such signage exists and if there is a symbol, what the symbol means.

Facilitators with children often read labels primarily so that they can have sufficient information to support the needs of their children.

Most Facilitating Parents work hard to translate and interpret the museum's exhibits for their children. Thus, helping adults play this role successfully should be a major goal of the museum. Conceptual advance organizers—information that allows an individual to know the big idea of an exhibition or exhibit element—are essential tools for Facilitating Parents. Placing this information in several places throughout an exhibition can make a huge difference in the likelihood that it will be seen, internalized, and used by the Facilitator.[7] If your museum attracts a high percentage of Facilitators with children, specific signage that helps parents interpret exhibits at an appropriate development level would be a real benefit. What would be wrong with having some labels written for young children, some for older children, and some for adolescents and adults as this is a situation where one "solution" is unlikely to work equally well for all visitors. There are also other ideas besides labels that museums can realize in order to support parents who are facilitating the experiences of their children. Museum researcher Minda Borun and her Philadelphia-based collaborators conducted a series of research studies on families in museums and suggested a range of strategies that museums can implement to better meet the needs of family visitors. They include the redesign of spaces and the use of interactives to better accommodate groups rather than just individuals.[8] Good exhibition design appears to be particularly important for the Facilitator Parent group of visitors, but as suggested above, the design issues of importance primarily are intergenerational interactions and labels that support parental involvement rather than lighting or placement of objects.

In institutions that attract many Facilitating Parents and their children, having friendly and knowledgeable floor staff who can relate well to the children, but also to multiage groups of adults and children, are essential. Many Facilitators will interact with floor staff primarily for directions to the restrooms or café since these necessities are high on their facilitating priority list. Having museum staff who can go the extra distance and help facilitate the learning experience will be greatly appreciated. Parents also love demonstrations, particularly those that include their children as volunteers. These are the kinds of high emotion experiences that are likely to be memorable for both child and adult for years to come. If a Facilitating Parent's child shows an interest, however fleeting, in the content of the museum, the Facilitator will happily sign their child up for additional programs in order to extend the good feelings of helping their child succeed in life. Take note that behind every child enrolled in a museum program is a Facilitating Parent!

Individuals with a Facilitating Socializer motivation represent a very interesting group of visitors. Since the visitor experience will likely revolve around the "chosen" adult, the basic trajectory and tenor of the visit will depend upon what kind of visitor that individual is with. If the "other" is an Explorer, then the visit will fit an Explorer model. If the "other" is an Experience seeker, then it will follow that model. If the "other" is also a Facilitator, then the two adults are likely to spend their time strolling through the museum chatting with each other about everything except, perhaps, the exhibits on display! In this book's opening vignette, I presented an example of this socializing in the visit of George and his father in-law to the National Aquarium in Baltimore. Both were happy to use the space and time to chat and catch up with each other rather than to look at fish and aquatic mammals.

Meeting the needs of a Facilitating Socializer is relatively easy. Since these Facilitators are primarily using the museum as a stage for their social agenda, the museum should keep the "stage" clean, friendly, and accommodating and create quiet and inviting spaces in order to generally support the visitor's social agenda. Often the most important parts of the "stage" may be the non-exhibit amenities of the museum such as the food service and restrooms. Facilitators, like Explorers, are likely to be regular patrons of these non-exhibit aspects of the museum. They avail themselves of museum gift shops and cafés, perhaps not on every visit, but frequently. The gift shop and café are often used by Facilitators as a final stop before departing. They represent a reward, as much for themselves as for their companions, for a day well-spent. Whereas many adult visitors to museums, including Facilitating Socializers, are seeking a slightly more upscale eatery, Facilitating Parents are delighted to find something similar to the food court at the shopping mall. Not necessarily McDonald's, but not Chez Panisse either, as long as it is good value for their money.

When Facilitating Parents visit the gift shop with their children, they have definite expectations. They expect that their children will make demands upon them to purchase a trinket or souvenir, but their hope is that it will be something of value. Similarly, they will be hoping to find an educational book, game, or toy at a reasonable price that they can use to carry on the educational experience at home. The best museum gift shops make these kinds of transactions easy to achieve both financially and psychically. Facilitating Socializers may at first avoid the gift shop since it's not really part of their visit goal, but after repeat visits, they may discover that it's a great place to pick up unusual gifts for friends and acquaintances. Developing promotional materials about the shop that is also available in the café can be a good way to entice Facilitating Socializers to pay their first serious visit to the shop.

Needs of Experience Seekers

The Experience seeker's goal in visiting the museum is not to become a subject matter expert, but to have a great experience. Invariably, what defines a great experience is feeling like they've seen and done what's important to see and do! Since many visitors with this kind of visit motivation lack extensive museum-going experience, as well as a good sense of what's important to see and do, the most important variables determining the nature and quality of their visit will be access to a good intellectual and physical orientation to the museum. In the absence of good orientation, most Experience seekers will have a tendency to just wander and/or follow the crowds; this may not help them achieve their visit goal. Thus, appropriate and early intervention with this group of visitors can really be helpful. Given that an Experience seeker most often comes to see the "highlights" of the museum, helping them accomplish this goal will significantly enhance their visitor experience. Creating one or more "Guides to the Museum's Best," each designed to highlight and help *appropriately* interpret museum exhibits for the different social groups of Experience seekers—families, all adult groups, foreign visitors—will be helpful to them. Although Experience seekers might drift by the information desk and pick up leaflets and floor plans, they will rarely stop and ask the museum staff for help. Consequently, proactive intervention by a trained staff member is essential such as a few well-designed questions, "I'd love to help make your visit as great as possible. Was there something you particularly hoped to see while here?" Also, given that it is not unusual for Experience seekers to be on a tight, pre-determined time budget, inquiring about the expected duration of their visit is extremely important. It will pay dividends to ask, "How long were you planning on spending with us today? I have some suggestions for different length visits and I can help you customize your experience to meet your needs."

Since Experience seekers are hoping to get an overview of the place rather than some "deep" understanding, museums that attract large numbers of these visitors should create interpretive aids that reflect this goal. Audio guides should be designed to give the "big picture" and a few salient facts, highlighted by interesting sound bites. Emphasizing the details, as many audio guides do, will be overkill for individuals with this type of visit motivation. Similarly, wall texts should be designed to be read quickly in headline fashion. Details should be in smaller print and not obstruct the Experience Seeker's goal of moving through the space relatively quickly. The exceptions to these suggestions are the few important iconic exhibits in the museum. These exhibits should have sufficient detail and be designed to answer the specific kinds of questions that a one-time Experience-seeking visitor might have. Through front-end and/or formative evaluation it should be relatively easy to determine what the frequently asked questions are for this group of visitors; the questions an Experience seeker is interested in knowing the answers to are not the kinds of questions a specialist thinks are important. However, if the goal is to satisfy the Experience-seeking visitor as opposed to the Professional/Hobbyist visitor, then the labels should be designed to address the questions of the former. Making a visitor feel inadequate and/or stupid is not a recipe for building future visits or good word-of-mouth recommendations to other potential visitors!

More than most visitors, Experience seekers care about the amenities of the museum. In addition to great signage and orientation to the exhibitions, they need to be able to easily find the washrooms, coatrooms, and café. They expect friendly floor staff, expect interactives to work, and they want the facilities to be clean, bright, and attractive. They want the area between the parking lot and the front door to be as engaging and attractive as the museum itself. In short, Experience seekers want the Disney experience—not the trivial and vacuous aspects of Disney, but the thing that Disney does so well, customer service. If your museum wants to attract large numbers of Experience seekers, then a week at the Disney Institute learning about guest services might not be a bad idea.[9]

Experience seekers are likely to be highly social visitors; their goal is "make memories." Not surprisingly then, Experience seekers love to take pictures of their museum visitor experience, memorializing this important social and cultural experience for themselves and for others when they get home. Instead of fighting this inclination, why not take advantage of it? Museums with large numbers of Experience seekers should create numerous and conspicuous settings for great photo opportunities. The museum should open up space and allow the Experience seekers to have their picture taken in front of a great iconic feature. Is it a crazy idea for museums with high numbers of Experience seekers to have staff available expressly for the purpose of taking pictures of these groups so everyone can be in the picture? Not if that's what this group of visitors wants, and your museum is serious about attracting and satisfying visitors with this visit motivation. In theory, great photos will be used to help promote the museum to others and form the foundation of great word-of-mouth promotion to future visitors; this is one of the things Disney does so well.

Like most visitors, Experience seekers will spend time utilizing the non-exhibit aspects of the museum; in fact, they may spend more time outside of the exhibit spaces than they do in them. These visitors are unlikely to see the café and gift shop or for that matter, parking, ticket purchasing, or restrooms as distinct and separate parts of the museum visitor experience. All of these spaces will be perceived as a single whole. Like the majority of visitors, Experience seekers will tend to visit the café and gift shop as their final stop before departing. Research shows that individuals with this visit motivation are likely to be the highest users of the museum's food services.[10] Some Experience seekers may actually start their visit at the gift shop and never get beyond it! That's okay, if you appreciate that Experience seekers do not view the gift shop as an irrelevant part of the museum. From their perspective, the gift shop is just as much the "museum" as are the exhibits or programs. This should reinforce how important it is for the gift shop to have intellectual integrity and be as good a representative of what the museum stands for as are the exhibitions and programs. It is necessary to resist the temptation to fill the gift shop with inexpensive items only remotely related to the content and mission of the museum. If a visit to the gift shop represents a major part of a visitor's museum visit experience, it should be designed to help facilitate the museum's mission; what is stocked in the store should require as much research and thought as does the best exhibition. The gifts purchased at the shop are likely to be one of the most salient aspects of the visit for Experience seekers; you want them to "spread the word" to others about this part of the experience just as for the exhibits, objects, and programs.

Needs of Professional/Hobbyists

If visitors with an Explorer motivation are like shoppers who love to browse and look for bargains, Professional/Hobbyist-motivated visitors are like shoppers who single-mindedly come into a department store just to buy a single pair of socks. They rush past all of the other store items, ignore the Point of Sale displays and solicitous sales people, and head straight to the socks section. Even then, they are not lured by a sale on argyles, they need sweat socks and that's what they look for and purchase. For many Professional/Hobbyists, the visit is not an excursion but a job to get done. What factors are most important for these visitors? Clearly, prior knowledge, experience, and interest are important, so too are interactions with professional staff and at least indirectly, orientation. How can we use this information to help such focused visitors make their museum experience better? The best way to help is to be proactive, make what they need easy to find and satisfactory to fulfilling their requirements, then get out of their way.

The Professional/Hobbyist is a visitor population highly unlikely to read labels or follow an exhibit pathway in the "prescribed" way. They are sufficiently capable in that they will be able to take what's available and use it for their own purposes and needs. They will generally expect, usually but not always correctly, that they already know what any label or wall text is likely to say. They will not be inclined to use any of the interpretive tools the museum provides, whether tours, audio guides, or brochures. Professional/Hobbyists will consider these tools to be too superficial or basic for them, and besides, it would make them look like tourists! Although students may read labels or look for support, most Professional/Hobbyists bring sufficient prior knowledge to the visit to make their own meanings. Ironically, "well-designed" exhibitions and programs—in other words, exhibitions that work well for most visitors—do not work as well for these visitors. On the other hand, the old "visual storage" model is perfect. What they are seeking is intense access to the objects or displays; particularly for those Professional/Hobbyists with a content objective, they'd love to get behind the scenes and see the objects up-close, without crowds and without disturbance.

Creating special behind-the-scenes tours or visits for Professional/Hobbyists are usually a great way to reach out to individuals with these kinds of motivations, as well to the communities with which they are associated. Individuals with a Professional/Hobbyist motivation are not likely to want to interact extensively with others in their own social group, but they are likely to want to interact directly with museum staff experts. Art-focused Professional/Hobbyists want to talk with professionals who know about art. History-focused Professional/Hobbyists want to talk with historians, politicians, artisans, or others with direct knowledge of the topic. Science-focused Professional/Hobbyists will want to talk with scientists. They'll attend lectures and seminars in order to gain access to these people. They'll also enroll in workshops and tutorials if it will allow them to hone their skills or gain access to the collections. Museums should work collaboratively with hobby organizations or professional groups to not only schedule, but design such experiences. This will both increase your institution's reach as well as ensure that what you create truly meets the needs of this audience. Experiences like these provide great satisfaction for the Professional/Hobbyist because they confirm the individual's self-perception of themselves as knowledgeable, special people. These individuals do not perceive themselves to be typical visitors; they consider themselves to be the *real* museum visitors while everyone else is just a "tourist." Not that you want to disparage other visitors, but anything you can do to help reinforce the Professional/Hobbyist's sense of identity with their specialty and help them feel as if they are special and important, will work wonders for building satisfaction and loyalty to your institution.

Since Professional/Hobbyists are typically repeat visitors, they normally require very little orientation support or guidance, particularly when utilizing their home museum. When on the road, these same visitors will be looking for good maps, orientation signage, and knowledgeable and responsive floor staff who can help guide them to the areas of the museum they wish to see. Since, unlike department stores, the layout of every museum is different and eclectic, even the most museum-savvy visitor requires some orientation help when visiting a new museum for the first time. Nothing frustrates a Professional/Hobbyist more than getting lost in a new museum. They think of their time as precious and getting lost means less time for accomplishing the purpose for which they came. They want to get where they're going as quickly and efficiently as possible and their expectation is that the museum will, and *should* support them in this effort.

Professional/Hobbyists will use the café and the gift shop, but not necessarily on every visit. Since they are likely to be quite intense during their visit, they will use the café as a recharging station—as a place to build up their caloric reserves before plunging back into their work. Like the rest of their visit, their use of the gift shop will be quite focused. The typical individual with a Professional/Hobbyist motivation will be looking for in-depth books on a topic of interest, reference materials, and specialized books or supplies that they believe they can't find anywhere else. Although stocking these kinds of materials can be quite expensive, if your museum has sufficient numbers of Professional/Hobbyists, it might warrant the cost. For some institutions, Professional/Hobbyists can be the single largest patron group of the shop.

Needs of Rechargers

As museum visitors go, individuals with a Recharger motivation are, in theory at least, relatively easy to please. They are not making huge demands upon the institution; all they want is a peaceful and aesthetically pleasing corner of the world in which to relax. More than for any other visitors, individuals seeking this kind of experience are highly attuned to the large-scale physical context of the museum. They are sensitive to the aesthetics of the space, and to crowding. If your museum is well-designed for Recharger behavior, it should be easy to help them satisfy their agenda. If your museum is not well-designed for such experiences, you'll need to do some work. What does every Recharger want? Visitors who wish to be renewed and reinvigorated are seeking a quiet place where they can sit without being disturbed—a space where they can recharge their personal "batteries." What is the one prop that so many museums lack that would enable this behavior? It is abundant benches strategically located in front of beautiful places and out of high-traffic areas. Why is it that benches are so hard to come by in so many institutions? They are relatively cheap, durable, and seem to always be in demand! Are we afraid that people might sit and stay too long? It's always amazing how adaptable people are—they will sit on ledges, on the floor, and some visitors will even bring their own seating if the museum will allow it. What does the lack of benches communicate to Recharger visitors? It certainly doesn't communicate "welcome" and that we understand your needs and are eager to accommodate them!

Although Rechargers may be thrilled to see what's on display, this is not the primary benefit they are seeking in a visit. They will pass up all the usual interpretive materials and only glance at labels when something really piques their interest. Individuals with this motivation are often looking for that special "at-one" experience with an often-viewed, much-loved object, scene or piece of art. Many art museum curators claim they are catering to these kinds of visitors when they minimize the size and content of labels. Although this may be true, I somehow doubt that label size really is the issue. As long as the labels don't significantly intrude upon the aesthetics of the art, Rechargers are quite content with labels of any size. They're much more likely to be distressed by crowds that get between them and the art than by the size and content of labels.

Like Professional/Hobbyists, individuals with a Recharger motivation are often repeat visitors and require very little orientation support or guidance. But when traveling, like any visitor who is visiting a place for the first time, good maps, orientation signage, and knowledgeable and responsive floor staff will also be appreciated. What they're seeking is not typically put on a map, so they are wont to wander the new museum, quite satisfied to discover for themselves the beautiful object, vista, or setting of their desires. However, like most visitors, Rechargers are delighted when they find helpful, friendly museum staff willing to support their journey and able to respond to a unique or specific request.

Rechargers are the group of visitors least likely to avail themselves of the non-exhibit aspects of the museum. They are unlikely to attend lectures and programs and they are disinclined to even visit the café or gift shop. As a group, Rechargers are visiting the museum in order to receive spiritual rather than physical or commercial nourishment. However, if they do go to the café, they'll expect food and drink to meet their high aesthetic standards as in the gift shop. In theory, it should be possible to drive Rechargers more to the café and gift shop if they knew that both settings had sumptuous offerings commensurate with their aesthetic tastes and interests. This would need to be a cost-benefit decision, determined by the number of Rechargers who visit your institution and the trade-offs required to cater to the needs of this audience as opposed to another.

Finally, it is worth re-emphasizing that Rechargers, as are other visitor groups, are not a type of person; they are people with a particular, situationally determined type of visit motivation. Each individual visitor is equally capable of enacting any of these visit motivations on any given day. The key to making your museum work is understanding what motivates each visitor to your museum on that particular day and then, ensuring that the experiences they have with exhibits, programs, staff, and museum amenities fulfill the needs determined by those motivations.

Expanding the Boundaries

All of these interventions make great sense and will help museums move towards the twenty-first century ideal of a personalized and customized museum visitor experience. However, restricting efforts to meeting visitors' needs to the time visitors are physically within the museum (or on-property if you're an outdoor facility) will limit the capacity for success. The museum visitor experience stretches beyond the museum in time and space—both prior to and subsequent to the visit. To make your museum really work for visitors requires engaging with visitors both *before* and *after* their visit.

Before Arrival

In an ideal world, visitors would arrive at the museum completely conscious of their true visit identity-related needs and already mindful of the ways that the museum could best support their visit motivations. In this "visitor-as-informed-consumer" scenario, each visitor would enter the museum with a concrete understanding of what their visit goals were together with the well-formulated knowledge of how to best utilize the resources of the museum for accomplishing them. If this scenario were true for all visitors, all museums would be able to almost fully meet the needs of each and every visitor. Unfortunately, presently only a small minority of museum visitors fully live out this scenario. Most museum visitors have only the vaguest understanding of their true needs and motivations upon entering the museum. Most visitors also enter the museum with only a vague sense of what the museum has to offer. The collective result is that the visitor is left to randomly attempt to play a matching game between their personal needs and the museum's capabilities. How much simpler this would be if both sides of the equation were better known! I am going to argue that we should strive to make this "ideal" scenario a reality.

Just as I discovered twenty-five years ago that schoolchildren's field trip experiences could be made significantly more successful if they were provided with a pre-visit orientation that focused on *their* agendas and needs,[11] we should also think of creating pre-visit orientations for regular visitors. In theory, this intervention could happen online as a pre-visit orientation, with the museum encouraging visitors to participate in these pre-visit experiences. Since the purpose of this pre-visit orientation is to measurably enhance the visitor's museum experience, why shouldn't visitors be willing to do this? If it isn't feasible to have everyone participate online prior to a visit, some kind of quick intervention just as the visitor enters the museum could be created by the museum staff. Perhaps, this intervention could even be tied to the ticketing process. Regardless, the long-term goal of this effort would be to begin to create an increasingly well-informed visiting population knowledgeable about both their needs and the museum's capacities to meet those needs.

Let's use the Facilitating Parents visitor group as an example how this might work. You might think that this type of visitor would understand their visit motivations and have a good sense of how the museum could support the museum visitor experience of their children. However, surprisingly enough, this is not the case. Although most Facilitating Parents do have a self-awareness about their visit motivations, few know how to optimally use a museum to support this visit goal. As we know, not every adult who arrives at the museum with children in tow is a Facilitating Parent, but many are. Thus, it should be possible to create some kind of intervention prior to the visit that would help these adults best support their museum visit experience. It would be wonderful to greet parents prior to their visit either online or at the front door and suggest possible ways that the museum might best support their visit on that day. It is perhaps surprising for most museum professionals to discover that most parents don't know how to provide engaging educational experiences for their children within a museum context.

Research that colleagues and I did at The Children's Museum, Indianapolis revealed that the majority of parents visiting with children, most of whom were well-educated, upper-middle-class mothers, had surprisingly narrow views about the possibilities for their children's learning in a museum. We had identified more than a dozen different types of learning outcomes that could be supported by the museum, including learning to be creative, learning to be curious, learning to be good observers, learning to think critically, and learning to ask good questions. When we asked parents what they thought the learning opportunities were available at the Museum, most parents could only think of one type of possible learning outcome for their children, and that was the usual suspect of learning new facts and concepts.[12] We recommended a variety of strategies that would be designed to help parents know about the full range of possible types of learning so that they could take full advantage of all the museum had to offer. In the absence of knowing what might be possible, the parents' ability to be a fully-engaged and supportive facilitator was limited. For example, we encouraged the Museum to run parent-educator training workshops for their regular family visitors to help parents get better at using the museum. We also encouraged the use of volunteer families as models in the galleries so other parents could adopt these strategies without the need of formal training. As The Children's Museum has begun to implement some of these ideas, the quality of parent-child interactions in the museum has markedly improved. Similar examples could be generated for the other types of visitor identity-related motivation categories. The bottom line is that an *informed* visitor is more likely than an uninformed visitor to be a satisfied visitor to your museum.

After Departure

As museum professionals come to fully appreciate the vital importance of visitors' pre-visit expectations and motivations, they will be forced to work at influencing these perceptions and understandings prior to the actual museum visit. In a similar way, the more we learn about how visitors make meaning from their museum visit experience, the more we come to appreciate that those memories are also "made" after the visit. Hence, museum professionals need to work at strategies to extend the museum visitor experience beyond the temporal and physical boundaries of the visit. As outlined in earlier chapters, these memories are only partially formed during the actual visit. Actual memories are laid down over time and typically include subsequent supportive and complementary experiences. Rather than leaving those subsequent experiences to chance, the museum should attempt to be directly involved in helping to support and, as much as possible, shape those experiences.

Virtually all museums currently believe they are actively addressing this issue. Nearly all have web sites and print materials that provide materials that support their exhibitions and programs, and nearly all also have gift shops that sell related materials. Although these efforts are part of the solution, they represent just a small part of what might be possible if museums invested as much time and energy in trying to reach the visitor after leaving the museum as they do trying to support them while in the museum. This seems heretical since museum professionals would argue that the only thing they can actually control is what happens inside the museum; after the visitor leaves they are beyond the "reach" of the museum. I would argue this is only true because museums have historically limited their view of what a museum is; if museums re-envisioned themselves as educational institutions with tools and ways to reach people across time and space, then other possibilities would become available. Take, for example, the development of virtual museums—institutions with no walls or actual onsite visitors. These museums have figured out how to engage visitors beyond traditional temporal and spatial boundaries! There are also myriad examples of collaborations between museums and other free-choice educational institutions such as public television, community organizations, and libraries, in which working together has been able to broaden how and when each institution reaches visitors.

But beyond just actively working to build long-term memories, museums have a vested interest in staying in contact with their visitors since this is the most cost-effective way to ensure future audiences. The most likely person to visit your museum today is someone who visited your museum previously. If you're going to spend money on marketing, then the least expensive and most effective use of those monies will be to invest in relationships with current users—trying to get each current user to visit once more rather than trying to convince people who have never visited to visit for the first time. The trick to getting any visitor to return is to make them feel good about their experience. Doing that transcends just ensuring that all the structures are there for a great museum experience; great experiences also require follow-up with the visitor after he or she leaves the museum. Museum professionals need to become better at communicating with visitors through email or on the Web; what needs to be communicated are things that help support and reinforce the visitor's identity-related needs. For example, to help ensure visitor satisfaction, museum professionals need to figure out how to continue to support the Explorer's need to have their curiosity satisfied and to support and reinforce how wonderful it was that the Facilitator invested their time and energy in helping to meet the needs of someone else.

What would it take to convince a person with a Recharger motivation to return again and again to the museum? Like all of us, Rechargers appreciate being invited. If we could identify our visitors who visit primarily in order to become rejuvenated and reinvigorated, we would want to say something like the following as they were leaving, or shortly after their visit, "Thank you so much for visiting us today. I hope we were able to provide you with that special moment you were seeking. Please let us know when next you come so we can help make your visit perfect. Perhaps, we can suggest a place you haven't discovered yet to visit that will meet your needs." By contrast, the communication goal for individuals with a Professional/Hobbyist motivation would be make them feel as if they were members of the museum's "inner family." The museum would want to identify these Professional/Hobbyist visitors and then go out of its way to keep them apprised of special lectures, courses, and events. .

The typical Experience seeker visitor is unlikely to return to your museum; however, if satisfied, they are highly likely to encourage others to visit. Rather than invest great effort in trying to convince Experience seekers to revisit, the smart museum would invest its energies in helping convert each and every Experience-seeking visitor into an ambassador for their museum. Why not give away postcards of the museum and set up a mailing station within the museum that encourages Experience-seeking visitors to send a postcard to loved ones? Using the latest technology, you could help visitors download their own images from cameras or cell phones and create a personalized postcard they could mail to their friends. Considering what traditional marketing to this audience costs, including the cost of postage might be one of the more cost-effective marketing strategies for a museum. An alternative strategy would be to create lapel buttons that say, "I visited the X Museum." These buttons could be given away to all visitors, but the only visitors likely to appreciate these would be those with Experience-seeking visit motivations who feel a sense of satisfaction at having actually accomplished their goal of "having been to the museum and seen this important place."

As I have suggested, the ultimate goal of the museum should be to personally interact with each and every visitor, either as they are leaving the facility or through some follow-up technique like email. The goal should be to personalize the experience for the visitor by making it more than just another anonymous leisure experience and more of an interaction with people who really care about them. For some groups of visitors, the most important thing you can say is, "Thank you for visiting today. I hope you had a wonderful time." However, if possible, you might also ask them, "Did you get to do and see what you hoped to today?" If the answer is "yes," then tell the visitor how thrilled you are and how much you hope that you can provide a comparable positive experience in the future. If the answer is "no," then try to determine the reason and how you can support a future experience that would ensure a better outcome.

As mentioned, the goal of the museum is to help visitors reinforce their entering identity-related motivation. Each and every one of us wants to feel special, whether it's because of our curiosity, our concern for our loved ones, our interesting hobbies or interests, our ability to discriminate the beautiful from the ugly, or just that we saw something important that only those who visit this place gets to see. I would assert that reinforcing these feelings and making sure that all visitors feel good about having accomplished their personal goals are as important as ensuring that visitors perceive they had a quality museum visitor experience. When visitors return home, they will think about returning, about becoming members, and will tell their friends and relatives about their wonderful museum visitor experience. The museum visitor experience is a dynamic process, a cycle with no real beginning, middle, or end—all parts of the process are equally important if the public is to have their needs satisfied.

CHAPTER 11

Institutional Value and Accountability

To be successful in the twenty-first century, museums will need to rethink how they define their purpose and measure their success. In order to be perceived as truly fundamental to their communities, museums will need to rewrite their mission and impact statements to more directly align with the identity-related visit motivations of their visitors.

I subscribe to the statement by the late Stephen Weil that, "In everything museums do, they must remember the cornerstone on which the whole enterprise rests: to make a positive difference in the quality of people's lives."[1] However, achieving this goal requires understanding not just the needs and wants of the public, but how the public can best be served by the resources and capabilities of the museum. The most successful museums are those who have found ways to merge their own interests and capabilities with those of their public and by appreciating that it's neither about just "giving them what they want" nor about just "giving them what they need." It's about understanding how these two ideas can merge into a single, unified action.

Although the criteria for determining success as a cultural institution at the beginning of the Knowledge Age are still evolving, there are a few universals that reflect the increasing value placed on leisure, learning, self-affirmation, and personalization that are hallmarks of this new age. Successful museums maximize the flexibility and ingenuity of their relationships both inside and outside the organization while responding to rapidly shifting economic, social, and political realities. Success is not limited to a single set of outcomes, but requires excellence in basic areas: (1) *support of the public good* which includes accomplishing one's cultural/ aesthetic mission, but also involves being a good community citizen; (2) *organizational investment* which includes building and nurturing staff;

supporting a climate and culture for creativity, innovation, collaboration, and research and development; and (3) *financial stability* which includes building organizational value and, when possible, generating annual financial surpluses that can be used to further support institutional learning and hence, the public good.[2] The issues of organizational investment and financial stability are beyond the scope of this book, but it is important to note that success cannot be achieved without them.[3] Supporting public good, though, can be reinterpreted in light of the ideas presented in this book.

SUPPORT OF THE PUBLIC GOOD

Every museum must be clear about why it exists and whom it is trying to serve. In other words, the museum must specify what specific needs (or wants) it is uniquely positioned to satisfy for each segment of the public it hopes to serve. In particular, the museum should assess what assets both it and the public bring to the table. Considerable debate in the United Kingdom has surrounded the issue of "cultural value." Cultural value has been characterized as having multiple dimensions; all of which are important components of what I would consider "public good."[4]

As highlighted in the opening quotation by Weil, creating public value, or ensuring that the public (or more likely publics) is better off after an institution's actions than it was before, are the hallmarks of an effective museum in the Knowledge Age. As Weil has also written, the goal of a museum can no longer be *about something*, whether that is art, history, science or nature; today, a museum must also set as its goal to be *for somebody*.[5] This transition must begin with the organization's mission and be reflected in all of its activities, including a sincere commitment to assessing the public good actually achieved by the organization. A corollary of this focus on public value is that museums have tried too hard to be all things to all people for too long. One of the important products of a focus on specifying and measuring the goal of public value is that it leads organizations to accept the limitations of their capacity to impact the public and requires that they target specific audiences in order to be strategic and optimize their impact.

Most museums argue that they exist to serve their community, to support civic engagement and build social capital, but many continue to focus on fairly traditional and self-serving ways of achieving these out-comes (for example, increase the number of underserved individuals who visit our museum, ensure the appropriate conservation and preservation of the objects under our care, and so on). To be truly viable organizations in the twenty-first century, museums need to not only talk about being part of a larger community, they also need to actually "walk the walk." For too long, most museums have thought and behaved as if they were iso-lated jewels, with their inherent value based on their longevity, privilege, or financial worth. Museums have come to appreciate that they are but one section of a large and complex community fabric, in fact, not just one fabric but multiple, intersecting community fabrics ——communities of geography (e.g., nation, state, and local), of purpose (e.g., education, so-cial service, culture, entertainment), of interest (e.g., art, history, science), and of commerce (e.g., tourism, education). As the financial challenges of the present reveal, many do not consider museums particularly essen-tial components of any of these various community fabrics. How, then, should museums define and measure their value?

I sincerely believe that the museum visitor experience model described in this book provides a unique and useful way for museums to critically re-examine their role in the communities they serve. In particular, I believe that it opens up new ways to think about issues of institutional impact.

INSTITUTIONAL IMPACT

Just as we have redefined the museum visitor experience as the interaction between visitors and museums, we must redefine how we think about a museum's impact. The museum is not an island onto itself, but a dynamic interaction between the public and society. As I've conceptualized in the figure on page 161, the museum's value as a composite of two separate, but interwoven sets of inputs—"visitor" and "museum" inputs. The mu-seum's impact in a community is the sum of the individual perceptions of the museum's value as determined by the museum visit experiences of thousands of visitors. It is also defined by an abstract societal construct determined by the experiences of visitors to the museum, but equally by the larger prevailing socio-cultural perceptions of what museums are and the potential roles they play in society. Thus, the task of defining as well as influencing, institutional value and impact over the long term need to begin with each institution analyzing how this dynamic relationship uniquely plays out for them. What is the actual value the museum currently provides to each individual through a visit, program, or some other effort? The museum also needs to understand the public perception of its value as an institution within the community. What do the various sectors of the community perceive the museum affords? While appreciating that museums are complex organizations and impact their communities through multiple mechanisms and efforts, for the sake of simplicity, I will focus my discussion primarily on one aspect of the museum—the general public's in-museum use of exhibitions.

If we knew the answers to the three basic questions of who goes to museums, what they do there, and what meaning they make from the experience, we would gain critical insights into how individuals derive value and benefits from their museum-going experience. Historically, museums have defined their impact from a top-down perspective. As museums over the past twenty-five years have become more educationally focused, institutional impact has increasingly been defined as involving changes in the public's understanding, attitudes, and behaviors. The leaders of the museum world have determined, usually expressed in their mission, that the goal of the institution is to improve the public's understanding, appreciation, and/or behavior of art, history, conservation, or science. To achieve this goal, the institution has created exhibitions designed to "educate," "inspire," and/or "enlighten" the public. In recent years, museums have engaged in the challenging task of evaluating their success at achieving these goals. For most museums, assertions of impact remain largely rhetorical rather than empirical, but increasingly museums are finding it not only useful, but possible to supplement their rhetoric with measurements of whether a museum visit resulted in changes in the public's knowledge, attitudes, or behaviors.

Perhaps not surprisingly, this is the same impact model used by the formal education system. In this system, authorities unilaterally determine what children should know and codify it within standards and curricula. These are then used by teachers as instructional guides to frame what and how children are taught. Finally, children are evaluated to determine whether or not they have learned what they were supposed to have learned. In the past, individual teachers exercised considerable discretion over what content to teach as well as how to evaluate individual children. Today, neither the content nor the student evaluations are primarily left to the discretion of the individual educator. The content and evaluations that really count are those devised and administered by individuals at the county, state, or national level and take the form of standardized, one-size-fits-all assessments. We could debate the pros and cons of this model for the schools, but I would assert that this model is wholly inappropriate for the free-choice learning context of a twenty-first century museum. Although the museum professional staff has a responsibility to define and prescribe the overall content and goals of the institution, the creation of such content and goals without the input and approval of the public makes little sense. In fact, as both the model and the actual data presented in this book demonstrate, the public utilizes museums to achieve the outcomes THEY deem important, NOT what the museum deems important.

What the museum visitor experience model should make clear is that the visiting public uses museums in order to achieve a range of personal goals. Different individuals on different days are motivated to use the museum in order to satisfy a range of different personal, often learning-related outcomes. Some of these personal outcomes involve learning facts and concepts related to art or history or science or conservation, but many do not. As a consequence, the kinds of personal meanings that the public seeks from museums only occasionally align with the kinds of learning outcomes museums profess they are designed to support. If we want to accurately measure the real impact museums achieve, we need to acknowledge these realities and strive to measure the full range of benefits visitors actually derive from their museum visitor experience, not just the benefits the museum supposes they receive.

Equally true is the realization that in order to truly maximize the impact museums have on the public (and by extension their community), it will require a major realignment of institutional goals so that those goals better mesh with the realities of visitor expectations and motivations. The alternative to this voluntary realignment of museum goals will be for funders and the public to come to realize that museums do not presently achieve much of what they claim to achieve—at least not for most of the people who visit, most of the time. We are perilously close to the moment when the "emperor is discovered to have no clothes."

As much as I admire and respect the job that museums do for all the millions of people they serve every year, I strongly believe that museums need to get better, not just for each visitor but better as institutions. In a world of ever-increasing competition for audience and resources, the two of which are inextricably bound together at the moment, museums need to get better at understanding and serving their visitors. Although museums continue to be extremely popular leisure venues, today's success cannot be taken for granted. This is particularly true for individual museums, since the success of "museums" as a leisure category has created a proliferation of museum-like entities, all vying for the same finite audiences and resources. If I can make any predictions about the future, it is that without considerable investment and constant improvement, museums are unlikely to retain their current lofty position in the leisure marketplace.

In the past decade we have witnessed a slow but steady erosion in the position of individual museums; visitor numbers have flattened out if not outright declined. Once abundant financial support is now more limited. Governments are cutting back funding and grant support is becoming ever more challenging to acquire. Even individual donations are becoming increasingly difficult to obtain and require more effort to maintain even constant levels. As I write this book in 2008, it seems unlikely that the next decade will be any kinder to museums. The current economic situation bodes poorly for all non-profits. By virtue of dwindling resources, it is almost certain that more emphasis will be placed on only supporting organizations that provide "essential services." If museums cannot make the case that they provide essential services, they will not receive funding. More problematic, if it is discovered that the museums do not actually deliver the services they currently claim to provide, that too will result in diminished funding if not an outright "closing of the doors."

Call me an optimist, but I believe that if we can change our focus and orientation to be truly visitor-centered, that is truly focused on meeting visitors' deepest and most important identity-related needs, museums can be viewed as an essential service. Make no mistake, accomplishing this goal will require major changes in the purposes and activities of museums. An enhanced understanding of current and potential audience has to be at the heart of every twenty-first century museum's rhetoric, actions, and business model.

Are museums currently essential institutions in their community? Ask any museum director, or museum professional and they will without hesitation say, "YES, ABSOLUTELY." Ask the local mayor or city councilperson the same question and you might get a more equivocal answer. More telling would be to ask the general public that question. Currently, do you as a museum professional want to go before the local government govern-ing board and play on a level playing field with the hospital, rubbish col-lection, and police force? Do you want to frame your argument by saying that the acquisition of a new work by contemporary artist Jenny Holzer, or the addition of a new giraffe to your breeding population, or the de-velopment of another special exhibition on nineteenth-century pioneers, are worth as much to the community as removing the trash, supporting emergency workers, or feeding the homeless? If you don't think this is what the future portends, then you haven't been paying attention to cur-rent events. Maybe you'll be lucky and always have sufficient wealthy benefactors who believe in "high culture" and "heritage" but, if not, then it comes back to meeting the needs of the general public.

What the museum visitor experience model tells us is that the public perceives that museums are good for five basic things: 1) the need to sat-isfy personal curiosity and interest; 2) the wish to engage in a meaningful social experience with someone you care about, in particular children; 3) the aspiration to experience that which is best and most important within a culture; 4) the desire to further specific intellectual needs; and 5) the yearning to immerse one's self in a spiritually refreshing environment. Of course, there will be a content-related twist to the specific public percep-tions for each individual museum, but a desire to acquire a deep and lasting knowledge of particular content, or develop the capacity to save the world, or any of the other lofty goals museums seem to espouse, will not rise to the top of most visitors' list of what they are primarily seeking in a museum visit. Although there are no doubt variations and possible things missing from this list of outcomes, at least in the English-speaking, developed world and in one Spanish-speaking, developing country, these five outcomes are what the vast majority of the public currently perceive that museums afford. And it goes without saying that not every museum is equally good at supporting all of these benefits. The question each and every museum needs to ask, after they determine how the public current-ly perceives their specific set of values, is whether this is how you want to be perceived and valued. Is this the niche you wish to be in? If it is not, then you have a lot of work to do. If you accept that it is a reasonable niche, which I believe it should be, then the challenge is how you ensure that your community appreciates that these outcomes are truly *essential*.

In theory, each of these needs could be viewed as essential functions of a society, but making the case and delivering on that case are what will be fundamental to long-term survival. What would a society be like if there was no place to satiate curiosity, or help children learn, or escape the pressures of a crazy urban world? And, if these are the amenities your institution provides the citizenry, then you need to make sure they are made available to *ALL* citizens. You need to ensure that each is delivered *REALLY* well. In the current economic situation, you need to clearly and unambiguously communicate to funders and supporters that these are indeed the benefits your organization provides and be able to back these assertions up with real data.

To be essential, museums need to bring their missions into alignment with the public's expectations. Then, museums must improve the fit between the needs the public perceives a museum is capable of delivering, presumably influenced by the museum's mission, and the actual benefits that the museum delivers. The museum visitor experience model doesn't answer the question of how to accomplish this, but it provides a framework for beginning to get the answers to these questions. The reason why this is true should be obvious. By knowing more about the real reasons visitors utilize our institutions, and more about the real benefits they perceive they derive from those experiences, we can more effectively meet their needs and ensure that they are satisfied customers. Satisfied customers will return and support the museum. Satisfied customers will also help the museum through word-of-mouth recommendations and politically support the museum in good times and bad. But I wouldn't be advocating this model if I thought all it was going to do was to provide superficial, short-term gains in popularity and support. Rather, I am enthusiastic about this new museum visitor experience model because it promises to give the museum community, for the first time, a truly deep and a valid way to understand how to effectively meet the needs of real, not just imagined museum visitors. Although the model suggests a range of ways to creatively move into the future, change will be difficult and challenging, not the least of these being the need for meaningful assessment.

ASSESSING IMPACT

One of the hallmarks of professional life in the twenty-first century, for both individuals and organizations, is accountability. Accountability is not just limited to ensuring that an organization follows prescribed accounting rules and ensures that all funds are appropriately spent; it is also about how organizations demonstrate they are achieving their goals. This is particularly true for non-profit organizations like museums. In the for-profit world, the ultimate accounting is the financial bottom line—the amount of money earned. In museums, accountability is increasingly measured in the good created. How do you reliably and credibly measure good created? Most museums have never actually done so, but in the twenty-first century, those that do not figure out how, will find themselves out of business. In an increasingly distrustful and competitive society, merely promising to do good no longer suffices.

Continued public and private funding for museums will ultimately be dependent upon evidence of public good accomplished by museums. Society increasingly is demanding that institutions evaluate their performance and provide concrete, tangible evidence of success. Such demands became a legislative reality at the U.S. federal government level with the passage of the Government Performance and Results Act (GPRA) in 1993. This Act required every government agency to establish specific objective, quantifiable, and measurable performance goals for each of its programs and report their success annually to Congress. In the U.K., government-supported museums (which means most museums) must now document Public/Cultural Value. Similar laws exist or are being considered in many other countries.

The demand for accountability is increasingly widespread. Many state and local government agencies have followed the lead of the federal government. Private foundations are including similar language in grants applications. From all sides, museums are receiving a clear message: to successfully compete for public or private funds in an accountability-driven environment, they must develop evaluation practices that provide a compelling picture of the impact of their services. Funders want evidence that something of quality actually happened as a consequence of the programs they support. Such outcomes-based assessments will require institutions to invest more money, more time, and more thought in the assessment process. To do less will not be an option.

Historically, it has been difficult to accurately and validly measure the impact of the museum visitor experience. This has been true for two reasons, the first of which was a lack of appropriate evaluation tools; most "standard" evaluation tools were designed for the realities of schooling rather than those of museums. Although recent advances in understanding how visitors learn within museums coupled with new and better measurement tools—tools specifically designed for use in free-choice learning settings —have helped, results have still not provided all of the ammunition necessary to allow museums to make a compelling case. I would assert the inability to make a clear case for museums has stemmed in large measure from the lack of a valid and reliable model of the museum visitor experience. It's hard to accurately measure something you don't understand! If we're measuring the wrong things, we will not get wonderful results! The museum visitor experience model promises to help overcome this second impediment by enabling museums to more fully and accurately predict and measure visitor outcomes. The model dictates that we need to develop strategies for effectively measuring things like enhanced curiosity, mental and physical rejuvenation, and satisfaction of a sense of cultural "competency."

It should be clear by now that I advocate determining institutional impact as a measure of the success an institution has in fulfilling each individual visitor's identity-related visit agenda. The greater the fit between each of hundreds of individuals' entering expectations and their long-term, post-visit outcomes, the greater the impact a museum could be determined to have achieved. If, as argued above, museums need to bring their missions into alignment with the public's expectations, then it follows that the goal of assessment will be to develop valid and reliable metrics that determine how successfully this has been accomplished. Implicit in this scenario is that museums will need to make the case to their funders that by aligning their institutional goals with the fundamental needs and expectations of the public, they are performing essential and invaluable service to the community—a service that few other organizations can do as well or as successfully.

The museum visitor experience model provides a clear and logical framework for improving how we as a profession value and measure the success of museums. The changes I have suggested here are unlikely to occur without considerable debate since not everyone will agree with what I have proposed. Should these outcomes really be defined as appropriate and worthy outcomes for museums? Should government and private funders actually be encouraged to re-evaluate their funding priorities to better match the realities described by this model? Currently few funders acknowledge, let alone support, the full range of museum visitor experience outcomes that is suggested by the model. Finally, should museums dramatically alter how they market and support their public activities? All of these changes of course depend ultimately on whether or not the model I have proposed is actually valid. The value of any good model is that it provides reliable and useful predictions. The predictions made by the museum visitor experience model are open to testing and should be tested. So far, the model has held up to scrutiny, but only additional test-ing will enable us to discover if it's a sufficiently robust model to justify making it the foundation of a whole new era in museum practice.

FINAL COMMENTS

I offer this model at this time not because I am convinced that it is perfect the way it is—quite the contrary. I know that the current model is a work in progress and, without question, will be found to have flaws. I offer this model because I think it is far enough along in its development to offer some important new insights to the museum community. As we look to the future, I know that there will be a need for changes and revisions, hopefully not to the core premise of the model, but certainly as to how it is applied. For example, I know that the strategies my colleagues and I have used to date for measuring an individual's identity-related motiva-tions are still quite crude and will need to be improved. As this book nears completion, my students and I have been working on several new approaches to this problem, but no ideal solution has yet emerged. Ob-viously, how one measures an individual's identity-related motivations, and thus assigns them to an identity-related category, is a critical issue. I am also not totally convinced that the way I have parsed the universe of museum identity-related motivations is completely correct. Would we be better served by having dozens of categories rather than just five? Is forcing individuals into a single category the best solution even within the current framework? If someone has multiple entering motivations, does a Facilitating Explorer have the same needs and interests as an Explor-ing Facilitator? Time and presumably, further study will tell the tale. At the moment, the current model seems to make sense and be supported by reliable data. However, more data and more testing of how the model actually works in practice are clearly required.

Without question, the current model has attempted to simplify a com-plex reality in order to be useable and generalizable. Greater detail and precision would undoubtedly ensure a closer fit to particular situations and types of museums, but it would also result in less fit for others. That might be a worthwhile tradeoff for a particular institution or group of museums to make, but it seems like a bad tradeoff when trying to create a model for something as diverse and heterogeneous as museums. Perhaps, the next generation of the museum visitor experience model would be a whole series of models, such as a zoo visitor experience model, an art museum visitor experience model, and a natural area/park visitor experience model. More useful, perhaps, would be a more fine-grained model, the "Museum X" visitor experience model which would be tightly focused on the unique set of visitors utilizing one institution.

I have no doubt that there will be changes in the use and design of the museum visitor experience model. Such changes are inevitable, particularly changes that enable the model to incorporate greater complexity and detail. Without question, there is need for additional research to determine if the model holds for visitors to the many museums located in the less-developed world. To date most of the research has been on visitors to museums in English-speaking parts of the developed world, though as mentioned above, these same categories seemed to work with individuals visiting art, history, and science museums in Medellin, Colombia as well. And even within this context, although there seems to be evidence that the model works for individuals from all manner of socio-economic and cultural affinities, this too requires further investigation.

Additionally, it is important to point out that the model as it currently exists is just a snapshot of the museum visitor and leisure preference realities of today. Over time, the identity-related needs and benefits the public perceives that museums support will undoubtedly shift. They may shift because of changes museums make or because of changes in society; either way they are unlikely to persist unchanged. I am hopeful that this book will result in changes in the nature of what museums offer the public that are more consistent with the perceived needs of their publics. In any case, return in twenty years, if not sooner, and the identity-related visit categories currently described by the model may well be quite different. However, if the basic outlines of this museum visitor experience model do indeed prove to be robust and useful, those shifts will be easy to track and the model will be easily modified to fit new realities.

Finally, I perceive several next steps. I have already stated that a major short-term goal will be to test the ability of the model to improve the experiences of real visitors in real museums. Even as I write this book, I am aware of many institutions that have begun to apply the principles of the model to everyday practice. It's still too soon to know how these efforts will work, but without question, these and other efforts will soon determine the worth of this model for improving museum practice. Similarly, if I am fortunate enough to have written a book that is noticed, than I can count on my colleagues in the research and evaluation community testing my ideas to determine if they are as reasonable as I have asserted. I look forward to these efforts to test and replicate my findings. Because this is the first really predictive model of the museum visitor experience, I envision researchers for the first time being able to begin to create computer-based simulations of the museum visitor experience; in fact, I hope to be one of those researchers. If successful, like any good computer simulation, these models would allow museum professionals to "electronically" test exhibit and program ideas, as well as marketing and fund-raising ideas prior to actually investing their time and resources in the real thing. And lastly, suspending disbelief and proceeding with the assumption that this is a worthwhile and robust model of the museum visitor experience, I believe that we will soon see the need for creating increasingly sophisticated strategies for measuring the public's entering identity-related motivations and devising strategies for adjusting, in real time, to this information.

No matter what happens, I am hopeful that the ideas presented in this book will stimulate discussions and possibly even debates within the museum community. Such conversations will certainly be interesting, and hopefully result in better museums. Since we are all going to spend the rest of our lives in the future, we might as well work towards making it as good and interesting a future as possible.

NOTES

PREFACE

1. Falk, J.H. & Dierking, L.D. (1992). *The museum experience.*Washington, DC: Whalesback Books.
2. Falk, J.H. & Dierking, L.D. (2000). *Learning from museums.* Walnut Creek, CA: AltaMira Press.

CHAPTER 1

1. All names of individuals described in this book are pseudonyms. All data is based upon extensive interviews collected by the author or his colleagues over the past seven years. The vignettes at the beginning of this first chapter are reconstructions of events based upon descriptions provided by the subjects.
2. For more information on the central role of audience in a museum's business model, see Falk & Sheppard, (2006).
3. And these days there is also a large permanent exhibition on the Australian outback.
4. Falk, J.H. (1993). *Factors Influencing Leisure Decisions: The Use of Museums by African Americans.* Washington, DC: American Association of Museums.().
5. Falk, J.H, Brooks, P., & Amin, R. (2001). Investigating the long-term impact of a science center on its community: The California Science Center L.A.S.E.R. Project. In: J. Falk (Ed.), *Free-Choice Science Education: How We Learn Science Outside of School.* pp. 115–132. New York, NY: Teacher's College Press, Columbia University.
   National Science Board (2004). *Science and engineering indicators: 2004.* Washington, DC: U.S. Government Printing Office.
   National Science Board (2006). *Science and engineering indicators: 2006.* Washington, DC: U.S. Government Printing Office.
   National Science Board (2008). *Science and engineering indicators: 2008.* Washington, DC: U.S. Government Printing Office.
6. Adams, G.D. (1989). *The process and effects of word-of-mouth communication at a history museum.* Unpublished master's thesis, Boston University, Boston, MA.
   McLean, F. (1997). *Marketing the museum.* London: Routledge.
   Bosman, J. (2006). Advertising is obsolete. Everyone says so. Business, *New York Times*, January 23.

7. Colonial Williamsburg Foundation. (1987). 1987 President's Report. Williamsburg, VA: Colonial Williamsburg Foundation.
8. American Museum of Natural History. (1986). Visitor profiles. Unpublished report.

    Balling, J.D., & Cornell, E.A. (1985). Family visitors to science-technology centers: Motivations and demographics. (Grant No.SED-8112927). Washington, DC: National Science Foundation.

    Biltmore Estate. (1987). *Survey of Biltmore Estate, Summer 1987.* Unpublished manuscript.

    Birney, B.A. (1990). Characteristics of Brookfield zoo visitors: five analyses of our audience. (Technical Rep.) Brookfield, IL: Zoological Society of Illinois.

    Bitgood, S., Patterson, D., & Nichols, G. (1986). Report of a survey of visitors to the Anniston Museum of Natural History. Jacksonville, AL: Jacksonville State University, Psychology Institute.

    Falk, J.H., Holland, D.G. & Dierking, L.D. (1992). A study of visitor expectations and their effect on visitation, Mystic Seaport Museum. Annapolis, MD: Museum Experience Associates.

    Hushion & Associates & Heath Consultants (1994). Mapping a future: An audience and stakeholder survey of the public art gallery network in Ontario. Toronto: Ontario Association of Art Galleries.
9. Falk, J.H., Koran, J.J., Dierking, L.D & Dreblow, L. (1985). Predicting visitor behavior. *Curator,* 28(4), 326–332.
10. Falk, J.H. & Storksdieck, M. (2005). Using the *Contextual Model of Learning* to understand visitor learning from a science center exhibition. *Science Education,* 89, 744–778.
11. Falk, J.H. & Dierking, L.D. (1997). School field trips: Assessing their long-term impact. *Curator,* 40(3), 211–218.
12. Anderson, D., Storksdieck, M. & Spock, M. (2006). Long-term impacts of museum experiences. In: J. Falk, L. Dierking and S. Foutz (eds.), *In Principle, In Practice,* pp. 197–216. Lanham, MD: AltaMira Press.
13. See review in Falk, J.H. & Dierking, L.D. (2000). *Learning from Museums,* Walnut Creek, CA: AltaMira Press. Also, Roschelle, J. (1995). Learning in interactive environments: Prior knowledge and new experience. In: J. Falk & L. Dierking (eds.), *Public Institutions for Personal Learning,* pp. 37–51. Washington, DC: American Association of Museums.
14. Falk, J.H. & Adelman, L.M. (2003). Investigating the impact of prior knowledge, experience and interest on aquarium visitor learning. *Journal of Research in Science Teaching,* 40(2), 163–176.

    Falk & Storksdieck, (2005).
15. Desolneux, A., Moisan, L. & Morel, J.M. (2008). *From Gestalt Theory to Image Analysis: A probabilistic approach.* New York: Springer.
16. Bickford, A., Doering, Z.D. & Smith, S.J. (1992). *Spiders are coming!: An*

exhibition background study for the National Museum of Natural History. (Institutional Studies Report 92–4). Washington, DC: Smithsonian Institution.

Doering, Z.D. (1991). *Across the river: A study of visitors to the Anacostia Museum.* (Institutional Studies Report No. 92-5). Washington, DC: Smithsonian Institution.

Doering, Z.D. & Bickford, A. (1994). *Visits and visitors to the Smithsonian Institution: A summary of studies.* (Institutional Studies Report No. 94–1). Washington, DC: Smithsonian Institution.

Doering, Z.D. & Black, K.J. (1989). *Visits to the National Air and Space Museum (NASM): Demographic characteristics.* (Institutional Studies Report No. 89–1). Washington, DC: Smithsonian Institution.

Hood, M.G. (1988). Arboretum visitor profiles as defined by the four seasons. In: S. Bitgood, J. Roper & A. Benefield (eds.), *Proceedings of the first annual visitor studies conference.* Jacksonville, AL: The Center for Social Design.

Horn, A. & Finney, J. (1994). *Bay area research report: A multi-cultural audience survey for Bay Area museums.* San Francisco, CSUSAN: Museum Management Consultants, Inc.

17. Birney, B.A. (1990). Characteristics of Brookfield zoo visitors: five analyses of our audience. (Technical Rep.) Brookfield, IL: Zoological Society of Illinois.

Dierking, L.D., Adams, M. & Spencer-Etienne, M. (1996). *Final Report: Lila Wallace/Reader's Digest Audience Development, Virginia Museum of Fine Arts.* Annapolis, MD: SLi.

DiMaggio, P. & Ostrower, F. (1990). Participation in the arts by black and white Americans. *Social Forces,* 68(3), 7537–78.

DiMaggio, P. & Ostrower, F. (1992). *Race, ethnicity and participation in the arts.* Washington, DC: Seven Locks Press.

Horn, A. & Finney, J. (1994). *Bay area research report: A multi-cultural audience survey for Bay Area museums.* San Francisco, CSUSAN: Museum Management Consultants, Inc.

Puckrein, G. (1991). The participation of African Americans in cultural leisure pursuits. Unpublished study produced for *American Visions,* Washington, DC.

Robinson, J.P., Keegan, C., Karth, M. & Triplett, T.A. (1986). *Public Participation in the arts: Final report on the 1992 survey, Volume 1, Overall project report.* Washington, DC: National Endowment for the Arts.

Robinson, J.P., Keegan, C., Karth, M. & Triplett, T.A. (1993). *Arts Participation in America: 1982–1992* NEA Research Division, Report #27. Washington, DC: National Endowment for the Arts.

18. Falk, J.H. (1993). *Factors Influencing Leisure Decisions: The Use of Museums by African Americans.* Washington, DC: American Association of Museums.

19. Fang, J., Madhavan, S. & Alderman, M.H. (1996). The association between

birthplace and mortality from cardiovascular causes among black and white residents of New York City. *New England Journal of Medicine,* 335(21), 1545–1551.

Gillum, R.F. (1996). The epidemiology of cardiovascular disease in black Americans. *New England Journal of Medicine,* 335(21), 1597–1598.

20. Falk, (1993).
21. e.g., Wilkening, S. (2008). *Audience Trends and Analysis: Drilling deeper.* Unpublished presentation. Slingerlands, NY: Reach Advisors.
22. Ulwick, A. (2005). What customers want: Using outcome-driven innovation to create breakthrough products and services. NY: McGraw-Hill, pp. 66–67.
23. Falk & Dierking, (1992; 2000).
24. e.g., Jacobsen, J.W. (2006). *Experiential Learning Museums.* (Forum '06). Marblehead, MA: White Oak Associates, Inc.
25. I first appreciated this reality in the mid-1980s as I was drafting the first versions of what was to become the *Museum Experience* (1992), this idea was later reiterated in *Learning from Museums* (2000) and again, the case was strongly made in a chapter I wrote as part of the edited volume, *In Principle, In Practice* (2006).
26. e.g., Bourdieu, P. (1989). Forms of capital. In: J.G. Richardson (ed.), *Handbook for theory and research for the Sociology of Education*, pp. 241–258. New York: Greenwood Press.

CHAPTER 2

1. Graburn, N. (1998). Quest for identity. *Museum International*, 50(3), p. 13.
2. e.g., Aguiar, M. & Hurst, E. (2006). *Measuring Trends in Leisure: The Allocation of Time over Five Decades*, Working Paper No. 06–2. Boston: Federal Reserve Bank of Boston.

    de Grazia, S. (1962). *Of Time, Work and Leisure.* New York: Twentieth Century Fund.

    Pearson, L.F. (1977). *Working, life and leisure.* Sunderland, UK: Sunderland Polytechnic.

    Roberts, K. (1999). *Leisure in Society.* Wallingford, UK: CBAI Publishing.

    Young, M. & Schuller, T. (1991). *Life after Work.* London: Harper Collins.
3. Kelly, J.R. & Freysinger, V.J. (2000). *21ˢᵗ Century Leisure: Current Issues.* State College, PA: Venture Publishing.

    Freysinger, V. J. & Kelly, J.R. (2004). *21ˢᵗ Century Leisure: Current Issues.* State College, PA: Venture Publishing.
4. Research Resolutions & Consulting Ltd. (2007). *U.S. Heritage Tourism Enthusiasts: A Special Analysis of the Travel Activities and Motivation Survey (TAMS).* Ottawa: The Canadian Tourism Commission.
5. See review by (Falk & Dierking, 2000).
6. Research Resolutions, 2007.
7. Maslow, A. (1943). A theory of human motivation. *Psychological Review,* 50, 370–396.

8. Roberts, K. (1999). *Leisure in Society*. Wallingford, UK: CBAI Publishing.
9. Sagon, C. 2004. Formerly known as Sutton Place. F1, *Washington Post*, April 7.
    Zuboff, S. & Maxmin, D. (2002). *The Support Economy: Why corporations are failing individuals and the next episode of capitalism*. New York: Viking Press.
10. Godbey, G. (1989). In Fred Coalter (ed.), *Anti-Leisure and Public Recreation Policy. In Freedom and Constraint—The Paradoxes of Leisure*. London: Routledge.
    Godbey, G. (2001). The use of time and space in assessing the potential of free choice learning. In: J.H. Falk (ed.), *Free-Choice Science Education: How we learn science outside of school*. New York: Teachers College Press.
11. Pine, J. & Gilmore, J. (2007). *Authencity: What consumers really want*. Boston: Harvard Business School.
12. Kelly, J.R. (1983). *Leisure identities and interactions*. London: George Allen & Unwin.
13. Bem, D. J. (1972). Self-perception theory. In: L. Berkowitz (ed.), *Advances in experimental social psychology* (Vol. 6. pp. 1–62). New York: Academic Press.
    Csikzentmihalyi, M. (1990a). *Flow: The psychology of optimal experience*. New York: Harper Collins.
    Samdahl, D.M. & Kleiber, D.A. 1989. Self-awareness and leisure experience. *Leisure Sciences*, 11, 1–10.
    Steele, C.M. (1988). The psychology of self-affirmation: Sustaining the integrity of the self. In: L. Berkowitz (ed.), *Advances in Experimental Social-Psychology* (Vol. 21, pp. 261–302). New York: Academic Press.
    Williams, D.R. (2002). Leisure identities, globalization, and the politics of place. *Journal of Leisure Research*, 34(4), 267–278.
14. Haggard, L. M. & Williams, D. R. (1992). Identity affirmation through leisure activities: Leisure symbols of the self. *Journal of Leisure Research*, 24(1), 1–18, p. 17.
15. Sandberg, J. (2006, July 19). It Doesn't Sound Like a Vacation to Me. *Wall Street Journal* online.
16. Graburn, N.H. (1977). The museum and the visitor experience. In: *The Visitor and the Museum*, pp. 5–32. Prepared for the 72nd Annual Conference of the American Association of Museums, Seattle, WA.
17. Kelly, J.R. (1977). *Situational and Social Factors in Leisure Decisions*. Technical Report. ERIC #:ED153143.
18. Beard, J.G. & Maunier, R. (1980). Measuring leisure satisfaction. *Journal of Leisure Research*, 12, 20–33.
19. Driver, B.L. & Tocher, S.R. (1970). Toward a behavioral interpretation of recreational engagements, with implications for planning. In: B.L. Driver (ed.),*Elements of outdoor recreation planning: Proceedings of a national short course held in Ann Arbor, Michigan, May 6-16, 1968*. Ann Arbor, MI: University of Michigan.
20. Manfredo, M.J. & Driver, B.L. (1996). Measuring leisure motivation: A meta-analysis of the recreation experience preference scales. *Journal of Leisure*

Research 28(3), 188–213.

21. Knopf, R. C., Driver, B. I, & Bassett, J. IL (1973). Motivations for fishing. In *Transactions of the 28th North American Wildlife and Natural Resources Conference* (pp. 191–204). Washington, DC: Wildlife Management Institute.

22. Manfredo, M.J. & Driver, B.L. (1996). Measuring leisure motivation: A meta-analysis of the recreation experience preference scales. Journal of Leisure Research 28(3), 188–213.

23. Hood, M. (1981). *Leisure Criteria of Family Participation and Non-Participation in Museums*. Technical Report. Columbus, OH: Hood Associates.

    Hood, M. (1983). Staying away: Why people choose not to visit museums. *Museum News*, 61(4), 50–57.

24. Falk, J.H. (1993). *Leisure decisions influencing African American use of museums*. Washington, DC. American Association of Museums.

25. Moussouri, T. (1997). *Family agendas and family learning in hands-on museums*. Unpublished doctoral dissertation, University of Leiscester, Leicester, England.

26. Falk, J.H., Moussouri, T. & Coulson, D. (1998). The effect of visitors' agendas on museum learning. *Curator,* 41(2), 106–120.

27. Paris, S.G. (1997). Situated motivation and informal learning. *Journal of Museum Education,* 22(2 & 3), 22–27.

28. Doering, Z.D. (1999). Strangers, guests or clients? Visitor experiences in museums. *Curator*, 42(2), 74–87.

    Pekarik, A.J., Doering, Z.D. & Karns, D.A. (1999). Exploring satisfying experiences in museums. *Curator,* 42, 152–173.

29. Packer, J. & Ballantyne, R. (2002). Motivational factors and the visitor experience: A comparison of three sites. *Curator*, 45, 183–198.

30. Morris Hargreaves McIntyre (2004). *Tate through visitor's eyes*. Technical Report. Manchester, UK: Morris Hargreaves McIntyre.

31. Bigley, J.D., Fesenmaier, D.R., Lane, M. & Roehl, W.S. (1992). The assessment of museum member motivations: A case study. In: A. Benefield, S. Bitgood & H. Shettel (eds.), *Visitor Studies: Theory, Research and Practice, Vol. 4*, pp. 72–81. Jacksonville, AL: The Center for Social Design.

32. I will assume that readers at this point are sufficiently familiar with the term *free-choice learning* so as not to need to extensively dwell on its definition. However, for those unfamiliar with this term, briefly, free-choice learning is the learning an individual does over the course of their life in which they get to exercise a strong measure of choice and control—choice and control over what, why, where, when, and how we will learn. The fact that free-choice learning happens, for the most part, outside of the imposed structure and requirements of schools, universities, or workplaces, makes it at once extremely interesting and chronically under-recognized and appreciated. For those wishing more information on free-choice learning, I'd refer them to Falk, J.H. & Dierking, L.D. (2002). *Lessons without limit: How free-choice*

learning is transforming education. Lanham, MD: AltaMira Press.

33. Lewington, J. (1998). More Canadians pursuing informal learning, survey reveals. *The Globe and Mail,* November 11, A13.

    Livingstone, D.W. (1999). Exploring the icebergs of adult learning: Findings of the first Canadian survey of informal learning practices. *Canadian Journal for the Study of Adult Education, 13*(2), 49–72.

34. Packer, J. (2006). Learning for fun: The unique contribution of educational leisure experiences. *Curator,* 49(3), 329–344.

35. Beard, J.G. & Maunier, R. (1980). Measuring leisure satisfaction. *Journal of Leisure Research,* 12, 20–33.

36. Holmes, L. (2000). Reframing learning: Performance, identity and practice. Presented at *Critical Contributions to Managing and Learning: 2nd Connecting Learning and Critique Conference,* Lancaster University, July 2000.

37. Falk, J.H. & Storksdieck, M. (in press). Science learning in a leisure setting. *Journal of Research in Science Teaching.*

38. Rounds, J. (2006). Doing identity work in museums. *Curator,* 49(2), 133–150.

39. Vygotsky, L. (1978). *Mind in society: The development of higher mental processes.* Cambridge, MA: Harvard University Press.

40. Penuel, W. & Wertsch, J. (1995). Vygotsky and identity formation: A sociocultural approach. *Educational Psychologist,* 30(2), 83–92.

41. Lave, J., & Wenger, E. (1991). *Situated learning. Legitimate peripheral participation.* Cambridge, U.K.: Cambridge University Press, p. 115.

42. Wenger, E. (1998). *Communities of practice: Learning, meaning, and identity.* Cambridge: Cambridge University Press, p. 239.

43. Ellenbogen, K. (2003). *From dioramas to the dinner table: An ethnographic case study of the role of science museums in family life.* Unpublished doctoral dissertation. Vanderbilt University, Nashville.

44. Falk, J.H. & Storksdieck, M. (2004). *A Multi-Factor Investigation of Variables Affecting Informal Science Learning.* Final Report to the National Science Foundation. Annapolis, MD: Institute for Learning Innovation.

    Falk, J.H. & Storksdieck, M. (2006). *Investigating the Long Term Impact of a Science Center on Its Community.* Final Report to the National Science Foundation. Annapolis, MD: Institute for Learning Innovation.

    Falk, J.H. & Storksdieck, M. (2005). Using the *Contextual Model of Learning* to understand visitor learning from a science center exhibition. *Science Education,* 89, 744–778.

    Falk, J.H. & Storksdieck, M. (in press). Science learning in a leisure setting. *Journal of Research in Science Teaching.*

    Falk, J.H. (2006). An identity-centered approach to understanding museum learning. *Curator,* 49(2), 151–166.

45. It should be noted for those who might have been following my writings on this subject for the past couple of years that I've relabeled the final category

from Spiritual Pilgrims to Rechargers. In so doing, I've bowed to the persistent and legitimate concerns raised by friends and critics alike, accepting that my own very secular view of "spirituality" and "pilgrim" are not universally shared. I believe the term "Recharger" better captures the visitor motivations I wish to convey.

CHAPTER 3

1. Goffman, E. (1959). *The presentation of self in everyday life.* New York: Doubleday, p. 75.
2. Packer, J. & Ballantyne, R. (2002). Motivational factors and the visitor experience: A comparison of three sites. *Curator*, 45, 183–198.
   Ballantyne, R., Packer, J. & Hughes, K. (2008). Environmental awareness, interests and motives of botanic gardens visitors: Implications for inter-pretive practice. *Tourism Management*, 29, 439–444.
3. Kaplan, S. (1995). The restorative benefits of nature: Toward an integrative framework. *Journal of Environmental Psychology*, 15, 169–182.
4. Kant, I. (1781/1997). *Critique of pure reason.* Cambridge: Cambridge University Press.
5. James, W. (1890). *Principles of psychology, Vol I & II.* New York: Holt.
6. James, W. (1890). p. 205.
7. Ashmore, R.D. & Jussim, L. (1997). Self and identity: Fundamental issues. In: R.D. Ashmore & L. Jussim (Eds.). *Rutgers series on self and social identity* (Vol. 1). Oxford: Oxford University Press.
   Baumeister, R. F. (1999.) The nature and structure of the self: An overview. In: *The Self in Social Psychology*, R. F. Baumeister, ed., 1–20. London: Psychology Press.
   Bruner, J. & Kalmar, D. (1998). Narrative and meta-narrative in the construction of self. In: *Self-Awareness: Its Nature and Development*, M. Ferrari and R. J. Sternberg, (eds.), 308–331. New York: The Guildford Press.
   Gee, J.P. (2001). Identity as an analytic lens for research in education. *Review of Research in Education*, 25, 99–125.
   McAdams, D. (1990). *The Person: An Introduction to Personality Psychology.* Orlando, FL: Harcourt Brace Jovanovich.
   Rounds, J. (2006). Doing identity work in museums. *Curator,* 49 (2), 133–150.
   Simon, B. (2004). *Identity in modern society: A social psychological perspective.* Oxford, UK: Blackwell. Wenger, 1998.
   Woodward, K. (2002). *Understanding identity.* London: Arnold.
8. Bruner, J. & Kalmar, (1998), p. 326.
9. Simon, B. (2004), p. 3.
10. Bronfenbrenner, U. (1979). *The Ecology of Human Development.* Cambridge, MA: Harvard University Press.
    Holland, D., Lachicotte, Jr., W., Skinner, D. & Cain, C. (1998). *Identity and*

Agency in Cultural Worlds. Cambridge: Harvard University Press.
Simon, (2004).

11. Gee, J.P. (2001). Identity as an analytic lens for research in education. *Review of Research in Education*, 25, 99–125.

Hall, S. (1992). The question of cultural identity. In: S. Hall & T. McGrew (eds.), *Modernity and its futures* (pp. 273–326). Cambridge: Polity Press.

Wenger, F. (1998). *Communities of practice: Learning, meaning, and identity.* Cambridge: Cambridge University Press.

Woodward, K. (2002). *Understanding identity.* London: Arnold.

12. Though most psychologists stop at these three "social science" levels of analysis, I'd suggest that there are also human "selves" at the "biological" level as well. These "selves" include our organs, tissues, and even the cells of our bodies; all of which have individual identities, all of which collectively influence our behaviors.

13. Bruner & Kalmar (1998). Narrative and meta-narrative in the construction of self. In: *Self-Awareness: Its Nature and Development,* M. Ferrari and R. J. Sternberg, (eds.), 308–331. New York: The Guildford Press.

Neisser, U. (1988). Five kinds of self-knowledge. *Philosophical Psychology* 1: 35–59.

14. Dweck, C. (2000). *Self-Theories: Their role in motivation, personality and development.* New York: Psychology Press.

15. cf., Cooper, C. R. (1999). Multiple selves, multiple worlds: Cultural perspectives on individuality and connectedness in adolescence development. In: A. Masten, (ed.), *Minnesota Symposium on Child Psychology: Cultural Processes in Development*, 25–57. Mahwah, NJ: Lawrence Erlbaum Associates.

McAdams, D. (1990). *The Person: An Introduction to Personality Psychology.* Orlando, FL: Harcourt Brace Jovanovich.

16. Calvin, W. H. (1997). *How Brains Think.* New York: Basic Books.

17. Was Macht eigentlich Martina Navratilova? (1996), *Stern*, 44, 250; translated by B. Simon (2004) 74.

18. Bruner, J. (1994). The 'remembered' self. In: U. Neisser & R. Fivush (eds.), *The remembering self: Construction and accuracy in the self-narrative,* pp. 41-54. New York: Cambridge University Press.

deCharms, R. (1968). *Personal causation: The internal affective determinants of behavior.* New York: Academic Press.

Simon, (2004).

19. Fiske, S.T. & Taylor, S.E. (1991). *Social cognition* (2nd ed.). New York: McGraw Hill.

Hoyle, R.H., Kernis, M.H., Leary, M.R. & Baldwin, M.W. (1999). *Selfhood: Identity, esteem, regulation.* Boulder, CO: Westview Press.

Maurus, H. & Wurf, E. (1987). The dynamic self-concept: A social psychological perspective. In: M. R. Rosenzweig & L.W. Porter (eds.), *Annual Review of Psychology*, 38, 299–337.

20. Higgins, E.T. (1987). Self-discrepancy: A theory relating self and affect.

Psychological Review, 94, 319–340.

Markus, H. & Nurius, P. (*1986*). Possible selves. *American Psychologist,* 41, 954–969.

21. Bandura, A. (1995). Introduction. In: A. Bandura (ed.), *Self-efficacy in changing societies.* New York: Cambridge University Press, p. 2.

22. For a reasonable overview of this remarkable body of work, I recommend two recent works by Bandura:

    Bandura, A. (1997). *Self-efficacy: The exercise of control.* New York: Freeman.

    Bandura, A. (2002). Growing primacy of human agency in adaptation and change in the electronic era. *European Psychologist,* 7, 2–16.

23. Stryker, S. (1987). The vitalization of Symbolic Interactionism. *Social Psychology Quarterly,* 50, 83–94.

24. Stryker, S. & Burke, P.J. (2000). The past, present, and future of an identity theory. *Social Psychology Quarterly,* 63, 284–297.

25. Bem, D.J. (1972) Self-perception theory. In: L. Berkowitz (ed.), *Advances in experimental social psychology* (Vol. 6. pp. 1–62). New York: Academic Press.

26. Simon, B. (2004). *Identity in modern society: A social psychological perspective.* Oxford, UK: Blackwell.

27. Simon, (2004), p. 45.

28. Linville, P.W. (1985). Self-complexity and affective extremity: don't put all your eggs in one cognitive basket. *Social Cognition,* 3, 94–120.

    Linville, P.W. (1987). Self-complexity as a cognitive buffer against stress-related illness and depression. *Journal of Personality and Social Psychology* 52, 663–676.

29. Linville, P.W. (1985). Self-complexity and affective extremity: don't put all your eggs in one cognitive basket. *Social Cognition,* 3, 94-120.

    Linville, (1987).

30. Simon, (2004), p. 46.

31. Simon, B. (1997). Self and group in modern society: Ten theses on the individual self and collective self. In: R. Spears, P.J. Oakes, N. Ellemera & S.A. Haslam (eds.), *The social psychology of stereotyping and group life* (pp. 318–335). Oxford, England: Basil Blackwell.

    Simon, B. (1998). Individuals, groups, and social change: On the relationship between individual and collective self-interpretations and collective action. In: C. Sedikides, J. Schopler & C, Insko (eds.) *Intergroup cognition and intergroup behavior* (pp. 257–282). Mahwah, NJ: Lawrence Erlbaum.

    Simon, B. (1999). A place in the world: Self and social categorization. In: T,R. Tyler, R.M. Kramer & O.P. John (eds.), *The psychology of the social self* (pp. 47–49). Mahwah, NJ: Lawrence Erlbaum.

    Simon, B. & Oakes, P. (2006). Beyond dependence: An identity approach to social power and domination. *Human Relations,* 59, 105–139.

32. Cantor, N., Mischel, W. & Schwarz, J. (1982). A prototype analysis of psychological situations. *Cognitive Psychology* 14: 45–77.

Schutte, N.S., Kenrick, D.T. & Sadalla, E.K. (1985). The search for predictable settings: Situational prototypes, constraint, and behavioral variation. *Journal of Personality and Social Psychology,* 51, 459–462.

33. Dweck, C. (2000). *Self-Theories: Their role in motivation, personality and development.* New York: Psychology Press.

34. Wegner, D.M. (2002). *The illusion of conscious will.* Cambridge, MA: MIT Press.

Edelman, G. & Tononi, G. (2000). Reentry and the dynamic core. In: T. Metzinger (ed.), *Neural correlates of consciousness: Empirical and conceptual questions,* pp. 121–138. Cambridge, MA: MIT Press.

Freeman, W. (2000). *How brains make up their mind.* New York: Columbia University Press.

35. cf., Galaburda & Kosslyn, S.M. (2002). *Languages of the brain.* Cambridge, MA: Harvard University Press.

Lieberman, P. (2000). *Human language and our reptilian brain: The subcortical bases of speech, syntax and thought.* Cambridge, MA: Harvard University Press.

Pinker, S. *The language instinct.* New York: Harper Collins.

36. Gutman, J. (1979). A means-end chain model based on consumer categorization processes. *Journal of Marketing* 46(2), 60–72.

Reynolds, T.J. & Gutman, J. (1984). Laddering: Extending the Repertory Grid Methodology to construct attribute-consequence-value hierarchies. In: *Personal Values and Consumer Psychology,* Vol II., R. Pitts and A. Woodside (eds.). Lexington, MA: Lexington Books.

37. Falk, J.H., Heimlich, J. & Bronnenkant, K. (2008). Using identity-related visit motivations as a tool for understanding adult zoo and aquarium visitor's meaning making. *Curator,* 51(1), 55–80.

38. Heimlich, J., Bronnenkant, K., Witgert, N. & Falk, J.H. (2004). *Measuring the Learning Outcomes of Adult Visitors to Zoos and Aquariums: Confirmatory Study.* Technical report. Bethesda, MD: American Association of Zoos and Aquariums.

39. Storksdieck, M. & Stein, J. (2007). *Using the visitor identity-related motivations scale to improve visitor experiences at the US Botanic Garden.* Paper presented at the Annual Meeting of the Visitor's Studies Association, July 19, 2007, Toronto, Canada.

Nickels, A.L. (2008). *An Exploration of Visitors' Conservation Attitudes, Expectations, and Motivations at Three Informal Education Institutions in Newport, Oregon.* Unpublished Master's Thesis. Corvallis, OR: Oregon State University.

Stein, J. (2007). *Adapting the visitor identity-related motivations scale for living history sites.* Paper presented at the Annual Meeting of the Visitor's Studies Association, July 19, 2007, Toronto, Canada.

40. J. Koke, personal communication, August 2008.
41. M. Storksdieck, personal communication, July 2008.
42. del Bosque, I. R. & Martin, H.S. (2008). Tourist satisfaction: A cognitive-affective model. *Annals of Tourism Research*, 35(2), 551–573.

CHAPTER 4

1. Hall, E.T. (1966). *The hidden dimension*. New York: Doubleday, p. 63.
2. For more information on the importance and role of advance organizers, see Falk & Dierking (2000), p. 117, 196–198.
3. Falk & Dierking, (1992; 2000).
4. For more information on these and other in-museum influences I would refer the reader to edited volume: Falk, J.H., Dierking, L.D. & Foutz, S. (2007). (eds.), *In Principle-In Practice: Museums as Learning Institutions*. Lanham, MD: AltaMira Press.
5. cf., Leinhardt, G., Crowley, K. & Knutson, K. (Eds.) (2002). *Learning conversations in museums*. Mahwah, NJ: Earlbaum.
   Falk, J.H. & Adelman, L.M. (2003). Investigating the impact of prior knowledge, experience and interest on aquarium visitor learning. *Journal of Research in Science Teaching*, 40(2), 163–176.
   Falk & Storksdieck, (2005).
6. Falk, J.H. & Balling, J.D. (1980). The school field trip: Where you go makes the difference. *Science and Children*, 18(3), 6–8.
   Maestro, R.H., Gallego, P.M. & Requejo, L.S. (2007). The moderating role of familiarity in rural tourism in Spain. *Tourism Management, 28,* 951–964.
7. Timmer, J. (2007). Product loyalty: consumers mistake familiarity with superiority. Ars techinica. http://arstechnica.com/news.ars/post/20070605-product-loyalty-consumers-mistake-familiarity-with-superiority.html
8. Tom Krakauer, 1999. Personal communication.
9. Falk & Storksdieck, (2005).
   Falk, J.H. (2008). Identity and the art museum visitor. *Journal of Art Education*, 34(2), 25–34.
   Falk, J.H., Heimlich, J. & Bronnenkant, K. (2008). Using identity-related visit motivations as a tool for understanding adult zoo and aquarium visitor's meaning making. *Curator*, 51(1), 55–80.
   Falk, J.H. & Storksdieck, M. (in press). Science learning in a leisure setting. *Journal of Research in Science Teaching*.
10. My assumptions about the content of the exhibition are based upon looking up the exhibition online (http://www.nga.gov/exhibitions/2007/hopper/hopper_brochure.pdf) as well as fleshing out this view with comments provided about the exhibition by Mara's partner, who I also interviewed.
11. See review by Bitgood, S. & Patterson, D. (1995). Principles of exhibit design. *Visitor Behavior*, 2(1), 4–6.
12. Serrell, B. (1998). *Paying attention: Visitors and museum exhibitions*.

Washington, DC: American Association of Museums.
13. Falk & Storksdieck, (2005).
14. Falk & Dierking, (1992; 2000).

Ellenbogen, K.M., Luke, J.J. & Dierking, L.D. (2007). Family learning research in museums: Perspectives on a decade of research. In: Falk, J.H., Dierking, L.D. & Foutz, S. (eds.), *In Principle, In Practice: Museums as Learning Institutions*. Lanham, MD: AltaMira Press.

15. Dierking, L.D. &. Falk, J.H. (1994). Family behavior and learning in informal science settings: A review of the research. *Science Education*, 78(1), 57–72.

Falk & Dierking, (2000).

16. Falk & Dierking, (2000).
17. Matusov, E. & Rogoff, B. (1995). Evidence of development from people's participation in communities of learners. In: J. Falk & L. Dierking (eds.), *Public Institutions for Personal Learning*, pp. 97–104. Washington, DC: American Association of Museums, p. 100.
18. Falk & Storksdieck, (2005).
19. Rounds, J. (2004). Strategies for the curiosity-driven museum visitor. *Curator*, 47(4), 389–412.
20. Rounds (2004), p. 389.
21. The challenge remains accurately gauging what an individual's entering identity-related motivation is. This is where we get into trouble doing this task pro-actively rather than retroactively. Retroactively, it is easy to see where an individual's tendencies lay. Pro-actively is much more challenging in large part because for many people, their true motivations lie below the level of consciousness and thus beyond their ability to articulate, let alone "know" their true feelings.

CHAPTER 5

1. Lewis, C.S. (1933). *The Pilgrim's Regress, Book 7*. Grand Rapids, MI: Eardmans. p. 128.
2. Barry, L. & Parasuraman, A. (1991). *Marketing services: Competing through quality*. New York: The Free Press.
3. Lee, B.K. & Shafer, C.S. (2002). The dynamic nature of leisure experience: An application of Affect Control Theory. *Journal of Leisure Research*, 34(2), 290–310.

Lee, B.K., Shafer, C.S. & Kang, I. (2005). Examining relationships among perceptions of self, episode-specific evaluations, and overall satisfaction with a leisure activity. *Leisure Sciences*, 27, 93–109.

Mannell, R. & Iso-Ahola, S.E. (1987). Psychological nature of leisure and tourism experience. *Annals of Tourism Research*, 14, 314–331.

Stewart, W.P. (1998). Leisure as multiphase experiences: Challenging traditions. *Journal of Leisure Research*, 30(4), 391–400.

Stewart, W.P. & Hull IV, B.R. (1992). Satisfaction of what? Post hoc versus

real-time construct validity. *Leisure Sciences,* 14, 195–209.
4. Graefe, A.R. & Fedler, A.J. (1986). Situational and subjective determinants of satisfaction in marine recreational fishing. *Leisure Sciences,* 8, 275–295.
    Whisman, S.A. & Hollenhorst, S.J. (1998). A path model of whiteriver boating satisfaction on the Cheat River of West Virginia. *Environmental Management,* 22(1), 109–117.
5. Lee, B.K., Shafer, C.S. & Kang, I. (2005). Examining relationships among perceptions of self, episode-specific evaluations, and overall satisfaction with a leisure activity. *Leisure Sciences,* 27, 93–109.
6. e.g., del Bosque, R., Martın, H.S. & Collado, J. (2006). The role of expectations in the consumer satisfaction formation process: Empirical evidence in the travel agency sector. *Tourism Management,* 27, 410–419.
    del Bosque, I. R. & Martin, H.S. (2008). Tourist satisfaction: A cognitive-affective model. *Annals of Tourism Research,* 35 (2), 551–573.
    Yoon, Y. & Uysal, M. (2005). An examination of the effects of motivation and satisfaction on destination loyalty: A structural model. *Tourism Management,* 26, 45–56.
7. del Bosque, I.R. & Martin, H.S. (2008). Tourist satisfaction: A cognitive-affective model. *Annals of Tourism Research,* 35 (2), 551–573.
8. Harmon-Jones, E. & Mills, J. (1999). *Cognitive Dissonance: Progress on a Pivotal Theory in Social Psychology.* Washington, DC: American Psychological Association.
9. Merton, R.K. (1957). Social theory and social structure, revised edition. New York: Free Press.
10. e.g., Finn, P. (2006). Bias and blinding: Self-fulfilling prophecies and intentional ignorance. *The ASHA Leader,* 11(8), 16–17, 22.
    Jussim, L. & Harber, K.D. (2005). Teacher expectations and self-fulfilling prophecies: Knowns and unknowns, resolved and unresolved controversies. *Personality and Social Psychology Review,* 9, 131–155.
    Madon, S., Guyll, M., Spoth, R.L., Cross, S.E. & Hilbert, S.J. (2003). The self-fulfilling influence of mother expectations on children's underage drinking. *Journal of Personality and Social Psychology,* 84, 1188–1205.
    Wong, J.T. & Hui, E.C.M. (2006). Power of expectations. *Property Management,* 24, 496–506.

CHAPTER 6

1. James, W. (1890), p. 645.
2. Falk, J.H. & Dierking, L.D. (1997) School field trips: Assessing their long-term impact. *Curator,* 40(3), 211–218.
3. Anderson, D., Storksdieck, M. & Spock, M. (2006). Long-term impacts of museum experiences. In: J. Falk, L. Dierking and S. Foutz (eds.) *In Principle, In Practice,* pp. 197–216, Lanham, MD: AltaMira Press.
4. Medved, M., & Oatley, K. (2000). Memories and scientific literacy:

Remembering exhibits from a science centre. *International Journal of Science Education,* 22(10), 1117–1132.
5. Falk, J.H., Scott, C., Dierking, L.D., Rennie, L.J. & Cohen Jones, M. (2004). Interactives and visitor learning. *Curator,* 47(2), 171–198.
6. McGaugh, J.L. (2003). *Memory & emotion: The making of lasting memories.* New York: Columbia University Press.
7. McGaugh, J.L. (2003).
8. Edelman, (1987).
9. Anderson, J.R. (1983). *The architecture of cognition.* Cambridge, MA: Harvard University Press.
  Baddeley, A. (1994). *Human memory: Theory and practice.* Hillsdale, NJ: Erlbaum.
  Barclay, Craig R. & Wellman, Henry M. (1986). Accuracies and inaccuracies in autobiographical memories. *Journal of Memory and Language,* 25(1), 93–103.
  McClelland, J.L. & Rumelhart, D.E. (1985). Distributed memory and the representation of general and specific information. *Journal of Experimental Psychology,* 114, 159–188.
  Neisser, U. & Hyman, Jr., I.E. (1999). *Memory observed: Remembering in natural contexts,* 2nd Edition. New York: Macmillan.
  Rumelhart, D.E., Hinton, G.E. & McClelland, J.L. (1986). A general framework for parallel distributed processing. In: D.E.Rumelhart, J.L. McClelland & the PDP Research Group (eds.), *Parallel distributed processing: Explorations in the microstructure of cognition* (Vol. 1, pp. 45–76). Cambridge, MA: MIT Press.
10. Geertz, C. (1973). *The interpretation of cultures.* New York: Basic Books.
11. cf., Olson, S. (2002). *Mapping human history: Genes, race, and our common origins.* Boston: Mariner Books.
12. Anzai, Y. & Yokohama, T. (1984). Internal models in physics problem solving. *Cognition and Instruction,* 1, 397–450.
  Chi, M.T.H., Feltovich, P.J. & Glaser, R. (1980). Categorization and representation of physics problems by novices and experts. *Cognitive Science,* 5, 121–152.
  Larkin, J.H. (1983). The role of problem representation in physics. In: D. Gentner & A.L. Stevens (eds.), *Mental models.* Hillsdale, NJ: Earlbaum.
  Trowbridge, D. & McDermott, L. (1980). Investigation of student understanding of the concept of velocity in one dimension. *American Journal of Physics,* 50, 242–253.
13. Vroom, V. (1964). *Work and Motivation.* New York: John Wiley & Sons.
14. e.g., Porter, L.W. & Lawler, E.E. (1968). *Managerial attitude and performance.* Homewood, IL: Irwin-Dorsey.
  deCharms, R. (1968). *Personal Causation: The Internal Affective Determinants of Behavior.* New York, NY: Academic Press.

Pinder, C.C. 1984. *Work Motivation: Theory, Issues, and Applications.* Glenview, IL: Scott, Foresman and Company.

15. Oliver, R. L. (1980). A cognitive model of the antecedents and consequences of satisfaction decisions. *Journal of Marketing Research,* 17, 460–469.

16. del Bosque & Martin, (2008).

17. The same phenomenon goes by the name "Hawthorne Effect"; a term coined in 1955 by Henry A. Landsberger when analyzing older experiments from 1924-1932 GE's Hawthorne Works.

18. Moerman, Daniel E. (2002). *Meaning, Medicine and the 'Placebo Effect.'* Cambridge, UK: Cambridge University Press.

    Price, D.D., Chung, S.K. & Robinson, M.E. (2005). Conditioning, expectation, and desire for relief in placebo analgesia. *Seminars in Pain Medicine* 3(1), 15–21.

    Thompson, W. Grant. (2005). *The Placebo Effect and Health-Combining Science and Compassionate Care.* New York: Prometheus.

19. Leuchter, A.F. (2002). Changes in brain function of depressed subjects during treatment with Placebo. *American Journal of Psychiatry,* 159, 122–129.

    Mayberg, H., Silva, A., Brannan, S.K., Tekell, J.L., Mahurin, R.K., McGinis, S. & Jerbek, P. (2002). The functional neuroanatomy of the placebo effect. *American Journal of Psychiatry,* 159, 728–737.

20. Kelly, J.R. (1983). *Leisure identities and interactions.* London: George Allen & Unwin.

21. McGaugh, (2003).

22. Bandura, A. (1989). Regulation of cognitive processes through perceived self-efficacy. *Developmental Psychology,* 25(5), 729–35.

    deCharms, R. (1968). *Personal causation: The internal affective determinants of behavior.* New York: Academic Press.

    Dweck, C. (2000). *Self-Theories: Their role in motivation, personality and development.* New York: Psychology Press.

    McCombs, B.L. (1991). Motivation and lifelong learning. *Educational Psychologist* 26(2), 117–127.

    Pearson, J. & Platt, M. (2008). Decision-making in the brain: Eavesdropping on neurons. *Scientific American,* August 5, 2008, (no page number), http://www.sciam.com/article.cfm?id=decision-making-in-brain&sc=rss

23. Pearson & Platt, (2008).

24. Perry, D. (1989). *The creation and verification of a developmental model for the design of a museum exhibit.* Unpublished doctoral dissertation. Indiana University.

25. Salami, H. (1998). *Motivation and meaningful science learning in informal settings.* Paper presented at the annual meeting of the National Association for Research in Science Teaching, April, San Diego, CA.

26. Rennie, L.J. & McClafferty, T.P. (1995). Using visits to interactive science

and technology centers, museums, aquaria, and zoos to promote learning in science. *Journal of Science Teacher Education*, 6(4), 175–185.

27. Griffin, J. (1998). *School-museum integrated learning experiences in science: A learning journey*. Unpublished doctoral dissertation. University of Technology, Sydney.

28. Griffin, (1998).

29. It is worth noting that recent research in Israel has shown that children on field trips seemingly can be given too much freedom as well. Researchers Yael Bamburger and Tali Tal found that providing children with some structure seemed to facilitate children's cognitive learning better than no structure at all or too many choices. Bamberger, Y. & Tali, T. (2007). Learning in a personal context: Levels of choice in a free choice learning environment in science and natural history museums. *Science Education*, 91(1), 75–95.

30. Falk, J.H. (2000). *An investigation of the educational impact of a science center high-entertainment, multi-media theater experience*. Unpublished Technical Report. Annapolis, MD: Institute for Learning Innovation.

31. Unfortunately, I don't currently have the data to support this statement, but it makes me want to collect it to see if it's true!

32. Sylwester, (1995); Calvin, (1997).

33. Calvin, (1997); Pearson & Platt, (2008).

34. Sylwester, (1995).

35. Rose, S. (1993). *The Making of Memory: From Molecules to Mind*. New York: Anchor Books/Doubleday.
    Hilts, P.J. (1995). *Memory's Ghost: The Strange Tale of Mr. M. and the Nature of Memory*. New York, NY: Simon & Schuster.
    Sylwester, (1995).

36. Rose, (1993); Sylwester, (1995).

37. Aggleton, J.P., (ed.), (1992). *The Amygdala: Neurological aspects of emotion, memory, and mental dysfunction*. New York: Wiley-Liss.

38. Damasio, A.R. (1994). *Descartes' Error: Emotion, Reasons, and the Human Brain*. New York: Avon Books.
    Piaget, J. (ed. and trans.), (1981). Intelligence and affectivity. Their relationship during child development. *Annual Reviews Monograph*. Palo Alto, CA: Annual Reviews.

39. Damasio, (1994).

40. Ben-Ze'ev, A. (2000). *The subtlety of emotions*. Cambridge, MA: MIT Press.
    Sylwester, (1995); Damasio, (1994).

41. Csikzentmihalyi, M. & Hermanson, K. (1995). Intrinsic motivation in museums: Why does one want to learn? In: J. Falk & L. Dierking (Eds.), *Public institutions for personal learning*. Washington, DC: American Association of Museums.

42. Lazarus, R.S. (1966). *Psychological stress and the coping process*. New York: McGraw-Hill, p. 16.

43. Turner, J.H. (2000). *On the origins of human emotions: A sociological inquiry into the evolution of human affect.* Stanford, CA: Stanford University Press, p. 59.

44. McGaugh, (2003).

45. Falk, J.H. & Gillespie, K. (in review). Measuring the relationship between emotion and learning in free-choice setting. *Science Education.*

46. Russell, J.A., Weiss, A. & Mendelsohn, G.A. (1989). Affect grid: a single-item scale of pleasure and arousal. *Journal of Personality and Social Psychology,* 57(3), 493–502.

47. Russell, J.A. (1979). Affective space is bipolar. *Journal of Personality and Social Psychology,* 37(3), 345–356.

48. cf., Falk, J.H. (2003). Personal Meaning Mapping. In: G. Caban, C. Scott, J. Falk & L. Dierking, (eds.), *Museums and Creativity: A study into the role of museums in design education,* pp. 10–18. Sydney, AU: Powerhouse Publishing.

49. Damasio, (1993).

50. Damasio, (1993).

51. According to Edelman, (1985), this is why dreams seem so nonsensical, it is because they are—dreams are mental patterns created in the absence of meaning-making external context.

52. Csikzentmihalyi & Hermanson, (1995).

    Clifford, G. (1981). The past is prologue. In: K. Cirincione-Coles (ed.), *The Future of Education: Policy Issues and Challenges.* Beverly Hills, CA: Sage Publications.

    Csikzentmihalyi, M. & LeFevre, J. (1989). Optimal experience in work and leisure. *Journal of Personality and Social Psychology* 56 (5): 815–822.

    Ellis, G.D., J.E. Voelkl & C. Morris. (1994). Measurement and analysis issues with explanation of variance in daily experience using the Flow model. *Journal of Leisure Research* 26(4), 337–356.

53. Csikzentmihalyi, M. (1975). *Beyond Boredom and Anxiety.* San Fransisco: Jossey-Bass.

    Csikzentmihalyi, M. (1990b). Literacy and intrinsic motivation. *Daedalus,* 119(2), 115–40.

54. Rohrkemper, M. & Corno, L. (1988). Success and failure on classroom tasks: Adaptive learning and classroom teaching. *Elementary School Journal,* 88, 297–312.

    Csikzentmihalyi & Hermanson, (1995).

55. Csikzentmihalyi & Hermanson, (1995), p. 70.

56. Rounds, (2006). p. 138.

57. Rounds, (2006), p.

CHAPTER 8

1. Lewin, K. (1951). *Field theory in social science; selected theoretical papers.* D. Cartwright (ed.). New York: Harper & Row, p. 169.

2. Falk, J.H. & Sheppard, B. (2006). *Thriving in the knowledge age: New business*

models for museums and other cultural organizations. Lanham, MD: AltaMira Press.

3. Treacy, M. & Wiersema, F. (1995). The discipline of market leaders. New York: Basic Books.

4. Falk & Sheppard, (2006).

CHAPTER 9

1. Falk, J.H. & Coulson, D. (2000). *Preliminary Analysis of Second Telephone Survey California Science Center L.A.S.E.R. Project.* Technical Report. Annapolis: Institute for Learning Innovation.

    Falk, J.H. & Needham, M. (in prep). Analysis of the Third Telephone Survey of the California Science Center.

2. cf., Adams, G.D. (1989). *The process and effects of word-of-mouth communication at a history museum.* Unpublished master's thesis, Boston University, Boston, MA.

    Bosman, J. (2006). Advertising is obsolete. Everyone says so. Business, *New York Times*, January 23.

    McLean, F. (1997). *Marketing the museum.* London: Routledge.

3. Packer, J. (2006). Learning for fun: The unique contribution of educational leisure experiences. *Curator*, 49, 329–344.

4. Falk, J.H. unpublished data.

5. Falk, J.H. unpublished data.

6. Falk, J.H. unpublished data.

7. Falk, J.H. unpublished data.

8. Falk, J.H. unpublished data.

9. Falk, J.H & Storksdieck, M. unpublished data.

10. Packer, (2006).

11. Falk, J.H. & Storksdieck, M. unpublished data.

12. Falk, J.H. unpublished data.

13. Falk, J.H. unpublished data.

14. Falk, J.H. unpublished data.

15. Falk, J.H. & Storksdieck, M. unpublished data.

16. And of course those who know me, know that I wear my "Spy" hat everywhere I go; so I must be "cool" too!

17. Falk, J.H. & Storksdieck, M. unpublished data.

18. Falk, J.H. unpublished data.

19. Packer, J. (2008). *Museums as restorative environments.* Paper presented at the Visitor Studies Association. Houston, TX, July 18, 2008.

    Ballantyne, R., Packer, J. & Hughes, K. (2008). Environmental awareness, interests and motives of botanic gardens visitors: Implications for interpretive practice. *Tourism Management*, 29, 439–444.

    Bennett, E.S. & Swasey, J.E. (1996). Perceived stress reduction in urban public gardens. *HortTechnology*, 6(2), 125–128.

    Kaplan, S. (1995). The restorative benefits of nature: Toward an integrative framework. *Journal of Environmental Psychology*, 15, 169–182.

20. Falk, J.H. unpublished data.
21. Packer, J. (2008). *Museums as restorative environments.* Paper presented at the Visitor Studies Association. Houston, TX, July 18, 2008.
22. Falk, J.H. & Dierking, L.D. (2000). *Learning from Museums.* Lanham, MD: AltaMira Press.
23. It should be noted, there were longstanding reasons for limited African American use of the VMFA, much of it related to long term discrimination and racism in Richmond.
24. Dierking, L.D., Adams, M. & Spencer-Etienne, M. (1996). *Final Report: Lila Wallace/Reader's Digest Audience Development, Virginia Museum of Fine Arts.* Unpublished Technical Report. Annapolis, MD: SLi.

CHAPTER 10

1. As quoted in Weil, S.E. (2002). *Making museums matter.* Washington, DC: Smithsonian Institution Press, p. 206.
2. Bandura, A. (1986). *Social foundation of thought and action: A social cognitive theory.* Englewood Cliffs, NJ: Prentice Hall. See also discussion in Chapter 3.
   Bandura, A. (1997). *Self-efficacy: The exercise of control.* New York: Freeman.
3. Zeldin, A.L., Britner, S.L. & Pajares, F. (2008). A comparative study of the self-efficacy beliefs of successful men and women in mathematics, science and technology careers. *Journal of Research in Science Teaching,* 45, 1036–1058.
4. Falk & Dierking, (2000).
5. Falk & Storksdieck, (2005).
6. Falk & Sheppard, (2006).
7. Falk, J.H. (1997). Testing a museum exhibition design assumption: Effect of explicit labeling of exhibit clusters on visitor concept development. *Science Education,* 81(6), 679–688.
8. Borun, M., Chamber, M.B., Dritsas, J. & Johnson, J.I. (1997). Enhancing family learning through exhibits. *Curator,* 40(4), 279–295.
9. www.Disneyinstitute.com
10. Morris Hargreaves McIntyre (2004). *Tate through visitor's eyes.* Technical Report. Manchester, UK: Morris Hargreaves McIntyre.
11. cf., Falk & Dierking, (1992; 2000).
12. Luke, J.J., Dierking, L.D. & Falk, J.H. (2001). *The Children's Museum of Indianapolis Family Learning Initiative: Phase I Baseline Report.* Unpublished technical report. Annapolis, MD: Institute for Learning Innovation.

CHAPTER 11

1. Weil, S.E. (2002). *Making museums matter.* Washington, DC: Smithsonian Institution Press, p. vii.
2. Falk, J.H. & Sheppard, B. (2006). *Thriving in the knowledge age: New business models for museums and other cultural institutions.* Lanham, MD: AltaMira

Press.

Falk, J.H. & Dierking, L.D. (2008). Re-envisioning success in the cultural sector. *Cultural Trends*, 17(4), 233–246.

3. I would recommend *Thriving in the Knowledge Age* (Falk & Sheppard, 2006) and its extensive bibliography for those interested in pursuing more information on these two issues.

4. cf., Holden, J. (2006). Cultural value and the crisis of legitimacy: Why culture needs a democratic mandate. London: Demos. http://www.demos.co.uk/files/Culturalvalueweb.pdf

5. Weil, S.E. (1999). From being *about* something to being *for* somebody: The ongoing transformation of the American Museum. *Daedalus*, 28(3), 229–258.

REFERENCES

Adams, G.D. (1989). *The process and effects of word-of-mouth communication at a history museum.* Unpublished master's thesis, Boston University, Boston, MA.

Aggleton, J.P., (Ed.) (1992). *The Amygdala: Neurological aspects of emotion, memory, and mental dysfunction.* New York: Wiley-Liss.

Aguiar, M. & Hurst, E. (2006). *Measuring Trends in Leisure: The Allocation of Time over Five Decades*, Working Paper No. 06–2. Boston: Federal Reserve Bank of Boston.

American Association of Museums. (1992). *Data report: From the 1989 national museum survey.* Washington, DC: American Association of Museums.

American Museum of Natural History. (1986). Visitor profiles. Unpublished report.

Anderson, D., Storksdieck, M. & Spock, M. (2006). Long-term impacts of museum experiences. In: J. Falk, L. Dierking, and S. Foutz (eds.), *In Principle, In Practice*, pp. 197–216. Lanham, MD: AltaMira Press.

Anderson, J.R. (1983). *The architecture of cognition.* Cambridge, MA: Harvard University Press.

Anzai, Y. & Yokohama, T. (1984). Internal models in physics problem solving. *Cognition and Instruction*, 1, 397–450.

Ashmore, R.D. & Jussim, L. (1997). Self and identity: Fundamental issues. In: R.D. Ashmore & L. Jussim (eds.), *Rutgers series on self and social identity* (Vol. 1). Oxford: Oxford University Press.

Baddeley, A. (1994). *Human memory: Theory and practice.* Hillsdale, NJ: Erlbaum.

Ballantyne, R., Packer, J. & Hughes, K. (2008). Environmental awareness, interests and motives of botanic gardens visitors: Implications for interpretive practice. *Tourism Management*, 29, 439–444.

Balling, J.D. & Cornell, E.A. (1985). *Family visitors to science-technology centers: Motivations and demographics.* (Grant No. SED–8112927). Washington, DC: National Science Foundation.

Bamberger, Y. & Tal, T. (2007). Learning in a personal context: Levels of choice in a free choice learning environment in science and natural history museums. *Science Education*, 91(1), 75–95.

Bandura, A. (1989). Regulation of cognitive processes through perceived self-efficacy. *Developmental Psychology*, 25(5), 729–35.

Bandura, A. (1995). Introduction. In A. Bandura (ed.), *Self-efficacy in changing societies*. New York: Cambridge University Press.

Bandura, A. (1997). *Self-efficacy: The exercise of control*. New York: Freeman.

Bandura, A. (2002). Growing primacy of human agency in adaptation and change in the electronic era. *European Psychologist*, 7, 2–16.

Barclay, Craig R., Wellman, Henry M. (1986). Accuracies and inaccuracies in autobiographical memories. *Journal of Memory and Language*, 25(1), 93–103.

Barry, L. & Parasuraman, A. (1991). *Marketing services: Competing through quality*. New York: The Free Press.

Baumeister, R.F. 1999. The nature and structure of the self: An overview. In: *The Self in Social Psychology*, R.F. Baumeister, (ed.), 1–20. London: Psychology Press.

Beard, J.G. & Maunier, R. (1980). Measuring leisure satisfaction. *Journal of Leisure Research*, 12, 20–33.

Bem, D. J. (1972). Self-perception theory. In: L. Berkowitz (ed.), *Advances in experimental social psychology* (Vol. 6. pp. 1–62). New York: Academic Press.

Ben-Ze'ev, A. (2000). *The subtlety of emotions*. Cambridge, MA: MIT Press.

Bennett, E.S. & Swasey, J.E. (1996). Perceived stress reduction in urban public gardens. *HortTechnology*, 6(2), 125–128.

Bickford, A., Doering, Z.D. & Smith, S.J. (1992). *Spiders are coming!: An exhibition background study for the National Museum of Natural History*. (Institutional Studies Report 92–4). Washington, DC: Smithsonian Institution.

Bigley, J.D., Fesenmaier, D.R., Lane, M. & Roehl, W.S. (1992). The assessment of museum member motivations: A case study. In: A. Benefield, S. Bitgood & H. Shettel (eds.). *Visitor Studies: Theory, Research and Practice*, Vol. 4, pp. 72–81. Jacksonville, AL: The Center for Social Design.

Biltmore Estate. (1987). *Survey of Biltmore Estate, Summer 1987*. Unpublished manuscript.

Birney, B.A. (1990). *Characteristics of Brookfield zoo visitors: five analyses of our audience*. (Technical Rep.) Brookfield, IL: Zoological Society of Illinois.

Bitgood, S. & Patterson, D. (1995). Principles of exhibit design. *Visitor Behavior*, 2(1), 4–6.

Bitgood, S., Patterson, D. & Nichols, G. (1986). *Report of a survey of visitors to the Anniston Museum of Natural History*. Jacksonville, AL: Jacksonville State University, Psychology Institute.

Borun, M., Chamber, M.B., Dritsas, J. & Johnson, J.I. (1997). Enhancing family learning through exhibits. *Curator*, 40(4), 279–295.

Bosman, J. (2006). Advertising is obsolete. Everyone says so. Business, *New York Times*, January 23.

Bourdieu, P. (1989). Forms of capital. In: J.G. Richardson (ed.), *Handbook for theory and research for the Sociology of Education*, pp. 241–258. New York: Greenwood Press.

Bronfenbrenner, U. (1979). *The Ecology of Human Development*. Cambridge, MA: Harvard University Press.

Bruner, J. (1994). The 'remembered' self. In U. Neisser & R. Fivush (Eds.), *The remembering self: Construction and accuracy in the self-narrative*, pp. 41–54. New York: Cambridge University Press.

Bruner, J. & Kalmar, D. (1998). Narrative and meta-narrative in the construction of self. In *Self-Awareness: Its Nature and Development*, M. Ferrari and R. J. Sternberg, eds., 308–331. New York: The Guildford Press.

Calvin, W.H. (1997). *How Brains Think*. New York: Basic Books.

Cantor, N., Mischel, W. & Schwarz, J. (1982). A prototype analysis of psychological situations. *Cognitive Psychology* 14: 45–77.

Chi, M.T.H., Feltovich, P.J. & Glaser, R. (1980). Categorization and representation of physics problems by novices and experts. *Cognitive Science*, 5, 121–152.

Clifford, G. (1981). The past is prologue. In: K. Cirincione-Coles (ed.), *The Future of Education: Policy Issues and Challenges*. Beverly Hills, CA: Sage Publications.

Colonial Williamsburg Foundation. (1987). 1987 President's Report. Williamsburg, VA: Colonial Williamsburg Foundation.

Cooper, C.R. (1999). Multiple selves, multiple worlds: Cultural perspectives on individuality and connectedness in adolescence development. In: A. Masten (ed.), *Minnesota Symposium on Child Psychology: Cultural Processes in Development*, 25–57. Mahwah, NJ: Lawrence Erlbaum Associates.

Csikzentmihalyi, M. (1975). *Beyond Boredom and Anxiety*. San Fransisco: Jossey-Bass.

Csikzentmihalyi, M. (1990a). *Flow: The psychology of optimal experience*. New York: Harper Collins.

Csikzentmihalyi, M. (1990b). Literacy and intrinsic motivation. *Daedalus*, 119(2), 115–40.

Csikzentmihalyi, M. & Hermanson, K. (1995). Intrinsic motivation in museums: Why does one want to learn? In: J. Falk & L. Dierking (eds.), *Public institutions for personal learning*. Washington, DC: American Association of Museums.

Csikzentmihalyi, M. & LeFevre, J. (1989). Optimal experience in work and leisure. *Journal of Personality and Social Psychology* 56 (5): 815–822.

Curry, A. & Stanier, R. (2002). *Filling the disappointment gap*. Paper presented at the Arts Marketing Association Annual Conference, 25 July, 2002, Glasgow, Scotland.

Damasio, A.R. (1994). *Descartes' Error: Emotion, Reasons, and the Human Brain*. New York: Avon Books.

deCharms, R. (1968). *Personal causation: The internal affective determinants of behavior*. New York: Academic Press.

de Grazia, S. (1962). *Of Time, Work and Leisure*. New York: Twentieth Century Fund.

del Bosque, I.R. & Martin, H.S. (2008). Tourist satisfaction: A cognitive-affective model. *Annals of Tourism Research*, 35(2), 551–573.

del Bosque, I.R., Martin, H.S. & Collado, J. (2006). The role of expectations in the consumer satisfaction formation process: Empirical evidence in the travel agency sector. *Tourism Management*, 27: 410–419.

Desolneux, A., Moisan, L. Morel, J-M. (2008). *From Gestalt Theory to Image Analysis: A probabilistic approach*. New York: Springer.

Dierking, L.D., Adams, M. & Spencer-Etienne, M. (1996). *Final Report: Lila Wallace/Reader's Digest Audience Development, Virginia Museum of Fine Arts*. Annapolis, MD: SLi.

Dierking, L.D. &. Falk, J.H. (1994) Family behavior and learning in informal science settings: A review of the research. *Science Education*, 78(1), 57–72.

DiMaggio, P. & Ostrower, F. (1990). Participation in the arts by black and white Americans. *Social Forces*, 68(3), 753–778.

DiMaggio, P. & Ostrower, F. (1992). *Race, ethnicity and participation in the arts*. Washington, DC: Seven Locks Press.

Doering, Z.D. (1991). *Across the river: A study of visitors to the Anacostia Museum*. (Institutional Studies Report No. 92–5). Washington, DC: Smithsonian Institution.

Doering, Z.D. (1999). Strangers, guests or clients? Visitor experiences in museums. *Curator*, 42(2), 74–87.

Doering, Z.D. & Bickford, A. (1994). *Visits and visitors to the Smithsonian Institution: A summary of studies*. (Institutional Studies Report No. 94–1). Washington, DC: Smithsonian Institution.

Doering, Z.D. & Black, K.J. (1989). *Visits to the National Air and Space Museum (NASM): Demographic characteristics*. (Institutional Studies Report No. 89–1). Washington, DC: Smithsonian Institution.

Driver, B.L. & Tocher, S.R. (1970). Toward a behavioral interpretation of recreational engagements, with implications for planning. In: B.L. Driver (ed.), *Elements of outdoor recreation planning: Proceedings of a national short course held in Ann Arbor, Michigan, May 6–16, 1968*. Ann Arbor, MI: University of Michigan.

Dweck, C. (2000). *Self-Theories: Their role in motivation, personality and development*. New York: Psychology Press.

Edelman, G. (1987). *Neural Darwinism: The theory of group selection*. New York: Basic Books.

Edelman, G. & Tononi, G. (2000). Reentry and the dynamic core. In: T. Metzinger (ed.), *Neural correlates of consciousness: Empirical and conceptual questions*, pp. 121–138. Cambridge, MA: MIT Press.

Ellenbogen, K. (2003). *From dioramas to the dinner table: An ethnographic case study of the role of science museums in family life.* Unpublished doctoral dissertation. Vanderbilt University, Nashville.

Ellenbogen, K.M., Luke, J.J. & Dierking, L.D. (2007). Family learning research in museums: Perspectives on a decade of research. In: Falk, J.H., Dierking, L.D. & Foutz, S. (eds.), *In Principle, In Practice: Museums as Learning Institutions,* pp.17–30. Lanham, MD: AltaMira Press.

Ellis, G.D., J.E. Voelkl & C. Morris. (1994). Measurement and analysis issues with explanation of variance in daily experience using the Flow model. *Journal of Leisure Research,* 26(4), 337–356.

Falk, J.H. (1986). The use of time as a measure of visitor behavior and exhibit effectiveness. In: S. Nichols, M. Alexander & K. Yellis (eds.), *Museum Education Anthology: 1973–1983.* Washington, DC: Museum Education Roundtable.

Falk, J.H. (1993). *Factors Influencing Leisure Decisions: The Use of Museums by African Americans.* Washington, DC: American Association of Museums.

Falk, J.H. (1997). Testing a museum exhibition design assumption: Effect of explicit labeling of exhibit clusters on visitor concept development. *Science Education,* 81(6), 679–688.

Falk, J.H. (2000). *An investigation of the educational impact of a science center high-entertainment, multi-media theater experience.* Unpublished Technical Report. Annapolis, MD: Institute for Learning Innovation.

Falk, J.H. (2003). Personal Meaning Mapping. In: G. Caban, C. Scott, J. Falk & L. Dierking, (eds.), *Museums and Creativity: A study into the role of museums in design education,* pp. 10–18. Sydney, AU: Powerhouse Publishing.

Falk, J.H. (2006). An identity-centered approach to understanding museum learning. *Curator,* 49(2), 151–166.

Falk, J.H. (2008). Identity and the art museum visitor. *Journal of Art Education,* 34(2), 25–34.

Falk, J.H. & Abrams, C. (1996). *Des Moines Art Center diversity initiative: Year Two Interim Report.* Annapolis, MD: Science Learning, Inc.

Falk, J.H. & Adelman, L.M. (2003). Investigating the impact of prior knowledge, experience and interest on aquarium visitor learning. *Journal of Research in Science Teaching,* 40(2), 163–176.

Falk, J.H. & Balling, J.D. (1980). The school field trip: Where you go makes the difference. *Science and Children,* 18(3), 6–8.

Falk, J.H, Brooks, P. & Amin, R. (2001). Investigating the long-term impact of a science center on its community: The California Science Center L.A.S.E.R. Project. In: J. Falk (ed.), *Free-Choice Science Education: How We Learn Science Outside of School,* pp. 115–132. New York, NY: Teacher's College Press, Columbia University.

Falk, J.H. & Coulson, D. (2000). *Preliminary Analysis of Second Telephone Survey California Science Center L.A.S.E.R. Project.* Technical Report. Annapolis: Institute for Learning Innovation.

Falk, J.H. & Dierking, L.D. (1992). *The museum experience.* Washington, DC: Whalesback Books.

Falk, J.H. & Dierking, L.D. (1997). School field trips: Assessing their long-term impact. *Curator, 40*(3), 211–218.

Falk, J.H. & Dierking, L.D. (2000). *Learning from Museums.* Walnut Creek, CA: AltaMira Press.

Falk, J.H. & Dierking, L.D. (2008). Re-envisioning success in the cultural sector. *Cultural Trends, 17*(4), 233–246.

Falk, J.H., Dierking, L.D. & Foutz, S. (eds.) (2007). *In Principle-In Practice: Museums as Learning Institutions.* Lanham, MD: AltaMira Press.

Falk, J.H. & Gillespie, K. (in review). Measuring the relationship between emotion and learning in free-choice setting. *Science Education.*

Falk, J.H., Heimlich, J. & Bronnenkant, K. (2008). Using identity-related visit motivations as a tool for understanding adult zoo and aquarium visitor's meaning making. *Curator, 51*(1), 55–80.

Falk, J.H., Holland, D.G. & Dierking, L.D. (1992). A study of visitor expectations and their effect on visitation, Mystic Seaport Museum. Annapolis, MD: Museum Experience Associates.

Falk, J.H., Koran, J.J., Dierking, L.D. & Dreblow, L. (1985). Predicting visitor behavior. *Curator, 28*(4), 326–332.

Falk, J.H., Moussouri, T. & Coulson, D. (1998). The effect of visitors' agendas on museum learning. *Curator, 41*(2), 106–120.

Falk, J.H., Scott, C., Dierking, L.D., Rennie, L.J. & Cohen Jones, M. (2004). Interactives and visitor learning. *Curator, 47*(2), 171–198.

Falk, J.H. & Sheppard, B. (2006). *Thriving in the Knowledge Age: New business models for museums and other cultural institutions.* Lanham, MD: AltaMira Press.

Falk, J.H. & Storksdieck, M. (2004). *A Multi-Factor Investigation of Variables Affecting Informal Science Learning.* Final Report to the National Science Foundation. Annapolis, MD: Institute for Learning Innovation.

Falk, J.H. & Storksdieck, M. (2005). Using the *Contextual Model of Learning* to understand visitor learning from a science center exhibition. *Science Education, 89,* 744–778.

Falk, J.H. & Storksdieck, M. (2006). *Investigating the Long Term Impact of a Science Center on Its Community.* Final Report to the National Science Foundation. Annapolis, MD: Institute for Learning Innovation.

Falk, J.H. & Storksdieck, M. (in press). Science learning in a leisure setting. *Journal of Research in Science Teaching.*

Fang, J., Madhavan, S. & Alderman, M.H. (1996). The association between birthplace and mortality from cardiovascular causes among black and white residents of New York City. *New England Journal of Medicine, 335*(21), 1545–1551.

Finn, P. (2006). Bias and blinding: Self-fulfilling prophecies and intentional ignorance. *The ASHA Leader,* 11(8), 16–17, 22.

Fiske, S.T. & Taylor, S.E. (1991). *Social cognition* (2nd ed.). New York: McGraw Hill.

Foot, D.K. & Stoffman, D. (1996). *Boom, bust & echo: How to profit from the coming demographic shift.* Toronto: Macfarlane, Walter & Ross.

Freeman, W. (2000). *How brains make up their mind.* New York: Columbia University Press.

Freysinger, V.J. & Kelly, J.R. (2004). *21ˢᵗ Century Leisure: Current Issues.* State College, PA: Venture Publishing.

Galaburda, A.M. & Kosslyn, S.M. (2002). *Languages of the brain.* Cambridge, MA: Harvard University Press.

Gee, J.P. (2001). Identity as an analytic lens for research in education. *Review of Research in Education,* 25, 99–125.

Geertz, C. (1973). *The interpretation of cultures.* New York: Basic Books.

Gillum, R.F. (1996). The epidemiology of cardiovascular disease in black Americans. *New England Journal of Medicine,* 335(21), 1597–1598.

Godbey, G. (1989). In: Fred Coalter (ed.) *Anti-Leisure and Public Recreation Policy. In Freedom and Constraint-The Paradoxes of Leisure.* London: Routledge.

Godbey, G. (2001). The use of time and space in assessing the potential of free choice learning. In: J.H. Falk (ed.), *Free-Choice Science Education: How we learn science outside of school.* New York: Teachers College Press.

Goffman, E. (1959). *The presentation of self in everyday life.* New York: Doubleday.

Graburn, N.H. (1977). The museum and the visitor experience. In: *The Visitor and the Museum,* pp. 5–32. Prepared for the 72ⁿᵈ Annual Conference of the American Association of Museums, Seattle, WA.

Graburn, N. (1998). Quest for identity. *Museum International,* 50(3), 13–18.

Graefe, A.R. & Fedler, A.J. (1986). Situational and subjective determinants of satisfaction in marine recreational fishing. *Leisure Sciences,* 8, 275–295.

Griffin, J. (1998). *School-museum integrated learning experiences in science: A learning journey.* Unpublished doctoral dissertation. University of Technology, Sydney.

Gutman, J. (1979). A means-end chain model based on consumer categorization processes. *Journal of Marketing* 46(2), 60–72.

Haggard, L.M. & Williams, D.R. (1992). Identity affirmation through leisure activities: Leisure symbols of the self. *Journal of Leisure Research,* 24(1), 1–18.

Hall, E.T. (1966). *The hidden dimension*. New York: Doubleday.

Hall, S. (1992). The question of cultural identity. In S. Hall & T. McGrew (eds.), *Modernity and its futures* (pp. 273–326). Cambridge: Polity Press.

Harmon-Jones, E. & Mills, J. (1999). *Cognitive Dissonance: Progress on a Pivotal Theory in Social Psychology*. Washington, DC: American Psychological Association.

Heimlich, J., Bronnenkant, K., Witgert, N. & Falk, J.H. (2004). *Measuring the Learning Outcomes of Adult Visitors to Zoos and Aquariums: Confirmatory Study*. Technical report. Bethesda, MD: American Association of Zoos and Aquariums.

Higgins, E.T. (1987). Self-discrepancy: A theory relating self and affect. *Psychological Review, 94*, 319–340.

Hilts, P.J. (1995). *Memory's Ghost: The Strange Tale of Mr. M. and the Nature of Memory*. New York, NY: Simon & Schuster.

Holden, J. (2006). *Cultural value and the crisis of legitimacy: Why culture needs a democratic mandate*. London: Demos. http://www.demos.co.uk/files/Culturalvalueweb.pdf

Holland, D., Lachicotte, Jr., W., Skinner, D. & Cain, C. (1998). *Identity and Agency in Cultural Worlds*. Cambridge: Harvard University Press.

Holmes, L. (2000). Reframing learning: Performance, identity and practice. Presented at *Critical Contributions to Managing and Learning: 2nd Connecting Learning and Critique Conference*, Lancaster University, July 2000.

Hood, M. (1981). *Leisure Criteria of Family Participation and Non-Participation in Museums*. Technical Report. Columbus, OH: Hood Associates.

Hood, M. (1983). Staying away: Why people choose not to visit museums. *Museum News*, 61(4), 50–57.

Hood, M.G. (1988). Arboretum visitor profiles as defined by the four seasons. In S. Bitgood, J. Roper & A. Benefield (eds.), *Proceedings of the first annual visitor studies conference*. Jacksonville, AL: The Center for Social Design.

Horn, A. & Finney, J. (1994). *Bay area research report: A multi-cultural audience survey for Bay Area museums*. San Francisco, CSUSAN: Museum Management Consultants, Inc.

Hoyle, R.H., Kernis, M.H., Leary, M.R. & Baldwin, M.W. (1999). *Selfhood: Identity, esteem, regulation*. Boulder, CO: Westview Press.

Hushion & Associates & Heath Consultants (1994). *Mapping a future: An audience and stakeholder survey of the public art gallery network in Ontario*. Toronto: Ontario Association of Art Galleries.

Jacobsen, J.W. (2006). *Experiential Learning Museums*. (Forum '06). Marblehead, MA: White Oak Associates, Inc.

James, W. (1890). *Principles of psychology, Vol I & II*. New York: Holt.

Jussim, L. & Harber, K.D. (2005). Teacher expectations and self-fulfilling prophecies: Knowns and unknowns, resolved and unresolved controversies. *Personality and Social Psychology Review, 9*, 131–155.

Kant, I. (1781/1997). *Critique of pure reason*. Cambridge: Cambridge University Press.

Kaplan, S. (1995). The restorative benefits of nature: Toward an integrative framework. *Journal of Environmental Psychology*, 15, 169–182.

Kelly, J.R. (1977). *Situational and Social Factors in Leisure Decisions*. Technical Report. ERIC #:ED153143.

Kelly, J.R. (1983). *Leisure identities and interactions*. London: George Allen & Unwin.

Kelly, J.R. (1991). Commodification and consciousness: An initial study. *Leisure Sciences*, 10, 7–18.

Kelly, J.R. & Freysinger, V.J. (2000). *21ˢᵗ Century Leisure: Current Issues*. State College, PA: Venture Publishing.

Knopf, R.C., Driver, B.L. & Bassett, J.L (1973). Motivations for fishing. In: *Transactions of the 28th North American Wildlife and Natural Resources Conference* (pp. 191–204). Wash., DC: Wildlife Management Institute.

Larkin, J.H. (1983). The role of problem representation in physics. In D. Gentner & A.L. Stevens (eds.), *Mental models*. Hillsdale, NJ: Earlbaum.

Lave, J. & Wenger, E. (1991). *Situated learning. Legitimate peripheral participation*. Cambridge, U.K.: Cambridge University Press.

Lazarus, R.S. (1966). *Psychological stress and the coping process*. New York: McGraw-Hill.

Lee, B.K. & Shafer, C.S. (2002). The dynamic nature of leisure experience: An application of Affect Control Theory. *Journal of Leisure Research*, 34(2), 290–310.

Lee, B.K., Shafer, C.S. & Kang, I. (2005). Examining relationships among perceptions of self, episode-specific evaluations, and overall satisfaction with a leisure activity. *Leisure Sciences*, 27, 93–109.

Leinhardt, G., Crowley, K. & Knutson, K. (Eds.). (2002). *Learning conversations in museums*. Mahwa, NJ: Earlbaum.

Leuchter, A.F. (2002). Changes in brain function of depressed subjects during treatment with Placebo. *American Journal of Psychiatry*, 159, 122–129.

Lewington, J. (1998). More Canadians pursuing informal learning, survey reveals. *The Globe and Mail*, November 11, A13.

Lewis, C.S. (1933). *The Pilgrim's Regress, Book 7*. Grand Rapids, MI: Eardmans.

Lieberman, P. (2000). *Human language and our reptilian brain: The subcortical bases of speech, syntax and thought*. Cambridge, MA: Harvard University Press.

Linville, P.W. (1985). Self-complexity and affective extremity: Don't put all your eggs in one cognitive basket. *Social Cognition*, 3, 94–120.

Linville, P.W. (1987). Self-complexity as a cognitive buffer against stress-related illness and depression. *Journal of Personality and Social Psychology* 52, pp. 663–676.

Livingstone, D.W. (1999). Exploring the icebergs of adult learning: Findings of the first Canadian survey of informal learning practices. *Canadian Journal for the Study of Adult Education*, 13(2), 49–72.

Luke, J.J., Dierking, L.D. & Falk, J.H. (2001). *The Children's Museum of Indianapolis Family Learning Initiative: Phase I Baseline Report*. Unpublished technical report. Annapolis, MD: Institute for Learning Innovation.

Madon, S., Guyll, M., Spoth, R.L., Cross, S.E. & Hilbert, S.J. (2003). The self-fulfilling influence of mother expectations on children's underage drinking. *Journal of Personality and Social Psychology*, 84, 1188–1205.

Maestro, R.H., Gallego, P.M. & Requejo, L.S. (2007). The moderating role of familiarity in rural tourism in Spain. *Tourism Management*, 28, 951–964.

Manfredo, M.J. & Driver, B.L. (1996). Measuring leisure motivation: A meta-analysis of the recreation experience preference scales. *Journal of Leisure Research*, 28(3), 188–213.

Mannell, R. & Iso-Ahola, S.E. (1987). Psychological nature of leisure and tourism experience. *Annals of Tourism Research*, 14, 314–331.

Markus, H. & Nurius, P. (1986). Possible selves. *American Psychologist*, 41, 954–969.

Markus, H. & Wurf, E. (1987). The dynamic self-concept: A social psychological perspective. In M.R. Rosenzweig & L.W. Porter (eds.), *Annual Review of Psychology*, 38, 299–337.

Maslow, A. (1943). A theory of human motivation. *Psychological Review*, 50, 370–396.

Matusov, E. & Rogoff, B. (1995). Evidence of development from people's participation in communities of learners. In: J. Falk & L. Dierking (eds.), *Public Institutions for Personal Learning*, pp. 97–104. Washington, DC: American Association of Museums.

Mayberg, H., Silva, A., Brannan, S.K., Tekell, J.L., Mahurin, R.K., McGinis, S. & Jerbek, P. (2002). The functional neuroanatomy of the placebo effect. *American Journal of Psychiatry*, 159, 728–737.

McAdams, D. (1990). *The Person: An Introduction to Personality Psychology*. Orlando, FL: Harcourt Brace Jovanovich.

McClelland, J.L., & Rumelhart, D.E. (1985). Distributed memory and the representation of general and specific information. *Journal of Experimental Psychology*, 114, 159–188.

McGaugh, J.L. (2003). *Memory & emotion: The making of lasting memories*. New York: Columbia University Press.

McLean, F. (1997). *Marketing the museum*. London: Routledge.

Medved, M., & Oatley, K. (2000). Memories and scientific literacy: Remembering exhibits from a science centre. *International Journal of Science Education*, 22(10), 1117–1132.

Merton, R.K. (1957). *Social theory and social structure, revised edition.* New York: Free Press.

Moerman, Daniel E. (2002). *Meaning, Medicine and the 'Placebo Effect.'* Cambridge, UK: Cambridge University Press.

Morris Hargreaves McIntyre (2004). *Tate through visitor's eyes.* Technical Report. Manchester, UK: Morris Hargreaves McIntyre.

Moussouri, T. (1997). *Family agendas and family learning in hands-on museums.* Unpublished doctoral dissertation, University of Leiscester, Leicester, England.

National Science Board (2004). *Science and engineering indicators: 2004.* Washington, DC: U.S. Government Printing Office.

National Science Board (2006). *Science and engineering indicators: 2006.* Washington, DC: U.S. Government Printing Office.

National Science Board (2008). *Science and engineering indicators: 2008.* Washington, DC: U.S. Government Printing Office.

Neisser, U. (1988). Five kinds of self-knowledge. *Philosophical Psychology* 1: 35–59.

Neisser, U. & Hyman, Jr. I.E. (1999). *Memory observed: Remembering in natural contexts,* 2nd Edition. New York: Macmillan.

Nickels, A.L. (2008). *An Exploration of Visitors' Conservation Attitudes, Expectations, and Motivations at Three Informal Education Institutions in Newport, Oregon.* Unpublished Master's Thesis. Corvallis, OR: Oregon State University.

Oliver, R.L. (1980). A cognitive model of the antecedents and consequences of satisfaction decisions. *Journal of Marketing Research,* 17, 460–469.

Olson, S. (2002). *Mapping human history: Genes, race, and our common origins.* Boston: Mariner Books.

Packer, J. (2006). Learning for fun: The unique contribution of educational leisure experiences. *Curator,* 49(3), 329–344.

Packer, J. (2008). *Museums as restorative environments.* Paper Presented at the Visitor Studies Association. Houston, TX, July 18, 2008.

Packer, J. & Ballantyne, R. (2002). Motivational factors and the visitor experience: A comparison of three sites. *Curator,* 45, 183–198.

Paris, S.G. (1997). Situated motivation and informal learning. *Journal of Museum Education,* 22(2 & 3), 22–27.

Pearson, J. & Platt, M. (2008). Decision-making in the brain: Eavesdropping on neurons. *Scientific American,* August 5, 2008, (no page number), http://www.sciam.com/article.cfm?id=decision-making-in-brain&sc=rss

Pearson, L.F. (1977). *Working, life and leisure.* Sunderland, UK: Sunderland Polytechnic.

Pekarik, A.J., Doering, Z.D. & Karns, D.A. (1999). Exploring satisfying experiences in museums. *Curator,* 42, 152–173.

Penuel, W. & Wertsch, J. (1995). Vygotsky and identity formation: A sociocultural approach. *Educational Psychologist*, 30(2), 83–92.

Perry, D. (1989). *The creation and verification of a developmental model for the design of a museum exhibit.* Unpublished doctoral dissertation. Indiana University.

Piaget, J. (ed. and trans.). (1981). Intelligence and affectivity. Their relationship during child development. *Annual Reviews Monograph*. Palo Alto, CA: Annual Reviews.

Pinder, C.C. (1984). *Work Motivation: Theory, Issues, and Applications.* Glenview, IL: Scott, Foresman and Company.

Pine, J. & Gilmore, J. (2007). *Authencity: What consumers really want.* Boston: Harvard Business School.

Pinker, S. *The language instinct.* New York: Harper Collins.

Porter, L.W. & Lawler, E.E. (1968). *Managerial attitude and performance.* Homewood, IL: Irwin-Dorsey.

Price, D.D., Chung, S.K. & Robinson, M.E. (2005). Conditioning, expectation, and desire for relief in placebo analgesia. *Seminars in Pain Medicine*. 3(1), 15–21.

Puckrein, G. (1991). The participation of African Americans in cultural leisure pursuits. Unpublished study produced for *American Visions*, Washington, DC.

Rennie, L.J. & McClafferty, T.P. (1995). Using visits to interactive science and technology centers, museums, aquaria, and zoos to promote learning in science. *Journal of Science Teacher Education*, 6(4), 175–185.

Research Resolutions & Consulting Ltd. (2007). *U.S. Heritage Tourism Enthusiasts: A Special Analysis of the Travel Activities and Motivation Survey (TAMS)*. Ottawa: The Canadian Tourism Commission.

Reynolds, T.J. & Gutman, J. (1984). Laddering: Extending the Repertory Grid Methodology to construct attribute-consequence-value hierarchies. In: *Personal Values and Consumer Psychology*, Vol II., R. Pitts and A. Woodside (eds.) Lexington, MA: Lexington Books.

Roberts, K. (1999). *Leisure in Society.* Wallingford, UK: CBAI Publishing.

Robinson, J.P., Keegan, C., Karth, M. & Triplett, T.A. (1986). *Public Participation in the arts: Final report on the 1992 survey, Volume 1, Overall project report.* Washington, DC: National Endowment for the Arts.

Robinson, J.P., Keegan, C., Karth, M. & Triplett, T.A. (1993). *Arts Participation in America: 1982-1992* NEA Research Division, Report #27. Washington, DC: National Endowment for the Arts.

Rohrkemper, M. & Corno, L. (1988). Success and failure on classroom tasks: Adaptive learning and classroom teaching. *Elementary School Journal*, 88, 297–312.

Rose, S. (1993). *The Making of Memory: From Molecules to Mind.* New York: Anchor Books/Doubleday.

Rounds, J. (2004). Strategies for the curiosity-driven museum visitor. *Curator*, 47(4), 389–412.

Rounds, J. (2006). Doing identity work in museums. *Curator*, 49(2), 133–150.

Rumelhart, D.E., Hinton, G.E. & McClelland, J.L. (1986). A general framework for parallel distributed processing. In: D.E.Rumelhart, J. L. McClelland & the PDP Research Group (eds.), *Parallel distributed processing: Explorations in the microstructure of cognition* (Vol. 1, pp. 45–76). Cambridge, MA: MIT Press.

Russell, J.A. (1979). Affective space is bipolar. *Journal of Personality and Social Psychology*, 37(3), 345–356.

Russell, J.A. Weiss, A., & Mendelsohn, G.A. (1989). Affect grid: a single-item scale of pleasure and arousal. *Journal of Personality and Social Psychology*, 57(3), 493–502.

Sagon, C. (2004). Formerly known as Sutton Place. F1, *Washington Post*, April 7.

Salami, H. (1998). *Motivation and meaningful science learning in informal settings.* Paper presented at the annual meeting of the National Association for Research in Science Teaching, April, San Diego, CA.

Samdahl, D.M. & Kleiber, D.A. (1989). Self-awareness and leisure experience. *Leisure Sciences*, 11, 1–10.

Sandberg, J. (2006, July 19) It Doesn't Sound Like a Vacation to Me. *Wall Street Journal* online.

Schutte, N.S., Kenrick, D.T. & Sadalla, E.K. (1985). The search for predictable settings: Situational prototypes, constraint, and behavioral variation. *Journal of Personality and Social Psychology*, 51, 459–462.

Serrell, B. (1998). *Paying attention: Visitors and museum exhibitions.* Washington, DC: American Association of Museums.

Simon, B. (1997). Self and group in modern society: Ten theses on the individual self and collective self. In: R. Spears, P.J. Oakes, N. Ellemera & S.A. Haslam (eds.), *The social psychology of stereotyping and group life* (pp. 318–335). Oxford, England: Basil Blackwell.

Simon, B. (1998). Individuals, groups, and social change: On the relationship between individual and collective self-interpretations and collective action. In: C. Sedikides, J. Schopler & C, Insko (eds.), *Intergroup cognition and intergroup behavior* (pp. 257–282). Mahwah, NJ: Lawrence Erlbaum.

Simon, B. (1999). A place in the world: Self and social categorization. In T.R. Tyler, R.M. Kramer & O.P. John (eds.), *The psychology of the social self* (pp. 47–49). Mahwah, NJ: Lawrence Erlbaum.

Simon, B. (2004). *Identity in modern society: A social psychological perspective.* Oxford, UK: Blackwell.

Simon, B. & Oakes, P. (2006). Beyond dependence: An identity approach to social power and domination. *Human Relations*, 59, 105–139.

Steele, C.M. (1988). The psychology of self-affirmation: Sustaining the integrity of the self. In: L. Berkowitz (ed.), *Advances in Experimental Social-Psychology* (Vol. 21, pp. 261–302). New York: Academic Press.

Stein, J. (2007). *Adapting the visitor identity-related motivations scale for living history sites*. Paper presented at the Annual Meeting of the Visitor's Studies Association, July 19, 2007, Toronto, Canada.

Stewart, W.P. (1998). Leisure as multiphase experiences: Challenging traditions. *Journal of Leisure Research*, 30(4), 391–400.

Stewart, W.P. & Hull IV, B.R. (1992). Satisfaction of what? Post hoc versus real-time construct validity. *Leisure Sciences*, *14*, 195–209.

Storksdieck, M. & Stein, J. (2007). *Using the visitor identity-related motivations scale to improve visitor experiences at the US Botanic Garden*. Paper presented at the Annual Meeting of the Visitor's Studies Association, July 19, 2007, Toronto, Canada.

Stryker, S. (1987). The vitalization of Symbolic Interactionism. *Social Psychology Quarterly*, 50, 83–94.

Stryker, S. & Burke, P.J. (2000). The past, present, and future of an identity theory. *Social Psychology Quarterly*, 63, 284–297.

Sylwester, R. (1995). *In celebration of neurons*. Alexandria, VA: Association for Supervision and Curriculum Development.

Thompson, W. Grant. (2005). *The Placebo Effect and Health-Combining Science and Compassionate Care*. New York: Prometheus.

Timmer, J. (2007). Product loyalty: consumers mistake familiarity with superiority. *Ars techinica*. http://arstechnica.com/news.ars/post/20070605-product-loyalty-consumers-mistake-familiarity-with-superiority.html

Treacy, M. & Wiersema, F. (1995). *The discipline of market leaders*. New York: Basic Books.

Trowbridge, D. & McDermott, L. (1980). Investigation of student understanding of the concept of velocity in one dimension. *American Journal of Physics*, 50, 242–253.

Turner, J.H. (2000). *On the origins of human emotions: A sociological inquiry into the evolution of human affect*. Stanford, CA: Stanford University Press.

Ulwick, A. (2005). *What customers want: Using outcome-driven innovation to create breakthrough products and services*. NY: McGraw-Hill, pp. 66–67.

Vroom, V. (1964). *Work and Motivation*. New York: John Wiley & Sons.

Vygotsky, L. (1978). *Mind in society: The development of higher mental processes*. Cambridge, MA: Harvard University Press.

Wegner, D.M. (2002). *The illusion of conscious will*. Cambridge, MA: MIT Press.

Weil, S.E. (1999). From being *about* something to being *for* somebody: The ongoing transformation of the American Museum. *Daedalus*, 28(3), 229–258.

Weil, S.E. (2002). *Making museums matter.* Washington, DC: Smithsonian Institution Press.

Wenger, E. (1998). *Communities of practice: Learning, meaning, and identity.* Cambridge: Cambridge University Press.

Whisman, S.A. & Hollenhorst, S.J. (1998). A path model of whiteriver boating satisfaction on the Cheat River of West Virginia. *Environmental Management,* 22(1), 109–117.

Wilkening, S. (2008). Audience Trends and Analysis: Drilling deeper. Unpublished presentation. Slingerlands, NY: Reach Advisors.

Williams, D.R. 2002. Leisure identities, globalization, and the politics of place. *Journal of Leisure Research,* 34(4), 267–278.

Wong, J.T. & Hui, E.C.M. (2006). Power of expectations. *Property Management,* 24, 496–506.

Woodward, K. (2002). *Understanding identity.* London: Arnold.

Yoon, Y. & Uysal, M. (2005). An examination of the effects of motivation and satisfaction on destination loyalty: A structural model. *Tourism Management,* 26, 45–56.

Young, M. & Schuller, T. (1991). *Life after Work.* London: Harper Collins.

Zeldin, A.L., Britner, S.L. & Pajares, F. (2008). A comparative study of the self-efficacy beliefs of successful men and women in mathematics, science and technology careers. *Journal of Research in Science Teaching,* 45, 1036–1058.

Zuboff, S. & Maxmin, D. (2002). *The Support Economy: Why corporations are failing individuals and the next episode of capitalism.* New York: Viking Press.

INDEX

Note: *Italicized page numbers indicate illustrations. Names of people interviewed are pseudonyms and are shown with first name followed by (pseud.).*

ABOUT THE AUTHOR

John H. Falk is a leading figure in free-choice learning, museum research, and science education in the United States. He holds the position Sea Grant Professor of Free-Choice Learning at Oregon State University. He is founder and President Emeritus of the renowned research firm, Institute for Learning Innovation in Annapolis, Maryland and has worked at a variety of other key positions in the museum world, including 14 years at the Smithsonian Institution. Falk earned a joint doctorate in Biology and Education from the University of California, Berkeley. He is the author of over one hundred scholarly articles and chapters in the areas of biology, psychology and education. He co-authored with Lynn Dierking of The Museum Experience, *Learning from Museums: Visitor Experiences and the Making of Meaning*, and *Lessons without Limit: How Free-Choice Learning is Transforming Education*; co-authored with Beverly Sheppard the volume *Thriving in the Knowledge Age: New Business Models for Museums and Other Cultural Institutions*; and has edited numerous books including *Free-Choice Science Education: How We Learn Science Outside of School*, and *In Principle-In Practice: Museums as Learning Institutions*.